John Osborne: *Look Back in Anger*   JOHN RUSSELL TAYLOR
Peacock: *The Satirical Novels*   LORNA SAGE
Pope: *The Rape of the Lock*   JOHN DIXON HUNT
Shakespeare: *Antony and Cleopatra*   JOHN RUSSELL BROWN
Shakespeare: *Coriolanus*   B. A. BROCKMAN
Shakespeare: *Hamlet*   JOHN JUMP
Shakespeare: *Henry IV Parts I and II*   G. K. HUNTER
Shakespeare: *Henry V*   MICHAEL QUINN
Shakespeare: *Julius Caesar*   PETER URE
Shakespeare: *King Lear*   FRANK KERMODE
Shakespeare: *Macbeth*   JOHN WAIN
Shakespeare: *Measure for Measure*   C. K. STEAD
Shakespeare: *'Much Ado about Nothing' and 'As You Like It'*   JOHN RUSSELL
BROWN
Shakespeare: *The Merchant of Venice*   JOHN WILDERS
Shakespeare: *Othello*   JOHN WAIN
Shakespeare: *Richard II*   NICHOLAS BROOKE
Shakespeare: *The Sonnets*   PETER JONES
Shakespeare: *The Tempest*   D. J. PALMER
Shakespeare: *Troilus and Cressida*   PRISCILLA MARTIN
Shakespeare: *Twelfth Night*   D. J. PALMER
Shakespeare: *The Winter's Tale*   KENNETH MUIR
Shelley: *Shorter Poems and Lyrics*   PATRICK SWINDEN
Spenser: *The Faerie Queene*   PETER BAYLEY
Swift: *Gulliver's Travels*   RICHARD GRAVIL
Tennyson: *In Memoriam*   JOHN DIXON HUNT
Thackeray: *Vanity Fair*   ARTHUR POLLARD
Webster: *'The White Devil' and 'The Duchess of Malfi'*   R. V. HOLDSWORTH
Virginia Woolf: *To the Lighthouse*   MORRIS BEJA
Wordsworth: *Lyrical Ballads*   ALUN R. JONES AND WILLIAM TYDEMAN
Wordsworth: *The Prelude*   W. J. HARVEY AND RICHARD GRAVIL
Yeats: *Last Poems*   JON STALLWORTHY

*Drama Criticism: Developments since Ibsen:* ARNOLD P. HINCHLIFFE
*The English Novel: Developments in Criticism since Henry James*   STEPHEN HAZELL
*The Metaphysical Poets*   GERALD HAMMOND
*The Romantic Imagination*   JOHN SPENCER HILL

TITLES IN PREPARATION INCLUDE
*Poetry Criticism: Developments since the Symbolists*   A. E. DYSON
*Tragedy:* R. P. DRAPER

# Yeats
## *Last Poems*

A CASEBOOK

EDITED BY

JON STALLWORTHY

First edition 1968
Reprinted 1975, 1980

*Published by*
THE MACMILLAN PRESS LTD
*London and Basingstoke*
*Associated companies in Delhi Dublin*
*Hong Kong Johannesburg Lagos Melbourne*
*New York Singapore and Tokyo*

ISBN 0 333 08317 2 (hard cover)
 0 333 02036 7 (paper cover)

*Printed and bound in Hong Kong*

# CONTENTS

# ACKNOWLEDGEMENTS

W. H. Auden, 'In Memory of W. B. Yeats', from *Collected Shorter Poems* (Faber & Faber Ltd, Random House Inc.); Winfield Townley Scott, 'Yeats at 73', from *Poetry*, LIII ii (Nov. 1938; Frederic Prokosch, 'Yeats's Testament', from *Poetry*, liv (Sept. 1939); 'W. B. Yeats: The Last Poems', from *The Times Literary Supplement*, 22 July 1939; J. J. Hogan, 'Last Poems and Plays', from *Studies*, vol. 29, no. 113 (The Editor); John Crowe Ransom, 'Old Age of a Poet', from *The Kenyon Review*, ii 3 (Summer 1940); Louis MacNeice, 'Yeats's Epitaph', from *The New Republic*, cii 26 (24 June 1940) (David Higham Associates Ltd); 'Yeats: Master of Diction', from *Saturday Review*, xxii (8 June 1940; © Saturday Review Inc. 1940) (W. H. Auden and Curtis Brown Ltd); Introduction and letters from *Letters on Poetry from W. B. Yeats to Dorothy Wellesley* (Miss Elizabeth Cleuer and Mr Raymond Barnett, Literary Executors of the late Dorothy Wellesley, and Oxford University Press); Curtis Bradford, 'Yeats's "Last Poems" Again', from *Dolmen Centenary Paper*, viii (The Dolmen Press Ltd); T. R. Henn, 'Last Poems' and 'Horseman, Pass by!', from *The Lonely Tower* (Methuen & Co. Ltd), and 'The Accent of Yeats's *Last Poems*', from *Essays and Studies*, 1956 (published by John Murray (Publishers) Ltd); J. R. Mulryne, 'Last Poems', from *An Honoured Guest* (Edward Arnold (Publishers) Ltd); Professor A. N. Jeffares, 'Notes on Yeats's "Lapis Lazuli" ', from *Modern Language Notes* (Nov. 1950); F. A. C. Wilson, 'The Statues', from *Yeats's Iconography* (Victor Gollancz Ltd); 'Times of Glory: Yeats's "The Municipal Gallery Revisited" ' (Professor A. M. Garab and *Arizona Quarterly*); Jon Stallworthy, 'The Black Tower', from *Between the Lines* (The Clarendon Press), and 'Under Ben Bulben',

*Review of English Studies* (Feb. 1966); Peter Ure, '*Purgatory*' and '*The Death of Cuchulain*', from *Yeats the Playwright* (Routledge & Kegan Paul Ltd, Barnes & Noble Inc.).

# GENERAL EDITOR'S PREFACE

EACH of this series of Casebooks concerns either one well-known and influential work of literature or two or three closely linked works. The main section consists of critical readings, mostly modern, brought together from journals and books. A selection of reviews and comments by the author's contemporaries is also included, and sometimes comments from the author himself. The Editor's Introduction charts the reputation of the work from its first appearance until the present time.

What is the purpose of such a collection? Chiefly, to assist reading. Our first response to literature may be, or seem to be, 'personal'. Certain qualities of vigour, profundity, beauty or 'truth to experience' strike us, and the work gains a foothold in our mind. Later, an isolated phrase or passage may return to haunt or illuminate. Where did we hear that? we wonder – it could scarcely be better put.

In these and similar ways appreciation begins, but major literature prompts to very much more. There are certain facts we need to know if we are to understand properly. Who were the author's original readers, and what assumptions did he share with them? What was his theory of literature? Was he committed to a particular historical situation, or to a set of beliefs? We need historians as well as critics to help us with this. But there are also more purely literary factors to take account of: the work's structure and rhetoric; its symbols and archetypes; its tone, genre and texture; its use of language; the words on the page. In all these matters critics can inform and enrich our individual responses by offering imaginative recreations of their own.

For the life of a book is not, after all, merely 'personal'; it is more like a tripartite dialogue, between a writer living 'then', a reader living 'now', and whatever forces of survival and honour link the two. Criticism is the public manifestation of this dialogue, a witness to the continuing power of literature to arouse and excite. It illuminates the possibilities and regards of the dialogue, pushing 'interpretation' as far forward as it can go.

And here, indeed, is the rub: how far can it go? Where does 'interpretation' end and nonsense begin? Why is one interpretation superior to another, and why does each age need to interpret for itself? The critic knows that his insights have value only in so far as they serve the text, and that he must take account of views differing sharply from his own. He knows that his own writing will be judged as well as the work he writes about, so that he cannot simply assert inner illumination or a differing taste.

The critical forum is a place of vigorous conflict and dis-agreement, but there is nothing in this to cause dismay. What is attested is the complexity of human experience and the richness of literature, not any chaos or relativity of taste. A critic is better seen, no doubt, as an explorer than as an 'authority', but ex-plorers ought to be, and usually are, well equipped. The effect of good criticism is to convince us of what C. S. Lewis called 'the enormous extension of our being which we owe to authors'. A Casebook will be justified only if it helps to promote the same end.

A single volume can represent no more than a small selection of critical opinions. Some critics have been excluded for reasons of space, and it is hoped that readers will follow up the further suggestions in the Select Bibliography. Other contributions have been severed from their original context, to which some readers may wish to return. Indeed, if they take a hint from the critics represented here, they certainly will.

A. E. DYSON

# INTRODUCTION

THE reader of Yeats's *Collected Poems* is given no indication that his *Last Poems* is other than a single book assembled by the same hand that, in *The Tower* and *The Winding Stair*, fitted poem to poem almost as carefully as stanza to stanza, word to word. The first thing to be said, therefore, about the *Last Poems* is that the first thirty-five (from 'The Gyres' to 'Are You Content?') were published in 1938 under the title *New Poems*, and that all but three of the rest appeared in July 1939, with *Purgatory* and *The Death of Cuchulain*, under the title *Last Poems and Two Plays*. Though this book, privately printed like *New Poems* by Yeats's sister at the Cuala Press, was published posthumously, the sequence of its contents followed a list in the poet's handwriting found among his papers. When in 1940, however, the poems from these two limited editions were brought together and published in *Last Poems and Plays*, those from the later book were drastically reshuffled and three were added that Yeats had omitted, one must assume deliberately, from his list of contents. So reshuffled, the *Last Poems* were incorporated into the *Collected Poems*, and no one appears to have appreciated the damage done to Yeats's thematic design until Curtis Bradford made his illuminating examination of this rearrangement (see pp. 75–97).

Although not many reviewers of *Last Poems and Two Plays* or *Last Poems and Plays* went as far as F. R. Leavis, who pronounced the latter 'a saddening volume' because of its 'slackening . . . tension', 'bitterness and an agonized sense of frustrate impotence',[1] most found these volumes lacking 'the brilliance and profusion of *The Tower* and *The Winding Stair*

[1] 'The Great Yeats and the Latest', in *Scrutiny*, VIII 4 (March 1940). Unfortunately, permission to reprint this review could not be obtained.

(presumably his two best books, certainly the ones which crystal-lized the superiority of his late work over his earlier)'.[1] The *Lis-tener*, the *Spectator*, the *Times Literary Supplement*, and a few other periodicals reviewed the Cuala Press edition, but not surprisingly – for private presses seldom distribute as many review copies as commercial publishers – the expanded and reshuffled *Last Poems and Plays* was the more widely noticed. One wonders how much better this book would have been received, and its author's intentions understood, if his grouping of its poems had been preserved. As it was – and indeed still is – the lack of the strong sequence that adds so much to the cumulative impact of *The Tower* and *The Winding Stair*, coupled with the nonchalant freedom of the *Last Poems* and their more colloquial style, suggested to many that the 'old man's eagle mind' had lost its sense of direction. If this was one principal source of the re-viewers' dissatisfaction, there was a second. The younger left-wing poets Auden and MacNeice undoubtedly spoke for their generation when they criticized certain of Yeats's social and political attitudes.[2] He was 'out of key with his time', they felt, not appreciating fully the differences between his time-scale and their own. With a war against the forces of fascism then newly begun, it was hardly surprising if his celebration of aristocratic traditions, authoritarian rule, and cosmic violence struck a jarring note. In view of the fact that most old writers' reputations fall at their death, and of the unfortunate timing of its publica-tion, *Last Poems and Plays* was perhaps fortunate to have been reviewed as sympathetically as it was. Not that it was reviewed in isolation, but, as Yeats would himself have wished, in the context of his total poetic output. There was an additional factor that had to be taken into consideration. As Louise Bogan put it in a perceptive 'portrait' written in June 1938:

The phenomenon of a poet who enjoys continued develop-ment into the beginning of old age is in itself rare. Goethe, Sophocles, and, in a lesser degree, Milton come to mind as men

[1] See p. 32. This notice appeared both in *Poetry* (Chicago) LIV (Sep-tember 1939) 338–42 and in *The Spectator*, CLXIII (4 August 1939) 190.
[2] But see the quotation from Yeats's letter to Ethel Mannin on p. 51.

whose last works burned with the gathered fuel of their lives. More often development, in a poet, comes to a full stop; and it is frequently a negation of the ideals of his youth, as well as a declination of his powers, that throws a shadow across his final pages.[1]

She reminds us that Yeats was himself well aware of the hazards of old age and wrote in 1917, when he was fifty-two:

A poet when he is growing old, will ask himself if he cannot keep his mask and his vision, without new bitterness, new disappointment. . . . Could he if he would, copy Landor[2] who lived loving and hating, ridiculous and unconquered, into extreme old age, all lost but the favour of his muses. . . . Surely, he may think, now that I have found vision and mask I need not suffer any longer. Then he will remember Wordsworth, withering into eighty years, honoured and empty-witted, and climb to some waste room, and find, forgotten there by youth, some bitter crust.

In 'Girl's Song' Yeats has the singer ask

> Saw I an old man young
> Or a young man old?

And there can be little doubt that he had himself in mind, though aware of Everyman at his shoulder. Old age, a common subject in Celtic mythology, was a recurrent theme in the poems of his youth. In the opening lines of the first poem of his first collection, Yeats has Saint Patrick say to the pagan poet:

> Oisin, tell me the famous story
> Why thou outlivest, blind and hoary,
> The bad old days.

And Oisin, 'sick with years', tells how, as a young man, he was 'led by the nose Through three enchanted islands, allegorical dreams',[3] until at last, falling from his faery horse, his three hundred years caught up with him and he became 'A creeping

---

[1] *Atlantic Monthly*, CLXI (5) 637.
[2] See also 'To a Young Beauty', written in 1918 (*Collected Poems*, 2nd ed. (1950) p. 157):
> And I may dine at journey's end
> With Landor and with Donne.
[3] 'The Circus Animals' Desertion'.

old man, full of sleep, with the spittle on his beard never dry'. In *The Wanderings of Oisin and Other Poems* (1889) we find also 'The Meditation of the Old Fisherman'. This was followed, at its second printing in book form, by 'The Ballad of Father O'Hart' (who 'died at ninety-four'), 'The Ballad of Moll Magee', and 'The Ballad of the Old Foxhunter' (who dies of old age, surrounded by his 'aged hounds and young'). The people of Faery in 'A Faery Song' are 'old, old and gay',[1] and in the free translation from Ronsard that was to become one of his most famous love poems Yeats bids his beloved

> When you are old and grey and full of sleep,
> And nodding by the fire, take down this book ...

Throughout his life he explored the theme of old age, its losses and its compensations. Far from being broken or silenced by his own advancing years, he turned them into poetry:

> Bodily decrepitude is wisdom; young
> We loved each other and were ignorant.

The young man writing of old age and the old man writing of 'the young in one another's arms' were both in search of wisdom, and as the old man came closer to what the young man had been seeking he wrote increasingly with the accent and authority of the prophet-poet. His earliest literary influences were Blake, whose Prophetic-Books he edited with Edwin Ellis; Shelley, whom he quoted approvingly as saying that 'Poets ... were called in the earliest epoch of the world legislators or prophets, and a poet essentially comprises and unites both these characters';[2] and Spenser, whose 'prophetic' fragment 'Mutabilitie' he singled out for special praise in his Introduction to the *Poems of Spenser* (1907). Shelley and Blake, though both religious in the widest sense, were united in their hatred of established religion, and it is clearly his masters' voices that one hears in Yeats's essay 'The Autumn of the Body' (1898): 'The arts are, I believe, about to take upon their shoulders the burdens that have fallen from the

---

[1] Compare the last lines of 'Lapis Lazuli'.

[2] Yeats, in his essay 'The Philosophy of Shelley's Poetry' (1900), is quoting from Shelley's *A Defence of Poetry*.

shoulders of the priests.' This theme of the artist assuming the lapsed authority of the priest he developed further as his early literary influences were complemented, and to some degree superseded, by personal and political influences – notably his friendship with Maud Gonne and the old Fenian leader, John O'Leary. Louis MacNeice, in his review of *Last Poems and Plays*, rightly speaks of 'Yeats's two passions – Ireland and Art' (see p.45 ). His faith in these he had proclaimed as long ago as 1901, in his essay 'Ireland and the Arts':

we must, I think, if we would win the people again, take upon ourselves the method and fervour of a priesthood. . . .
I would have our writers and craftsmen of many kinds master this history and these legends, and fix upon their memory the appearance of mountains and rivers and make it all visible again in their arts, so that Irishmen, even though they had gone thousands of miles away, would still be in their own country.

There can be little doubt that, consciously or unconsciously, Yeats was modelling himself on his bardic forerunners, whose traditions – so unlike those of Spenser, Shelley, and Blake – were influencing him at this time:

according to the early metrical tracts the *bard* was simply a poet and versifier; the *fili* a poet, but also a scholar and guardian of traditional knowledge; he is especially a prophet and a seer and can wield supernatural powers. In short, he somewhat resembles in his functions the druid of pre-Christian Gaul.[1]

The romantic figure of the prophet-poet dominated Yeats's imagination from the 1880s to his death, and in his fears for his failing eyesight he was clearly a little comforted by the long tradition of blind but visionary poets: Homer, Milton, Raftery. Of all the bards and gleemen that appear in his early stories, the most fully described is Red Hanrahan. Like Michael Gillane in *Cathleen Ni Houlihan*, he forsakes and forgets an earthly love for an unearthly woman, 'the most beautiful the world ever saw'. His love songs are succeeded by – or transformed into – 'songs about Ireland and her griefs', as were Yeats's own. On the top of Ben Bulben he sees a vision of 'tall beautiful young men, and of

[1] Eleanor Knott, *Irish Classical Poetry* 2nd ed. (1960) p. 7.

queen-women . . . and Hanrahan knew them by their whirling flight to be the Sidhe, the ancient defeated gods'. At last he dies, in a high cabin on a hillside, hearing about him 'faint, joyful voices' and 'the continual clashing of swords'.[1] Like Raftery on his deathbed, he is engulfed in a blinding light 'full of great shadowy figures'. The prophet-poet enters his ultimate revelation on the mountain.

In 1917 Yeats married Georgina Hyde-Lees and began to restore the Norman tower at Ballylee that was to become their home and the central symbol of his later poetry. In his fine elegy, 'In Memory of Major Robert Gregory', he says:

> I'll name the friends that cannot sup with us
> Beside a fire of turf in th'ancient tower
> And having talked to some late hour
> Climb up the narrow winding stair to bed:

Like a prophet to his mountain top, or a priest to his pulpit, Yeats for the next twenty years was to 'climb to the tower-top and lean upon broken stone'. The increasingly prophetic poems of these years abound in images of climbing – the Wild Swans at Coole, the Irish Airman, the Fisherman 'Climbing to a place Where stone is dark under froth'. Stone and rock replace the water that dominated the poetic landscape of the early poems. The wild swans 'delight men's eyes'; Major Robert Gregory is driven by 'a lonely impulse of delight' to the fatal 'tumult in the clouds'; and Yeats, in his elegy on his 'dear friend's dear son', reflects that 'all things the delighted eye now sees Were loved by him'. Delight – a rare emotion in the early poetry – from the year of his marriage takes the place of 'sorrow', a dominant word in the early poems appearing in only two written after 1900. Mrs Yeats, it is clear, brought her husband his new delight. This he acknowledges in 'The Gift of Harun Al-Rashid', a poem whose drafts contain the cancelled lines: 'And that was my first news of her that now Is my delight & comfort.'[2] Literature owes more to

[1] Cf. 'To Some I have Talked with by the Fire' and *At the Hawk's Well*, lines 241 and 245.

[2] See Stallworthy, *Between the Lines: W. B. Yeats's Poetry in the Making* (1963) p. 78.

Georgina Hyde-Lees, whose automatic writing provided Yeats
with the framework for most of the finest poems of his last
twenty years, than to Maud Gonne. The change from sorrow to
delight seems the more remarkable when one considers the
private griefs and public disappointments that beset him and his
growing awareness of death. Further light is shed on this
apparent paradox by his poem 'Upon a Dying Lady'. Section VI
of that elegy on Mabel Beardsley is entitled 'Her Courage', and
in it the poet asks that her soul, after death, should

> come face to face,
> Amid that first astonishment, with Grania's shade, . . .
> Aye, and Achilles, Timor, Babar, Barhaim, all
> Who have lived in joy and laughed into the face of Death.

The more Yeats saw of death the more he became convinced that

> Whether man die in his bed
> Or the rifle knock him dead,
> A brief parting from those dear
> Is the worst man has to fear.

Armed with this belief in an afterlife, he came to the conviction
that one must live in joy and – like the ancient heroes – laugh
into the face of Death; 'come Proud, open-eyed and laughing to
the tomb'.[1]

He saw beyond his own terrible vision of 'The Second
Coming'. Ahasuerus, in Shelley's *Hellas*, is said to have 'survived
Cycles of generation and of ruin', and Yeats was, I am sure,
deliberate in following 'The Second Coming' with 'A Prayer for
my Daughter', in which the storm symbolic of the coming fury
is preceded and succeeded by images of generation.

In 1934 he introduced Shri Purohit Swami's translation of *The
Holy Mountain*. This book gave him his material for 'Meru', the
poem that ends both his sequence of 'Supernatural Songs' and *A
Full Moon in March*. In this sonnet Yeats, through the eyes of
the oriental ascetic, sees that man

[1] For the influence of Nietzsche's concept of 'laughter' on Yeats,
see S. B. Bushrui, '*The King's Threshold*: A Defence of Poetry', in
*A Review of English Literature*, IV (3) 81–94.

despite his terror, cannot cease
Ravening through century after century,
Ravening, raging, and uprooting that he may come
Into the desolation of reality:

One might consider this a conclusion of total despair, but for
the strongly buoyant – even exultant – rhythm of the line that
follows: 'Egypt and Greece, good-bye, and good-bye, Rome!'[1]
There is a similar movement in the opening line of 'The Gyres',
the first of the *Last Poems*: 'The gyres! the gyres! Old Rocky
Face, look forth;' and one must here admire the skill with which
Yeats links not only poem with poem, but also book with book.
Old Rocky Face – glossed in Mrs Yeats's copy of *Last Poems* as
'Delphic Oracle'[2] – is clearly a development of the hermit upon
Mount Meru 'Caverned in night'. In the drafts of 'The Gyres'
Old Rocky Face even appears as 'Old cavern man, old rocky
face'.[3] He is also described as 'wrinkled rocky face',[4] an anticipation of the 'eyes mid many wrinkles' that look out 'On all the
tragic scene' from the carving of lapis lazuli in the poem of that
name. It is generally agreed that the Rocky Face of 'The Gyres',
the Rocky Voice of 'The Man and the Echo', is compounded of
Delphic oracle, oriental ascetic, the cave-dwelling Ahasuerus, and
an echo or recollection of the phrase 'rockie face' in Ben Jonson's
poem 'My Picture Left in Scotland' (see p. 140). T. R. Henn has
called attention to what, I am convinced, must have been a fifth
element in its composition: 'the carved stone head, high in the
S.E. wall of Thoor Ballylee' (see p. 113). Yeats would naturally
have identified himself with the weathered face staring out
towards Coole Park, whose ruin he had correctly prophesied in
'Coole Park, 1929'. Extending this line of thought, it is tempting
to speculate on whether he may not have had Robert Gregory in
mind when he wrote: 'Hector is dead and there's a light in Troy.'
Old Rocky Face can afford to 'laugh in tragic joy', just as
the ascetic could exclaim with something approaching gaiety,

[1] Cf. *The Resurrection*, lines 401–2: 'O Athens, Alexandria, Rome,
something has come to destroy you.'
[2] Curtis Bradford, *Yeats at Work* (1965) p. 148.
[3] Ibid. p. 145.                               [4] Ibid. p. 143.

'Egypt and Greece, good bye,' because he sees the alternation of the 'Cycles of generation and of ruin', and knows that the one would be impossible without the other. The ascetic's illumination comes upon him, in the time-honoured neo-Platonic tradition, when he is 'Caverned in night'. Related to this concept is Yeats's belief that as day follows night the new gyre rises from darkness,

> From marble of a broken sepulchre,
> Or dark between the polecat and the owl. ...

Similarly, 'The Statues' ends with an assertion of magnificent arrogance worthy of Yeats's bardic predecessors:

> We Irish, born into that ancient sect
> But thrown upon this filthy modern tide
> And by its formless spawning fury wrecked,
> Climb to our proper dark ...

The sibylline voice that introduced *New Poems* (1938), speaking from a mountain summit, and the unshuffled *Last Poems and Two Plays* (1939), speaking from 'Under Ben Bulben', makes perhaps its most eloquent statement in 'Lapis Lazuli'. There can be no doubt that Yeats identifies himself with the Chinamen climbing their mountain. He 'delights' to imagine them staring 'On all the tragic scene': that it is tragic does not annul his delight.

> One asks for mournful melodies;
> Accomplished fingers begin to play.

As Keats's imagination conjured music from the marble pipes and timbrels of the Grecian urn, so Yeats's accomplished fingers bring the lapis lazuli to life, and his melody is far from mournful.

The voice that sings 'Of what is past, or passing, or to come' in 'The Gyres',[1] 'Lapis Lazuli', 'The Statues', 'The Black Tower', and 'Under Ben Bulben' is not the only voice of the *Last Poems*, of course, though it is the one that carries furthest. T. R. Henn argues convincingly that this section of the *Collected Poems* falls into four main, but interrelated, divisions: the 'cosmic' poems, the Cuchulain group, the ballads, and the so-called 'lust and rage'

---

[1] The three stanzas of this poem consider, respectively, past, present, and future.

poems (see p. 99). If one considers not their range of subject but their range of voice, one discovers three distinct tones of the one distinct voice: that of the old poet who speaks as an old poet, whether in the high, bardic tone of 'The Gyres'; the middle, personal tone of 'The Municipal Gallery Revisited'; or the low, 'gleeman' tone of the ballads. It is one and the same voice that celebrates Cuchulain and the Irish heroes of a later age – Parnell, Casement, Pearse, and The O'Rahilly; one and the same man who 'holds dear Lovers of horses and of women', is 'mad about women', and intended his *Last Poems* to end with 'Politics':

> And maybe what they say is true
> Of war and war's alarms,
> But O that I were young again
> And held her in my arms!

In assembling the contents of this *Casebook* I have had one guiding principle of selection: that each review, letter, and article should contribute to as balanced an historical survey of informed critical opinion on the *Last Poems* as is possible within the limits of a short anthology. I have allowed myself a generous sampling of reviews, being anxious to represent the full range of immediate critical reaction – in Ireland, England, and America – to Yeats's poetic last will and testament; and because reviews tend now to be less accessible in libraries than the more important articles and books. One cannot expect the judgement of reviewers to be final. Through no fault of their own they have frequently to pass sentence after little more (and not infrequently a little less) than a single reading; and when the book before them is by as complex a poet as Yeats, it is not surprising if some of their verdicts are reversed by later generations of critics. Few would now agree, for instance, that *Purgatory* and *The Death of Cuchulain* are 'worthless' (Auden), 'flat failures' (MacNeice). Though a poet's critics usually seem wiser – after the event – than his reviewers, there is much to be learnt from an age's first reaction to the art it has produced.

Kathleen Raine, herself a fine poet of the generation that

followed Yeats, in her Introduction to the 1964 reissue of *Letters on Poetry from W. B. Yeats to Dorothy Wellesley*, paints a skilful portrait of Yeats as he appeared to the poets of the thirties, and so explains his unpopularity at that time. It should perhaps be added that Yeats, especially in his later years, was as combatant and uncompromising as his natural courtesy would allow and did nothing to court the popularity of those whose views he did not respect. However, 'the wild old wicked man' who, proudly declaring his bias, denounced democratic values and advocated eugenic reform in *On the Boiler*, is revealed as a gentle and generous friend in his letters to Dorothy Wellesley. I have included a considerable number of these, both for the picture they give of Yeats in old age and for the fascinating light they shed on the process of poetic composition.

In my selection of chapters and articles for the latter part of this anthology, I have tried to represent what seem to me the half-dozen most rewarding avenues of approach to the *Last Poems*. First of three critics whose work I have chosen for its view of the book as a whole, Curtis Bradford examines the inter-relationship, both thematic and musical, of poem with poem. T. R. Henn, with his unrivalled knowledge of Yeats's background and sources, relates the *Last Poems* to the events, ideas, objects, and *dramatis personae* that prompted them. In 'The Accent of Yeats's *Last Poems*' he examines the 'lust and rage' that certain reviewers found so distasteful, not perceiving the philosophical and satirical implications behind so many seemingly personal poems. J. R. Mulryne shows how the poet achieves his victory over the 'incoherence' and 'tragedy' of the actual world, imposing upon it an imaginative transformation whereby the living and impermanent attain the condition of sculpture. Each of the next five articles is concerned with one of the more complex poems: 'Lapis Lazuli', 'The Statues', 'The Municipal Gallery Revisited', 'The Black Tower', and 'Under Ben Bulben'. The first two are approached through their roots, as it were, in Yeats's reading; the third – not, I think, a great poem, but one central to an understanding of the poet – through an elucidation of its references; and the last two through his revealing manuscript drafts. Though it is clearly right that the poems and the plays should now be segregated in their separate volumes, we should not overlook the extent to which they are interrelated, or ignore the fact that Yeats intended *Purgatory* and *The Death of Cuchulain* to be published with his *Last Poems*. Peter Ure, in his discussion of the ironies that underlie the action of these plays, shows them to be far from 'flat failures'.

The anthologist who can truthfully 'wish not one man more' is a rare and happy man. I have not his luck or judgement, but unlike many less fortunate anthologists I have the consolation of a Select Bibliography in which to make partial atonement for my sins of omission. This I commend to the attention of anyone interested in mining the deeper levels of the *Last Poems*.

*January 1967*                                    JON STALLWORTHY

PART ONE

Contemporary Opinions
1939-40

## W. H. Auden

## IN MEMORY OF W. B. YEATS (1939)
*(d. January 1939)*

I

He disappeared in the dead of winter:
The brooks were frozen, the airports almost deserted,
And snow disfigured the public statues;
The mercury sank in the mouth of the dying day.
O all the instruments agree
The day of his death was a dark cold day.

Far from his illness
The wolves ran on through the evergreen forests,
The peasant river was untempted by the fashionable quays;
By mourning tongues
The death of the poet was kept from his poems.

But for him it was his last afternoon as himself,
An afternoon of nurses and rumours;
The provinces of his body revolted,
The squares of his mind were empty,
Silence invaded the suburbs,
The current of his feeling failed: he became his admirers.

Now he is scattered among a hundred cities
And wholly given over to unfamiliar affections,
To find his happiness in another kind of wood
And be punished under a foreign code of conscience;
The words of a dead man
Are modified in the guts of the living.

But in the importance and noise of to-morrow
When the brokers are roaring like beasts on the floor of the
     Bourse,
And the poor have the sufferings to which they are fairly
     accustomed,
And each in the cell of himself is almost convinced of his freedom,
A few thousand will think of this day
As one thinks of a day when one did something slightly unusual.
O all the instruments agree
The day of his death was a dark cold day.


## II

You were silly like us: your gift survived it all;
The parish of rich women, physical decay,
Yourself; mad Ireland hurt you into poetry.
Now Ireland has her madness and her weather still,
For poetry makes nothing happen: it survives
In the valley of its saying where executives
Would never want to tamper; it flows south
From ranches of isolation and the busy griefs,
Raw towns that we believe and die in; it survives,
A way of happening, a mouth.


## III

Earth, receive an honoured guest;
William Yeats is laid to rest:
Let the Irish vessel lie
Emptied of its poetry.


Time that is intolerant
Of the brave and innocent,
And indifferent in a week
To a beautiful physique,

Worships language and forgives
Everyone by whom it lives;
Pardons cowardice, conceit,
Lays its honours at their feet.

Time that with this strange excuse
Pardoned Kipling and his views,
And will pardon Paul Claudel,
Pardons him for writing well.

In the nightmare of the dark
All the dogs of Europe bark,
And the living nations wait,
Each sequestered in its hate;

Intellectual disgrace
Stares from every human face,
And the seas of pity lie
Locked and frozen in each eye.

Follow, poet, follow right
To the bottom of the night,
With your unconstraining voice
Still persuade us to rejoice;

With the farming of a verse
Make a vineyard of the curse,
Sing of human unsuccess
In a rapture of distress;

In the deserts of the heart
Let the healing fountain start,
In the prison of his days
Teach the free man how to praise.

# Winfield Townley Scott

## YEATS AT 73 (1938)*

THE pleasantest sight in the contemporary literary scene is the continuing vigor of William Butler Yeats's poetry. Many an aging poet must take the fair or the unfair disregard of newer men; but Yeats at seventy-three continues to command the homage of mature craftsmen and of the very children in the craft. He seems, to readers and writers alike, our best example of the integrated, triumphant artist. I saw an immediate illustration of this, one August night last summer. The Abbey at Dublin produced for the first time a new, brief play by Yeats called *Purgatory*. The play's merits are those of a well-written soliloquy; its dramatic moments were frankly theatrical and its total effect was one of confusion. Yet the ovation that followed was right. Yeats sat there in the audience and the enormous applause was for everything he has ever said and, so, for what he is. The delight of paying honor is sweet but rarely so justified as when Mr Yeats – tall, grave, gray, weary, and I may say beautiful – at last stood up in the Abbey Theatre.

Such honor is accumulative; it becomes fact and history – and an impediment to criticism. Even without Yeats in the flesh, *New Poems* cannot be read plain: the poet's fame is a nearly unavoidable distraction between the reader and the book. Reviewers have maintained an unbroken rule of writing 'Yeats-the-greatest-living-poet' as one word until anyone who admires the sentiment (and I do) finds it difficult to judge, if he tries, just where Yeats's work is great and how great. If a man is fortunate enough to have a long and widely admired career, it follows to the last that anything he says commands interest if for no other reason than that

* A review of *New Poems*.

he is saying it. And this is especially true when the artist has
sustained the strength and variety of his art.

In this new collection of poems 'The Municipal Gallery
Revisited' is a pertinent example of a Yeats poem whose specific
value is hard to estimate. We proceed with Mr Yeats, hear his
nostalgic comments upon Casement, the Gregorys, John Synge
and others, and he says:

> You that would judge me do not judge alone
> This book or that, come to this hallowed place
> Where my friends' portraits hang and look thereon;
> Ireland's history in their lineaments trace;
> Think where man's glory most begins and ends
> And say my glory was I had such friends.

It is moving – as autobiography from a source we cannot choose
but hear. As poetry, it is excellent prose rather wilfully rhymed.

Yeats's poetry began with this tune:

> The woods of Arcady are dead,
> And over is their antique joy;
> Of old the world on dreaming fed;
> Grey Truth is now her painted toy...

To use his own later word, the embroidery of that tune proceeded
in lavish and seductive detail; his eventual conviction that the
woods of Arcady were the painted toy and Grey Truth the real
rock saved a distinguished poet to far greater statement. The
growing liveliness of his mind created an increasing simplicity
and eloquence of poetry and, in such recent books as *The Tower*
and *The Winding Stair*, achieved a rich, passionate utterance.
The expression in poetry of a mind, a personality, has seldom
been so direct; it has seemed unimpeded by poetic form – as
though the outpouring of thought were indeed the creation of
poetry. This is lyric art. We are not lacking in lyric art in this
century; we have samples and they can be analyzed, like wines,
by those who study to be wise – ingredient, taste, density, age
can be stated. But what can those learned in wines say of clear,
cold water?

Like most poets, Yeats probably has not a great mind. – No,
of course I cannot define a 'great mind'; I suggest it must be

more departmental and purer than a poet's. The purity of Yeats' most excellent verse flowers in equations of thought and feeling Thus when he says that, thinking of the things he used to say and do or things he did not do or say: 'My conscience or my vanity appalled', I doubt if mood alone could go that deep, or if thought alone could condense pathos and humor to such a flash of revelation. Where poetry is deepest and simplest it is most anonymous and universal; in the achievement of that, Yeats has repeatedly triumphed.

But as to the *New Poems* in particular. Grey Truth begins to break the artistry here and there, as though by itself it were enough.

The most frequent mood of *New Poems* is that of an old man. Yeats returns again to thinking of his father, of Lady Gregory and Maud Gonne: 'All the Olympians; a thing never known again.' In the opening poem he says 'A greater, a more gracious time has gone'; and in the Municipal Gallery piece, 'The Curse of Cromwell', and others, the tone is the same. Dependent upon the same mood are the occasional examples of determined, half-mad balladry of lusty living – 'The Wild Old Wicked Man' is a good sample – as though, since much that was noble and fine has perished, whatever is truly alive is a violence of the flesh. A four-line poem, 'The Spur', is a commentary:

> You think it horrible that lust and rage
> Should dance attendance upon my old age;
> They were not such a plague when I was young;
> What else have I to spur me into song?

Yeats expends tight-lipped rage in several political songs: of Roger Casement, Parnell, and in one delightful ballad of 'The O'Rahilly' who couldn't stay away from the Trouble and ended in Henry Street, his R.I.P. written by himself in his own blood on the doorway where they found him. Two or three of these poems show Yeats's larger conclusions:

> Parnell came down the road, he said to a cheering man;
> 'Ireland shall get her freedom and you still break stone.'

and, 'The Great Day':

Hurrah for revolution and more cannon shot;
A beggar upon horseback lashes a beggar upon foot;
Hurrah for revolution and cannon come again,
The beggars have changed places but the lash goes on.

That is flat statement, not unusual among the elders who have seen the world, but most unfashionable among younger poets who, these days, are so intent upon seeing a better world. From the 'big bones of Yeats' these are 'disappointed, middle-aging words'. I should like wholeheartedly to believe in Archibald MacLeish – but then, for that matter, I should be glad to believe in Jesus Christ. 'Come unto me all ye that labor and are heavy-laden, and I will give you rest'; poetry, Mr MacLeish – yet we are not delivered. Whatever our hopes and whatever the end, Mr Yeats's quatrain is thus far the fact.

The deeper occurrences of poetry in *New Poems* are not infrequent. Most of the writing is pitched to the level of plain-speaking most characteristic of the later Yeats; some of it, as in 'Lapis Lazuli', is ruminative and delightful; some of it is more formal. 'The Three Bushes' is a formal ballad of the lady who loved a man yet loved her virginity more: and so sent her maid to the lover's bed. In the ballad and in several brief, dependent songs, Yeats plays freshly on the symbols of body and soul. Here and there in these pages, too, there occur those sudden liftings of language:

Stretch toward the moonless midnight of the trees
As though that hand could reach to where they stand

– and on, through a strange, magic poem.

Yeats says many things in these *New Poems*, all of them of compelling interest. The notes of age and farewell sound in many of the poems, yet with the vigor of the un-contented old man Yeats says he is. The total of the poetry lessens, still the clean diction is here, the words are set by the hand of a master of English; and the tone is still one of authority unmatched in the lyric verse of this century.

# Frederic Prokosch

## YEATS'S TESTAMENT (1939)*

THE importance of this collection of Yeats's poems (aside from its quite peculiar flavor – the testament of an isolated, violent poet about to die) lies in its value as an index: the validity of his time-worn manner, the continued upward curve of his career, the great freshening power that even old age might conceivably provide – they are here put to the test. It is usual with a posthumous work either listlessly to overpraise or benignly to dismiss. With this particular volume, at least, there is no occasion for either.

There are sixty pages in the book: twenty poems, two short plays. It is impossible, if one reads them at all carefully, to read them through without a novel and intense excitement. Probably it would be irrelevant to argue that these poems are his best – as it would be irrelevant to argue that 'Guernica' is a finer painting than Picasso's early clowns and absinthe drinkers. This much can be said safely: they include, astoundingly, almost every variety of form and tone he has used before; and of the twenty at least ten are as masterly as any poem he has written.

Subsequent to the brilliance and profusion of *The Tower* and the *Winding Stair* (presumably his two best books, certainly the ones which crystallized the superiority of his late work over his earlier) it seemed that a further development occurred, in the direction of the angular, bleak, acrid Crazy Jane poems. Then a certain confusion appeared to set in; the 'foolish passionate man' grew into one intermittently torn by 'lust and rage'. The collection which appeared some two years ago was pinched and comfortless indeed.

However, in these final poems there are echoes of the earlier, more rounded and grandiloquent manner. They are highly lyrical

* A review of *Last Poems and Two Plays*.

and eyen ornate, more richly colored, more deftly patterned. Sometimes clear and elegiac in sound, they are never really clear or elegiac.

> When a man grows old his joy
> Grows more deep day after day,
> His empty heart is full at length,
> But he has need of all that strength
> Because of the increasing Night
> That opens her mystery and fright.

In such lines, seemingly direct, one presently perceives the thrilling and frightful *double entendre* – the uncompromising self-disgust and humiliation of his old age sharpening every edge. The effect of these pages, frantically emphasizing as they do all that has gone before, is at times terrifying. It is a sort of magnificence I have met nowhere else.

The old images recur – like ghosts: self-admitted effigies –

> . . . and yet when all is said,
> It was the dream itself enchanted me.

The old figures appear once again, rubbing shoulders, acquiring a bizarre freshness from propinquity and the dreamy self-identifying loyalty Yeats felt toward them: Michael Angelo, Oisin, Pearse and Connolly, Pythagoras, Cuchulain, Parnell. And the old décor too – the Post Office, the tower, the dolphins, the ruined house, ancient Ireland. They are juxtaposed and brought into focus with a dexterity and pertinence no surrealist could surpass. It is the terrible burden of old age, that 'foul rag-and-bone shop of the heart', again and again impelled into activity by the glamour which his ceaseless brooding cast over his former passions, his own lost youth and beauty, the qualities of beauty, pride, belligerence and learning in his dead friends.

The best poems are 'The Man and the Echo', 'A Bronze Head', 'News for the Delphic Oracle', 'The Statues', and 'The Circus Animals' Desertion'. In these exist most conspicuously the unique and flawless music, as well as the vigor and virtuosity with which he produces in a single daring image the whole luxuriance of a highly elaborate idea.

No! Greater than Pythagoras, for the man
That with a mallet or a chisel modelled these
Calculations that look but casual flesh, put down
All Asiatic vague immensities. ...

The two plays are very short – a dozen pages or so. Both are
spasmodic, fragmentary, horrible. Both deal with the linked
themes of passion and death – or rather, lust and homicide. Old
men 'about to die' (a phrase which is a haunting refrain throughout the book) are the protagonists. In *The Death of Cuchulain*,
there is a frightful scene in which the blind man, knife in hand,
fumbles upward along the dying Cuchulain's body, fastened to a
pillar to keep him from falling. Finally he reaches the neck, and
Cuchulain cries,

There floats out there
The shape that I shall take when I am dead,
My soul's first shape, a soft feathery shape,
And is not that a strange shape for a soul
Of a great fighting man?

Yeats seemed to have attained to an almost legendary view of
humanity, in which could be projected in their full horror acts
which in a less remote and rarefied atmosphere would be
unacceptable.

It is interesting to contrast Yeats with that other awe-inspiring
poet of old age, his opposite in every way: Walt Whitman.
Shrewd contemporary minds might see foreshadowed, in these,
two well-known opposing ideologies. Yeats drew continually
from the vast, energetic phantoms of his mind; Whitman only
from the quasi-photographic, masculine figures of his own landscape. Yeats brought to perfection certain rigid verse forms of his
own; Whitman exploited every variety of looseness, reluctant
ever to repeat an image or pattern (though in the end presenting
a far greater uniformity of impulse than Yeats). Yeats ended his
days in despair, unsated passion, and intense disgust with the
contemporary world; Whitman with an oddly unimpaired
optimism, and (paradoxically) every evidence of satisfied desire.
Of the two Yeats ended more impressively, and it may be said
that no poet has ever worked so relentlessly and sublimely

toward a close. Though far less expansive and perhaps less remunerative than Whitman, it appears that his unfaltering preference for an ugly truth rather than a palatable hypothesis, deeply rooted in the richness of his experience, together with his life-long veneration for his craft, involved in the end a corresponding sharpness of intellect and eye. He will never date; if he were ever to do so, he would already, for his ways of thinking are unfashionable in 'this foul world in its decline and fall'.

*Times Literary Supplement*

# W. B. YEATS: THE LAST POEMS (1939)*

CIRCUMSTANCE gives a melancholy interest to these last poems and plays from the hand of William Butler Yeats, for all of them were written during the last year or so of his life. Some of the poems, including the poetic testament, 'Under Ben Bulben', have already appeared in periodicals, but others are printed here for the first time. The remarkable vigour of thought and of imagination, which increased with the poet's years, is shown here once more. A few of the passing snatches were perhaps too hastily written, and at times one cannot help feeling that the great inspiration was flagging. We watch the poet brooding over the symbols and imaginative signs which prevailed in his work for so many years. Occasionally it is clear that he was too easily intoxicated by that musical rhetoric which he invented for himself in his last period. But sudden line or stanza still surprises us, as if 'the eddying cat-headed bird', which always fascinated the poet's thought, suddenly had struck.

In many of these retrospective poems the labour of composition becomes its own drama and difficulties resolve themselves in song.

> I sought a theme and sought for it in vain,
> I sought it daily for six weeks or so.
> Maybe at last, being but a broken man,
> I must be satisfied with my heart, although
> Winter and summer till old age began
> My circus animals were all on show,
> Those stilted boys, that burnished chariot,
> Lion and woman and the Lord knows what.

Such lines as these, even if they are disturbing to those who expect a deeper commentary on life or on art, must attract the

* Unsigned review of *Last Poems and Two Plays*.

young by their fine gesture. The contrast between youth and age, heroic dream and the commonplaces of outer reality are once more pushed to extremes. We note the further development of plain derogatory images, 'man's dirty slate', 'the foul rag-and-bone shop of the heart'. Helen has come to the gutter at last and her feet

> Practise a tinker shuffle
> Picked up on a street.

In choosing beggarly, down-at-heel images rather than the brand-new inventions of a modern world, the poet was essentially a romantic and therefore his comment on European tension is set in the terms of a past imagery.

> That civilization may not sink,
> Its great battle lost,
> Quiet the dog, tether the pony
> To a distant post;
> Our master Caesar is in the tent
> Where the maps are spread,
> His eyes fixed upon nothing,
> A hand under his head.

In form and length the two plays are little more than dramatic episodes. In *The Death of Cuchulain* Yeats returned to a theme which he had never expressed with complete satisfaction. The Prologue in prose is spoken by a very old man 'looking like something out of mythology'. The little speech, for all its humour, shows that the poet was too self-conscious of the fact that the heroic mood receives scant attention today. In the Epilogue it is made quite clear that Yeats wished to give body and substance to the mood by linking it with the new national symbols of the 1916 Rising. *Purgatory*, which was produced at the Abbey Drama Festival last year and caused much irrelevant controversy, is less successful. Its theme is the decline of the old landed families; but that theme is mingled with the oddities of other-worldly cycles. Both subjects are forced rather violently into a small dramatic framework of event, but the treatment lacks that interplay of human emotion which alone makes violent action tolerable on the stage.

# J. J. Hogan

## ON *LAST POEMS AND PLAYS* (1940)*

THE wrapper of *Last Poems and Plays* quotes a critic declaring that these 'include, astoundingly, almost every variety of form and tone he has used before, and of the twenty at least ten are as masterly as anything he has written'. This is to say too much, I think. The varieties of form and tone hardly go beyond those of Yeats's other late work. The poem are of the kinds he had been writing latterly, and few of them are equal to the best of those kinds. We frequently get flashes of power and beauty in pieces that are not altogether satisfying, probably because they are vaguer echoes of others written a few years earlier; in some cases it may be that the poems are unfinished. Two sorts of poem figure more largely than in the earlier collections, poems of crude animality and poems in the Irish ballad manner. The former are mostly artistic mistakes. The ballads are better art; but they will hardly rank very high in his work as a whole.

The real things in the book are the personal things, the old man's memories, his judgments on what he has seen, his preparation for the end – the cold eye cast on life and death. They are, of course, second recollections and second testaments these, but the subject – Yeats's strong personality, aloof and yet both richly friended and self-enriching – sustains them, and they will be remembered among his utterances. In six or seven poems we see the old man striving still to remake himself more worthy of his own esteem:

> Grant me an old man's frenzy,
> Myself I must remake
> Till I am Timon and Lear
> Or that William Blake

* A review.

> Who beat upon the wall
> Till Truth obeyed his call.

Such as these, and Michael Angelo, are the models he sets before him, and with these the ancestors whom his self-forged religion canonises:

> Sandymount Corbets, that notable man
> Old William Pollexfen,
> 'The smuggler Middleton, Butlers far back,
> Half legendary men.

And ever the refrain recurs, *But I am not content.* Memories and former selves no less than ancestors embody themselves to question and reproach this man whose eye is always turned inward:

> I lie awake night after night
> And never get the answers right.
> Did that play of mine send out
> Certain men the English shot?
> Did words of mine put too much strain
> On that woman's reeling brain?
> Could my spoken words have checked
> That whereby a house lay wrecked?
> And all seems evil until I
> Sleepless would lie down and die.

The last piece of all, 'Under Ben Bulben', is Yeats's final testament to his kind, who are not 'the sort now growing up'. Stoicism, re-incarnation, the reality of images alone and their command over all else, these are flung into coldly glowing words for the last time. The Irish poets, as makers of controlling images for our race, are exhorted to

> Scorn the sort now growing up
> All out of shape from toe to top,
> Their unremembering hearts and heads
> Base-born products of base beds.
> Sing the peasantry, and then
> Hard-riding country gentlemen,
> The holiness of monks, and after
> Porter-drinkers' randy laughter;
> Sing the lords and ladies gay

> That were beaten into the clay
> Through seven heroic centuries;
> Cast your mind on other days
> That we in coming days may be
> Still the indomitable Irishry.

The poem ends with the words he commands to be cut on his tombstone, as true to himself and almost as striking as Swift's:

> Cast a cold eye
> On life, on death.
> Horseman, pass by!

# J. C. Ransom

# OLD AGE OF A POET (1940)*

YEATS had as fine a personal endowment as a poet requires, and sometimes his successes were complete. Perhaps he was as great a lyric poet as our time permitted, and less than the greatest poets in the language only because of the special handicap under which modern poets must have labored. The last two centuries have been bad ones for the poets. I make the usual remark that we live in the age of science, but I will try to find a few words that will be a little more explicit than that.

Modern science is the only strict science. It seems fair to say that it has achieved its brilliant successes by means of resolutely simplifying its program, and limiting the act of free imagination that might otherwise muddle it. Science attacks its problem by defining its problems, and proceeding seriatim: *divide et impera*; one thing at a time; and, in every distinct operation, suppression of the ranging imagination. For modern science operates with images just as poetry does, or just as did old science, which was poetico-science. It handles the images harshly in order to focus and make them manageable; regularly reducing them till they become bare patterns, or stereotypes, as clean and useful as they are void of the diffuse interest which is called aesthetic. So the brilliant successes came duly to crown the new technique, and that was splendid. But then, unduly, the successes over-impressed the poets, and seriously determined their practice too. We may be sure now that the scientific imagination and the poetic imagination are not of the same kind, and that the kinds of knowledge which they intend are not the same; and that it is just as impossible in the modern world for poetry to flourish in the practice of a pseudo-scientific imagination as it was impossible in the old

* A review of *Last Poems and Plays.*

world for a real science to arise unless it would repudiate the imaginative processes of poets. Yet that was the role which poetry assumed deliberately in the eighteenth century, and continued, in spite of desperate efforts to find another one, in the nineteenth and early twentieth centuries. In all that period no poet has been more detached from the low standards prevailing in his art, better aware of its state of demoralization, than was Yeats. For fifty years he explored the possibilities of recovery.

Of the new poems, written during the last three years of his old age and gathered and published now since his death . . . few will compete for a place within the canon of Yeats's best poems. Briefly, they are little, and casual; or they are personal, and nostalgic or vituperative, and miss the delicate strategy of the imaginative process. What they do have is the style; they are all by Yeats. I quote from 'A Bronze Head':

> No dark tomb-haunter once; her form all full
> As though with magnanimity of light,
> Yet a most gentle woman; who can tell
> Which of her forms has shown her substance right?
> Or maybe substance can be composite,
> Profound McTaggart thought so, and in a breath
> A mouthful held the extreme of life and death.

Here there is an idiom that writes the poet's signature unmistakably; a distinctiveness of the sort that we might receive from the passage by Shakespeare, or Milton, or Keats. Yet it is not quite as good as it sounds. The item that disturbs me is the one about the profound McTaggart. The most important aspect of Yeats's genius, I imagine, was his carefully nurtured gift for pure intrinsic particularity, for committing himself even in his 'noblest' moments to the image with absolutely local detail; a feat whose secret had been all but lost to English poetry. (The ranging of the poetic imagination expresses itself most characteristically in lighting upon the absolute unmediated detail; it would not belong in the scientific operation.) But McTaggart is an unhappy particularity to rest the case on. Whatever the admirable Hegelian scholar may have meant to Yeats, he is not Pythagoras, and in fact he is defined for most of us by those footnotes that call his name in the academic treatises in ethics and metaphysics; in other words, as an item of the scientific rather than the poetic imagination.

I will quote also the short poem, 'Beautiful Lofty Things':

Beautiful lofty things: O'Leary's noble head;
My father upon the Abbey stage, before him a raging crowd:
'This Land,of Saints,' and then as the applause died out,
'Of plaster Saints'; his beautiful mischievous head thrown back.
Standish O'Grady supporting himself between the tables
Speaking to a drunken audience high nonsensical words;
Augusta Gregory seated at her great ormulu table,
Her eightieth winter approaching: 'Yesterday he threatened my
    life.
I told him that nightly from six to seven I sat at this table,
The blinds drawn up'; Maud Gonne at Howth station waiting a
    train,
Pallas Athene in that straight back and arrogant head:
All the Olympians; a thing never known again.

Here one has the feeling that the detail is local in some sense without being local in the real or philosophical sense; that it is self-glorifying, which is being not local but parochial; that it is too typical, and too neatly assembled; that it is put together just as other co-ordinate data are often put together by science to make out a 'case'; and that the case is, namely, that Yeats's Ireland has had its Olympian moment too. This poet at his best would not have confused the innocent poetic fact with its assertive generalization.

# Louis MacNeice

## YEATS'S EPITAPH (1940)*

DURING the last ten years, Yeats has had more bouquets from the critics than any other poet of our time. It was refreshing to see these critics and also many of the younger poets committing themselves to enthusiasm for an older contemporary; their praise, however, was sometimes uncritical and sometimes, on a long-term view, injurious to its subject. There were reviewers who felt Yeats was a safe bet – safe because he was an exotic; anyone can praise a bird of paradise, but you have to have some knowledge before you go buying Rhode Island Reds. There is a double point that needs making – first that Yeats was not so exotic as is popularly assumed, second that on the whole his exoticism was not an asset but a liability. He was partly aware of this himself; in his middle period he fought clear of the dead hand of Walter Pater and deliberately set out to make his poetry less 'poetic' and in his later years (the years when he was a devotee of Balzac) he paid at least lip-homage to the principle of 'Homo sum. . . .' His failure fully to practise this principle was due to a constitutional inhumanity.

I say this in honor to his memory. If you believe a man was a genius, it is an insult to him to ignore his deficiencies and peculiarities. One of the most peculiar poets in our history, Yeats was also extraordinarily lacking in certain qualities which the greater poets usually possess; in so far as he achieved greatness it proves, not the power of inspiration or any other such woolly miracle – all that it proves is the miracle of artistic integrity. For this was a quality he possessed even though as a man he may sometimes have been a fraud. His more naïve enemies regard him as knave or fool all through – at best as a 'silly old thing'; his

* A review of *Last Poems and Plays*.

more naïve admirers regard him as God-intoxicated and therefore impeccable. It is high time for us to abandon this sloppy method of assessment; if poetry is important it deserves more from us than irresponsible gibes on the one hand or zany gush on the other.

Take Yeats's two passions – Ireland and Art. We have to remember that, in regard to both, his attitude was conditioned by a comparatively narrow set of circumstances and that, in judging his services to Ireland and Art, we shall be very shortsighted if we reapply his own heavily blinkered concepts of either; it is a lucky thing for the artist that his work usually outruns his ideology. Yeats talked a good deal about magic and beauty and mysticism, but his readers have no right to gabble these words like parrots and call what they are doing appreciation. Beauty is *not* the mainspring of poetry and, although a few poets have been genuine mystics, Yeats, unlike his friend A. E., was certainly not one of them; he had what might be called a mystical sense of value, but that is a different thing and a thing which perhaps for *all* artists is a *sine qua non*.

Yeats's poetry reached its peak in *The Winding Stair* (1933). The *Last Poems* now published represent the Indian summer of his virile, gossipy, contumacious, arrogant, magnificently eccentric old age. Although the book as a whole certainly lacks the depth and range of *The Tower* or *The Winding Stair*, although the septuagenarian virility is sometimes too exhibitionist, although he overdoes certain old tricks and falls into needless obscurities, and although the two plays here included are flat failures, there is still enough vitality and elegance to compensate for certain disappointments. Few poets in English literature have been able to write lyrics after thirty-five; the astonishing thing about Yeats is that he remained essentially a lyric poet till the last. Even the enormous cranky pseudo-philosophy of *A Vision* only served as an occasion for further lyrics. Yeats's ingredients became odder and odder but, because they were at least dry and hard, they helped him to assert a joy of life which was comparatively lacking in his early Celtic or pre-Raphaelite twilights. The great discovery of the later Yeats was that joy need not imply softness and that boredom is something more than one gets in dreams. Axel has been refuted; 'Hamlet and Lear are gay'.

Ireland is very prominent in these last poems. Yeats had for a long time regarded the essential Ireland as incarnate in the country gentry and the peasantry, his ideal society being static and indeed based upon caste. The Irish 'Troubles', however, evoked in him an admiration, even an envy, for the dynamic revolutionary. His thought, in assimilating this element, became to some extent dialectical; he began to conceive of life as a developing whole, a whole which depends upon the conflict of the parts. He even began to write in praise of war, a false inference from a premise which is essentially valid –

> when all words are said
> And a man is fighting mad,
> Something drops from eyes long blind,
> He completes his partial mind. . . .

Physical violence being a simple thing, the Yeats who honored it took to writing in ballad forms, while the contemplative Yeats continued to use a grand rhetorical manner and a complex inlay of esoteric ideas and images; there are good examples of both in this book. There are also, as in the preceding volumes, a number of poems about himself and his friends; once again he goes around with a highly colored spotlight; it is amusing to turn from one of these poems, 'Beautiful Lofty Things', which contains a reference to a public banquet in Dublin, to George Moore's account of the same banquet in *Ave*. The most revealing poem in this book is 'The Circus Animals' Desertion', where Yeats with admirable ruthlessness looks back on his various elaborate efforts to project himself on to the world – Celtic legend, Maud Gonne, symbolic drama. In this excellent and moving poem a self-centered old man rises above his personality by pinning it down for what it is.

# W. H. Auden

## YEATS: MASTER OF DICTION (1940)*

'EVERYTHING he wrote was read,' Yeats said in one of his last poems, and, indeed, he was unusually fortunate, for few poets have so managed to complete their career without suffering any reverses of reputation, at least with the young, and still fewer have written their most widely acclaimed work in the second half of their life. The universal admiration which his later poems have commanded is all the more surprising when one remembers how antagonistic were both his general opinions and his conception of his art to those current in recent literary movements.

> Sing the peasantry, and then
> Hard-riding country gentlemen,
> The holiness of monks, and after
> Porter-drinkers' randy laughter;
> Sing the lords and ladies gay
> That were beaten into the clay
> Through seven heroic centuries;
> Cast your mind on other days. . . .

This shows scant sympathy with the Social Consciousness of the thirties, and

> Processions that lack high stilts have nothing that catches the
>     eye. . . .
> Because piebald ponies, led bears, caged lions, make but poor
>     shows,
> Because children demand Daddy-long-legs upon his timber toes,
> Because women in the upper storeys demand a face at the pane.

is far removed from those who, reacting during the twenties against inflated Victorian rhetoric, made understatement their

* A review of *Last Poems and Plays.*

God, and sacrificed grammar to terseness. I find it encouraging that, despite this, Yeats was recognized as a great poet, for it indicates that readers are less bigoted, less insistent upon the identity of the poet's beliefs with their own, and, when they can find some that is not completely trivial in subject, more appreciative of poetry that sounds well, that *sings*, than they sometimes appear.

The first thing that strikes one about Yeats is that he really enjoyed writing poetry. Some moderns make one feel that they regard it merely as a necessary means to some other end, the communication of ideas, mystical experience, self-analysis, castigation of abuses or what-have-you, and that the medium in which they work, the sounds and patterns of words, irrespective of the subject, give them little or no pleasure. Yeats, on the other hand, was always more concerned with whether or not a phrase sounded effective, than with the truth of its idea or the honesty of its emotion.

Both attitudes, the Puritanical and the Esthetic, have their dangers. The first, in forgetting that poetry is an *art*, i.e. artificial, a *factibile* not an *agibile*, may defeat its own purpose by producing drab stuff which is so harsh to the ear and lacking in pattern, that no one can take any pleasure in reading it; the second, by ignoring the fact that the artist is a human being with a moral responsibility to be honest, humble, and self-critical, may leave the poet too easily content with ideas which he finds poetically useful and effective. Not bothering to re-examine them, to throw out the false elements and develop the rest further, he is prevented from reaching his full potential poetic stature, and remains playing variations on the old tune which has served him so well in the past.

It cannot be said that Yeats completely escaped this second temptation. There are, particularly in this volume, more frequent echoes from his own previous work, both in phrasing and rhythm, than there ought to be, and, though every short poem, no doubt, expresses an attitude which in so far as it is one out of many possible moods may be called a pose, its singularity should not obtrude, and on occasion Yeats indulges in an embarrassing insistence upon an old man's virility, which some one who was more self-critical, not as a poet, but as a man, would have avoided.

Further, his utter lack of effort to relate his esthetic Weltan-schauung with that of science, a hostile neglect which was due, in part at least, to the age in which he was born when science was avidly mechanistic, was perhaps the reason why he never suc-ceeded in writing a long poem. For, as he himself says so beauti-fully in 'The Circus Animals' Desertion',

> Character isolated by a deed
> To engross the present and dominate memory.
> Players and painted stage took all my love,
> And not those things that they were emblems of.
>
> Those masterful images because complete
> Grew in pure mind, but out of what began?
> A mound of refuse or the sweepings of a street,
> Old kettles, old bottles, and a broken can,
> Old iron, old bones, old rags, that raving slut
> Who keeps the till. Now that my ladder's gone,
> I must lie down where all the ladders start,
> In the foul rag-and-bone shop of the heart.

But it was just this that he never did.

Much of his best work, such as the poem just quoted or 'Ego Dominus Tuus', is concerned with the relation of Life and Art. In this relation he had, like Thomas Mann and Valéry, a profound sense of what Kierkegaard called the Dialectic, but his vision of other kinds of relations was two-dimensional. Hence his one-sided determinist and 'musical' view of history, and the lack of drama which not all his theater can conceal. I cannot but feel, for instance, that the two plays in this volume are worthless.

Yet how little we care. For it is the lyrics we read. In lyric writing what matters more than anything else, more than subject-matter or wisdom, is diction, and of diction, 'simple, sensuous and passionate', Yeats is a consummate master.

*Kathleen Raine*

INTRODUCTION TO
*LETTERS ON POETRY FROM W. B.
YEATS TO DOROTHY WELLESLEY*
(1964)

WHEN, a quarter of a century ago, W. B. Yeats died, his greatness was recognized almost with reluctance by the generation
whose views on poetry then prevailed; views so different from
his own that it seems even surprising that the best-known writer
of that school, W. H. Auden, wrote a poem on the occasion of
Yeats's death. Perhaps few people at the time were very clear
about what Yeats really did think about poetry, or about anything else, for that matter. *A Vision*, republished in 1937, barely
two years before Yeats's death, whose metaphysical subtleties are
veiled (in the best tradition of mythological discourse) in
allegory almost playful, was certainly incomprehensible at the
time to all but a handful of esoteric students. The Mysteries
formed no part of the initiation of my crude generation, and we
lacked the knowledge even to assess our own ignorance, still less
to fathom Yeats's understanding. T. S. Eliot was then at the
height of his prestige as a critic, but as a writer on poetry Yeats
was hardly taken seriously at all by the young poets of the day.

The current notion was, as I remember, that it was astonishing
considering the nonsense that he read (Thomas Taylor, Plotinus
and the Upanishads in preference to Freud, Marx or Lancelot
Andrews, Shelley and Blake rather than Shaw and Hopkins) that
Yeats wrote verse so obviously magnificent; curiously enough
we did not draw the obvious conclusion that effect must be
related to cause. Far from concluding a connection so obvious,
Auden in his poem summed up the view of his school: that
although Yeats was 'silly like us' (and surely 'like us' was put in
to temper the accusation of 'silliness') he would be 'pardoned'
under 'a foreign code of conscience' for 'writing well'. It was also
fashionable to make a distinction between the 'early Yeats' of the

Celtic Twilight, embroidered, mythological and coloured by a
romantic view of love, and the 'late Yeats' for whom his one-
time secretary Ezra Pound was given much credit. Social realists,
the political left-wing, and those influenced, through Pound,
Eliot and others, by the American Imagist style, could recognize
in 'late Yeats' certain stark images, crude words and ragged
personages which might have appeared in works of their own
school. They had not looked closely enough to see that these
were but a new embodiment of those 'heroic and religious
themes, passed down from age to age, modified by individual
talent, but never abandoned' which Yeats had declared to be the
unchanging substance of sublime poetry. Against the rising tide
of realism, political verse and University wit, Yeats upheld the
innocent and the beautiful, the traditional and the noble. 'The
young Cambridge poets write out of their intellectual beliefs and
that is all wrong,' he wrote to Mrs Llewelyn Davies in 1937. 'I
have no such pleasant world as they seem to do. Like Balzac, I see
decreasing ability and energy and increasing commonness, and
like Balzac I know no-one who shares the premises from which I
work. What can I do but cry out, lately in simple peasant songs
that hide me from the curious?'

Yeats's adherence (in art, politics and human relationships) to
the aristocratic and traditional values was indeed resented as an
affront to the rising lower classes then first becoming articulate
and powerful. To question the values of the new era was, at that
time, to invite the accusation of 'Fascism'. *On the Boiler*,
published shortly before his death, was perhaps Yeats's most unpopular publication; yet his concern was to safeguard precisely
those aspects of life which are threatened by politics. 'Do not try
to make a politician of me,' he wrote to Ethel Mannin in 1936. 'As
my sense of reality deepens, and I think it does with age, my
horror at the cruelty of governments grows greater, and if I did
what you want, I would seem to hold one form of government
more responsible than any other, and that would betray my
convictions. Communist, Fascist, nationalist, clerical, anticlerical, are all responsible according to the number of their
victims.' Three important men are indifferent to politics: the

sculptor, the flute-player, and the man in a woman's arms; and perhaps that other unfashionable triad he elsewhere names, 'workman, noble and saint'.

Unpopular too was his *Oxford Book of Modern Verse*. It was generally felt that the *avant-garde* political poets had been neglected in favour of such names as Edith Sitwell, W. H. Davies, W. J. Turner, Herbert Read. The name of Wilfrid Owen, omitted, rightly or wrongly, on the grounds that passive suffering is not a theme for poetry, was waved like a banner behind which much ignorance mustered. The warnings of his Introduction, dictated not by fashionable opinion, but by a considered view of poetry, were ignored.

But now there have been second thoughts, afterthoughts; Auden's poem reads strangely now, and the 'foreign code of conscience' has undergone the judgment of time, which tries all codes, be they native and complacent, or foreign and frightening. We have come to realize that however silly 'we' may have been, 'we' were not at all like Yeats. When in 1939 Lady Gerald Wellesley published the correspondence between W. B. Yeats and herself, covering the last four years of the poet's life, Yeats's view of poetry was at the height of its unpopularity. In some letters he reminds his correspondent that they and their circle have few friends on the newspapers, where political values were sitting in judgment upon works of the imagination. Perhaps the publication of the letters at that moment was untimely; Dorothy Wellesley as the champion of an unfashionable view of poetry, and of Yeats himself, exposed herself to criticism while lacking the weapons to defend herself or her great poet from his enemies and her own. Now it is Yeats and the values of 'unageing intellect' which pass judgment upon that vanished *avant-garde*; and the rich harvest of poetry Yeats reaped from his friendship with her vindicates Dorothy Wellesley herself. A minor poet, a not always perceptive judge of Yeats's poems, she gave him the food his genius needed at that time of life when the friends of youth are becoming few. Lady Gregory had died in 1932, and his lifelong friend Olivia Shakespear in 1936. In Dorothy Wellesley Yeats found at once a symbol and a charming embodiment of the traditional aristocratic culture he admired. He found in her, besides, a woman with talent enough to deserve his friendship and to evoke and respond to some of his best thoughts. At Penns in the Rocks he found again a house, where, as once at Coole Park, 'all's accustomed, ceremonious'. In an early letter he writes that he finds in her poems 'the noble style'; and if this was so of her work, still more was it true of the quality of the friendship which grew up between them; in a more refined age it might have been called love perhaps, for the relationship went beyond the mere exchange of ideas and civilities and possessed that magical quality which belongs to a deeper level of imagination, the level which we sound in certain dreams, and from which poetry itself springs.

The main subject-matter of the letters is poetry. The relation-ship is that of teacher to pupil, but in such a relationship neither the giving nor the receiving is all on one side. A great deal of the early correspondence is about a poem, first written by Dorothy Wellesley, which Yeats appropriated, worked upon, and pub-lished as 'The Three Bushes' and its accompanying Songs. The first draft of the poem, shown him by his pupil, a reverie upon the grave of a trio of lovers, caught and held Yeats's imagination as a theme worthy of a poet nearing his grave but still afire with the life of this world. Presently we see the craftsman getting to work, arranging 'the natural words in the natural order', giving ever greater complexity to the thought, simplicity to the form. As in a film made by Picasso, we see the artist's hand at work. It was Yeats's aim, during the last years of his life, to embody the highest possible thought in the simplest possible form. 'I have recovered a power of moving the common man I had in my youth', he wrote to Dorothy Wellesley, 'the poems that I can now write will go into the general memory.' In another letter he quotes Tagore, 'not the poet but the poem'; in this high anony-mity he knew he would be remembered.

Yeats was magnanimous, but sometimes the master let it be seen that his role was to advise not to be advised on how to write poems. Will he not, the pupil writes, remove that coarse 'worm' from the Chambermaid's Song? Yeats replies that the worm

must stay; he strengthens, even coarsens, the offending phrase.
At other times the pupil 'fishes' for reassurance, perhaps praise;
and in general Yeats is full of kind encouragement, as he habi-
tually was to younger writers. But – all honour to her honesty in
recording the episode – Dorothy Wellesley notes that on one
occasion 'he says testily: "you have written a flawless lyric" ' and
adds, 'He does not really care for my poem which I call Poem...'.

Dorothy Wellesley, on the other hand, did not always approve
of Yeats's Irish politics and was shocked at the possibility of his
song on Roger Casement being sung in Oxford. Parnell, however (so Yeats evaded), belonged not to politics but to history;
he might have said, to heroic legend. She was distressed, too, at
his indifference to 'nature' in poetry, flowers and animals
especially, so dear to English poets. She had little appreciation,
on the other hand, of the importance, for him, of esoteric
religious themes and those myths which are the clothing of
metaphysical thought. A man of Yeats's many-sided greatness
cannot reveal the whole of himself to any single person, and
certainly Dorothy Wellesley's picture of her revered magician
(so she once saw him in a dream) is not the whole Yeats. It is
evident from a reading of the collection of his letters edited by
Allan Wade and published in 1954, that he would reveal a certain
side of himself to one or another friend, corresponding with one
on political, with another on theatrical, another on esoteric
subjects. He was, in this respect, a sensitive friend, never overriding his correspondent.

The interest of this volume lies in the presentation of a group
of Yeats's letters within the context of the correspondence which
elicited them. The letters throw light upon the aims Yeats set
himself as a poet during the last years of his life, the years in
which he wrote his play *Purgatory* (he knew it for a masterpiece) and his last volume of poems, some of them his finest.
They remind us that the soil from which great poetry grows is
remote from these aridities which occupy the pens of critics; the
beauty of a woman, the charm of her house and her com-
panionship, friendship, dreams and kindness, these nourish
immortal poetry.

# Yeats and Dorothy Wellesley

## LETTERS ON POETRY (1936)*

Riversdale
July 2nd, 1936

My dear Dorothy,

I dictated to my wife a business letter which she wanted about *The Broadsides*. This must have reached you some days ago. Here however is the emotional diary of my week. Saturday night sleepless; thought I fell asleep for only a few minutes. Dreamed I was in a great country house. Dorothy came to my room in the middle of the night. She was in some trouble about Dante, thought of turning Catholic. I was furious. Rest of the night tried vainly to sleep. Next morning finish my play. Triumphant; believe I have written a masterpiece. That night, sleeping draft, artificially quieted, good sleep. Next morning begin ballad about the poet the lady and the servant. Bad night. Next morning finish ballad in the rough. Triumphant; believe I have written a masterpiece. Twelve verses, six lines each. Will take a whole Broadside. That afternoon – despair. Reject my wife's suggestions for next *Cuala* book. Beg her to take over press. She explains that my name is necessary. I say I am incapable of facing practical life. Ill. Doctor told to hurry his visit. Good night. Then on Wednesday I finish ballad in the smooth and decide to do no serious work for some days. Good night and this morning perfectly well; capable of facing anything. What the devil is that doctor coming for?

There is an account which you will recognise from your own experience as a normal four or five days of the poetical life. To me you turn only the convex side of the work, and there is content and peace when I think about you.

*Extracts from *Letters on Poetry from W. B. Yeats to Dorothy Wellesley*, first published 1940 and re-issued in 1964 with the Introduction by Kathleen Raine printed above, pages 50–4.

I am longing to read your ballad. I will not send you mine until yours is finished.

Yours with love and affection,

W. B. Yeats.

PS. Just come.*


My dear,

Here you have a masterpiece. (I have just put in the rhymes, made it a ballad.)

### I

She sent her maid unto the man
That would her leman be
'O Psyche mimic me at love
With him I will not lie
'Tis sweetly done, 'tis easy done
So child make love for me'.

### II

'Why will you never meet the dawn,
Nor light the torch my child?'
Said lover to the serving maid
'Lie down, lie down you are wild,
O you are wild for love of me
And I with love am wild'.

### III

The black death came or another death
And took the lady and lord,

* D. W.'s ballad. D. W.'s own words are published in the Cuala Broadsides, 1937, first incorrectly, with three final verses which were cut out because of W. B. Y.'s criticism, and then correctly on an erratum slip. – D. W.

The serving maid, the sewing maid
Sat down to hem the shroud.
'O all goes well, O all goes well
And I can sing it aloud'.


IV

She that did what she was bid
Sang to the feather stitch,
'What of the man and the lady
No matter which is which,
All goes well with a man in the dark
And well with the feather stitch'.


This is far better than my laboured livelier verses. This is complete, lovely, lucky, born out of itself, or born out of nothing. My blessing upon you and it.


\*     \*     \*


Riversdale
[July 10, 1936] Friday

My dear Dorothy,
Here is another version of second & third stanzas. I start changing things because the rhyme of 'lord' & 'loud' etc. is not admissible in any prosody, then went on to the rest.

Yrs,
W. B. Yeats.


'I go if that candle is lit'
'Lie down, lie down you are wild'
'O you are wild for love of me
And I with love am wild'
'I came to lie with a man in the dark'
'Lie down again dear child'

or

But the black death took the lady & lord
'I sew but what I am bid
And all goes well O all goes well'
But why does she sing so loud
The serving maid, the sewing maid
She that hems the shroud.

Penns in the Rocks
July 14

My dear W. B.,

I send the revised version of the Ballad, and except for a minor change here or there I regard it as written. Have added lines to fit an air.

May I have yours now? I long to see it.

Loving
**D.**

PS. I like my ballad; anyway for the moment.

\*      \*      \*

Riversdale
[A] Tuesday [in July, 1936]

I have added 'The Three Bushes', etc.

My dear Dorothy,

I send to you what seems to me a better version of the little poem. There is no reason why you should not write a separate poem on the Rose Bushes or rather put what you have written into ballad rhyme. Forgive me for my work on the present poem. I thought from what you wrote that you meant to leave it un-rhymed & I wanted to prove you wrong. Perhaps it will go well with the 'Street Corner Songs' – it has their mood. I have re-covered from the shock of your archaic modernity, which for a moment made me lose faith in myself. I now like my long Ballad of the Three Bushes again. I have written two other poems on the same theme. I will send all as soon as I can. I think them among my best things. Now that I have shut off external activity (the theatre board & 'The Academy' threaten to meet here but so far I waved them off) I live in excitement. A mass of new subjects (not now on sex) are crowding upon me. I waked tired after the imaginative feeling of some hour of the night. But I must not bore you with the concave of my mask.

I thank you for the ballad book* which I keep beside my bed & read at intervals of my morning's work.

Ottoline came here a few days ago for tea. She was a hen who had layed a very big white egg & wanted all the yard to know. The egg was our friendship, which was not only 'important' to me & you but to my wife (this when she got George to herself for a moment) for I would be safe in your hands 'You were no minx'.

Now that I have had all my Anthology in galley proof I am astonished at the greatness of much of the poetry, & at its sadness. Most of the 'moderns' – Auden, Spender, etc. seem thin beside the more sensuous work of the 'romantics'.

I am well – my blood pressure very low & my heart is well. I can now sleep lying flat but I am physically but not mentally weak. At last I shall, I think, sing the heroic song I have longed for – perhaps my swan song.

> Yours affectionately,
> W. B. Yeats.

### Poem by Dorothy Wellesley†

#### I

She sent her sewing girl to the man
That would her leman be
'O Psyche mimic me at love
With him I will not lie
'Tis sweetly done, 'tis easy done
So child make love for me.'

#### II

'I go, should you light a candle'
'Lie down, lie down you are wild,

---

* *The Oxford Book of Ballads*, which I sent him. – D. W.
† A second version, by W. B. Y.

O you are wild for love of me
And I with love am wild'
'I came to lie with a man in the dark'
'Lie down again, dear child.'

### III

But the black death took the lord & the lady
'Who is singing so loud'
'A sewing girl, a sewing girl
That sings hemming a shroud
'All goes well, O all goes well
And all that I did she bid.'

### IV

High up lady, or sewing girl
What does it matter which!
Has found it sweet to lie in the dark
Nor cared who made the match;
O all goes well in the dark with a man
And well with the feather stitch!


# THE THREE BUSHES

## (By W. B. Y.)

### I

'Man's love that lacks its proper food
None can rely upon
And could you sing no more of love
Your genius would be gone
And could that happen what were you
But a starving man'
        *O my dear, O my dear.*

### 2

'Light no candles in your room'
That lovely lady said
'When twelve o'clock is sounding
I shall creep into your bed
But if I saw myself creep in
I think I should drop dead'
    *O my dear, O my dear.*

### 3

'I love a man in secret
Dear chambermaid,' said she.
'I know that I must drop down dead
If he stop loving me,
Yet what could I but drop down dead
If I lost my chastity?'
    *O my dear, O my dear.*

### 4

'So you must lie beside him
And let him think me there
Maybe we are all the same
Where no candles are,
Maybe we are all the same
When the body's bare.'
    *O my dear, O my dear.*

### 5

'No, not another song' said he
'Because my lady came
A year ago for the first time
At midnight to my room

And I must lie between the sheets
  the clock*
When bells* begin to boom'
   *O my dear, O my dear.*


6

'A laughing, crying, sacred song
A leching song' said they.
Did ever man hear such a song?
No not before that day.
Did ever man ride such a race?
Not till he rode away.
   *O my dear, O my dear.*


7

But when his horse had put its hoof
Into a rabbit hole,
He dropped upon his head and died
His lady that saw it all
Dropped and died thereon for she
Loved him with her soul.
   *O my dear, O my dear.*


8

The chambermaid lived on and took
Their graves into her charge
And there two bushes planted,
That when they had grown large
Seemed sprung from but a single root
So did their roses merge.
   *O my dear, O my dear.*

* These are alternative readings. – D. W.

### 9

When she was old and dying
The priest came where she was
She made a full confession
Long looked he in her face,
And O he was a good man
And understood her case.
    *O my dear, O my dear.*

### 10

He bade them take and bury her
Beside her lady's man
And set a rose tree on her grave
And now none living can
When they have plucked a rose there
Know where its roots began.
    *O my dear, O my dear.*

## THE LADY TO HER CHAMBERMAID
### (By W. B. Y.)

### 1

What manner of man is coming
To lie between your feet?

What matter we are but women;
Wash, make your body sweet,

I shall find a perfume
To scatter on the sheet.

    The Lord have mercy on us.

He shall love my soul as though
Body were not all

He shall love your body
Untroubled by the soul

Love crams his two divisions
Yet keeps his substance whole

    The Lord have mercy on us.

Soul must learn a love that is
Proper to my breast

Limbs a love in common
With every noble beast

If soul may look and body touch
Which is the more blest?

    The Lord have mercy on us.


II

When you and my true lover meet
And he plays tunes between your feet,

If you dare abuse the soul,
Or think the body is the whole

I must, that am his daylight lady,
Outrageously abuse the body;

Swear that he shall never stray
From either neither night and day,

That I may hear, if we should kiss,
That contrapuntal serpent hiss,

You, should hand explore a thigh,
All the labouring heaven sigh.


Riversdale
[postmark, July 18, 1936] Thursday

My dear Dorothy,

You have got me down to fundamental rock. I cannot say the good is bad or the bad good, even though the good is by my bitterest enemy, the bad by my dearest friend. When I got your first sketch I went down stairs humming over the opening stanzas, getting the rhymes regular & said to somebody 'I have something here that will not die'. Yet what you send me is bad. What has the beginning to do with the end? 'With him I will not lie' can only mean (I thought it a masterly simplification) left unqualified that she is not in love with the man, that she does not want him at all. Why then should she in her talk with the briar lament that he was never hers. Why should this be 'truth after death'. Then why should the fact that she never gave herself cause the squire to lose not the lady but Psyche. Then in the last stanza I do not understand why Psyche has a living heart & why she can rise & deck their graves. Of course you know why, but it is not in the poem.

Then look through any old book of ballads & you will find that they have all perfectly regular rhyme schemes.

'O my dear, O my dear'

W. B. Y.

Perhaps your mind is meditative not narrative. I am putting your little poem with its music in one number with my ballad.

Penns in the Rocks<br>July

My dear W. B.

I have this minute received your letter, slanging my 'ballad'. I take your points as they come.

1. It is not obvious that the lady was a minx, a demi-vierge, an 'allumeuse', leading the young man on, letting him down? A mental baggage, a jade, hussy, slut, demirep, and so on?

2. *Argument.* So she left it to her maid, when it came to grips.

3. You say why then when the rose tells her the truth does she mind? Because she, like all the women described above, regrets what she never knew she wanted.

4. The squire of course minded. He had been cheated. (Psyche is merely a symbol.) And he lamented after death. It disturbed his sleep.

5. Why has Psyche a 'living heart'?

Because she loved the man and got what she wanted, and even the bitter truth after death could not destroy her memories. So she rose to deck all their graves.

6. Now as to technical errors about riming ballads. I hadn't attempted a true ballad. Had tried to graft a modern form upon the skeleton of the old. That is all. I don't believe in 'going back' in any sense, but this was an experiment. The modern mind cannot perhaps avoid short cuts, the assumption being that the reader has jumped to it.

I thought your verses very beautiful. Some I thought as fine as anything you have done. All yesterday I was in despair about the Muse.

Will you send back that false ballad? Just stick it into an envelope. I might rewrite it or not. There is something false in any case about archaic modernity.

Yrs. with affection,<br>D.

PS. Have you kept the first version of my 'ballad'? I destroyed mine. You called it a 'masterpiece' in your letter of that date, a fortnight or so ago. I was certainly astonished at your praise. Could I have that version back too?

Riversdale
July 21st, 1936

Dear Lady Dorothy,

I enclose your first draft, which does not differ much from the second. When I read it I think I only glanced at the end about the thorntree. I thought that you had put it in because it was part of the story, and would as a matter of course leave it out. The first part surprised me, the new point of view and the absence of rhyme. Just as I thought you would leave out the end, so I was certain you either intended or could be persuaded to add rhyme. I ended the poem at 'Sang sewing maid to shroud'. In those first four verses I found something that had never been sung. The maid who had seemed 'wild with love' was able to 'sing aloud' as she hemmed the shroud 'All goes well, Oh all goes well, No matter who she be, All in the dark unto a man' (I read this to mean 'in the dark with a man'). She was gay. She was without grief. —— said once to George Moore 'I wish I had a slave to do this for me. I would not have to think of him afterwards.' Your sewing maid gets the same result by being a slave – she had not to think of him afterwards. He was merely a man in the dark. In my excitement I began using my acquired skill to make your meaning plainer than you had made it. I sent you a first version with rhymes – I thought you would use it as quarry for rhyme. Then against my first intention I sent you what I thought a finished version.

Regular rhyme is needed in this kind of work. The swing of the sentence makes the reader expect it. 'Said lover to the serving maid', ' 'Tis sweetly done, 'tis easy done' and so on are ballad cadences, and then the six line stanzas suggest ballad stanzas. There is another reason. In narrative verse we want to concentrate the attention on the fact or the story, not on the form. The form must be present as something we all accept – 'the fundamental sing-song'. I do not know a single example of good narrative where the rhyme scheme is varied.

I have left out the poem you have asked me to leave out, but I will write later about that and other things. I have begun my new long poem, and now I must get up. After lunch I have letters to dictate. I am in a great whirl of work and my working day is crushed into a short space. One letter is to the B.B.C. accepting their request that I should deliver the 'National Lecture' on poetry. They give me £100 which put my finances right, but my wife would not let me accept until I had read aloud with suitable expression for three quarters of an hour to judge of the strain. There was no strain, and I picked an average day when I was already tired by shouting for an hour at a deaf man.

Ah my dear how it added to my excitement when I re-made that poem of yours to know it was your poem. I re-made you and myself into a single being. We triumphed over each other and I thought of *The Turtle and the Phoenix*.

Yours,<br>W. B. Yeats.

Riversdale<br>July 26, 1936

Dear Lady Dorothy,

I did not write because I have been busy mainly writing poetry. I get up every morning about 4, work at proof sheets until about 5.30, then go to bed again, breakfast at 7.30, and then write poetry, with interruption for rest, till 12. The rest of the day I try to do this or that but generally cannot. I remain sunk in indolence. Yesterday I finished my longer poem 'Lapis Lazuli'[1] and so to-day have come down full of energy having done nothing but my proof sheets in the small hours. Higgins came in last night and I showed him your poem, which he likes as much as I do. Turner has sent three poems of his own set by himself which my wife will send you in a couple of days together with a song by York Powell which I delight in. Would you care to go through the poems of Davies and see if there is anything that you think suitable?

The poem 'Lapis Lazuli' is almost the best I have made of recent years, I will send it when I can get it typed. To-morrow I write a story to be added to the Michael Robartes series (a prelude to *A Vision* which I am now revising in proof). It is almost an exact transcript from fact. I have for years been creating a group of strange disorderly people on whom Michael Robartes confers the wisdom of the east.

I have not put anything in place of 'The Thorn Tree'. I did my best, I went through your 'Selections' and your 'Poems of Ten Years' but found myself vacilating. I have an idea that I left out the nature poems because I wanted your poems to give an impression of rapidity. Rapidity is returning, it is no longer left to the popular poetry. I try to arrange the selections from each poet so that they will have unity of effect. I had great trouble with ——— who wanted a more 'representative' selection, even wrote to the publishers. I have changed my selection from Turner to increase its unity.

Can I come to you in October? They have fixed my broadcast for Oct. 11. If I cannot come then I will do it from Belfast. But Oh my dear, my dear.

Yours affectionately,<br>W. B. Yeats.

PS. Have *Selections* been reviewed?

*　*　*

1st August, 1936

TO  D. W.²

Reach towards the moonless midnight of the trees
As though that hand could reach to where they stand,
As though they were but famous upholsteries
Velvet under the touch; tighten that hand
As though to draw them closer yet; rammed full
Of that most sensuous silence of the night,
For since you bought the horizon all is still,
Climb to your chamber full of books and wait,
No books upon the knees and no one there
But some great dog that long had bayed the moon
But now lies sunk in sleep.
What climbs the stair?
Nothing a common woman could ponder on

If you are worth my hope; neither content
Nor satisfied conscience, but that great family
Some ancient famous authors misrepresent,
The proud Furies each with her torch on high.

W. B. Y.

Riversdale

Received August 2, 1936.

*Corrections in 'To D. W.'*

line 7    instead of 'all is still' read 'strange dogs are still'
line 10  instead of 'great' read 'old'
   Will write on Saturday or Sunday.

W. B. Y.

Riversdale
August 5 [1936]

My dear Dorothy: I began a letter to you on Saturday and began
it with some new corrections in 'To D. W.' Then I changed my
mind about the corrections and tore it up. I meant to write on
Sunday but my wife offered to type my play if I would read out
the MS. That took us Sunday and Monday and now I am free
again. Here are my latest corrections in 'To D. W.'

Reach towards the moonless midnight of the trees,
As though that hand could reach to where they stand,
As though they were but famous upholsteries
Velvet under the touch; tighten that hand
As though to draw them closer yet    etc.

Higgins says the poem is 'terrific' which I like as an adjective. He
seems to like it best of all my recent poetry. . . . We have all
something within ourselves to batter down and get our power
from this fighting. I have never 'produced' a play in verse without showing the actors that the passion of the verse comes from
the fact that the speakers are holding down violence or madness –
'down Hysterica passio'. All depends on the completeness of the
holding down, on the stirring of the beast underneath. Even my

poem 'To D. W.' should give this impression. The moon, the moonless night, the dark velvet, the sensual silence, the silent room and the violent bright Furies. Without this conflict we have no passion only sentiment and thought.

My wife will send you the Turner poems and their setting and also a poem by Hugh MacDaermid – there are so many ways of spelling that name – I would like to use,* partly because its subject, Noah and his beasts, would be a good theme for the artist. The poem of yours that Higgins liked is that which goes to music by Turner.

About the conflict in 'To D. W.' I did not plan it deliberately. That conflict is deep in my subconsciousness, perhaps in everybody's. I dream of clear water, perhaps two or three times (the moon of the poem), then come erotic dreams. Then for weeks perhaps I write poetry with sex for theme. Then comes the reversal – it came when I was young with some dream or some vision between waking and sleep with a flame in it. Then for weeks I get a symbolism like that in my Byzantium poem or in 'To D. W.' with flame for theme. All this may come from the chance that when I was a young man I was accustomed to a Kabalistic ceremony where there were two pillars, one symbolic of water and one of fire. The fire mark is $\triangle$, the water mark is $\nabla$, these are combined to make Solomon's seal $\varhexagon$. The water is sensation, peace, night, silence, indolence; the fire is passion, tension, day, music, energy.

Yours in love
W. B. Yeats.

Riversdale
August 6th, 1936

Dear Lady Dorothy,

This is a letter from George and W. B. Y. She has been so busy getting off galley proofs of the anthology that she has been unable to write. We enclose Turner's three poems with his music, we also send a York Powell, 'The Pretty Maid' and 'Parley of Beasts' by M'Diarmid; we could probably get the music for the

* For the Broadsides. – D. W.

last two done here. If you agree to these poems please let us
know as soon as possible and send them back so that we can give
them to the artists.

Yours,

George Yeats.

W. B. Yeats.

PS. (by W. B. in his own hand) My lecture is on October 11th.
I should probably be in London by (say) October 9th (Friday).
May I come to you at the end of September? If so what day?

I think I have got the third line right at last:

'And they but famous old upholsteries' etc.

## NOTES

1. See *Last Poems and Plays* (1940).

2. This poem, with some important revisions, was printed in the
*London Mercury*, March 1938, under the title 'To a Friend' and in the
Cuala Press edition of *New Poems* (Dublin, 1938). It is published
under the title 'To Dorothy Wellesley' in *Last Poems and Plays* (1940).

# PART TWO

# Recent Studies

# Curtis Bradford

# ON YEATS'S *LAST POEMS* (1965)

## I: PRELIMINARIES

THIS re-reading of *Last Poems* has to begin by rejecting their very heading as used in the collected editions for all the poems Yeats wrote after *A Full Moon in March*. Starting with 'The Gyres' and ending with 'Are You Content?' these are Yeats's *New Poems*. That is what he called them when he had them published by the Cuala Press in 1938, and that is what they are. The final poems in *A Full Moon in March* are 'Supernatural Songs'; Yeats at his most difficult. He wrote to Dorothy Wellesley of the book, saying, 'I don't like it – it is a fragment of the past I had to get rid of. The swift rhythm of "Fire", and the study of rhythm my work for the anthology entailed [*The Oxford Book of Modern Verse*], have opened my door.'[1] The door opened on to *New Poems*, which are perhaps the simplest, most direct that Yeats has written since *The Green Helmet*; the preponderance of ballad meters gives the work a new tone. After correcting the proofs of *New Poems* in January 1938, Yeats wrote of them to Dorothy Wellesley, 'It is all nonchalant verse', which could hardly be said of *The Tower* or of *The Winding Stair* or of the actual *Last Poems*. The heading 'Last Poems' – and I do not know its source – can be properly applied only to those poems Yeats wrote or finished during the last year of his life, between January 1938 and January 1939, as they were published by the Cuala Press in the order Yeats intended in July of 1939. *New Poems* first appeared under the heading 'Last Poems' in Macmillan's *Last Poems and Plays* published in 1940, hence their inclusion under that heading could not have had Yeats's sanction.

During the last days of his life Yeats arranged the work he had completed since *New Poems* by number and title in a manuscript table of contents. His arrangement is masterly, though at the outset it will be disturbing to most of his readers who know these poems only in the order given them by the Macmillan editors. We can recover Yeats's arrangement and at the same time grow aware of the extent of the displacement by cancelling the heading 'Last Poems' in *Collected Poems* and replacing it by 'New Poems'; then, after 'Are You Content?', we should re-introduce the heading 'Last Poems'. We shall have also to relegate to an appendix the three poems Yeats had put in *On the Boiler*: 'Why should not Old Men be Mad?' 'Crazy Jane on the Mountain' and 'The Statesman's Holiday' – this will give them the order in which they appear in *On the Boiler*; then renumber the actual *Last Poems* as follows: 2, 6, 7, 8, 5, 9, 10, 11, 13, 12, 14, 15, 16, 18, 19, 17, 4, 3, 1.

The expansion of the title *Last Poems* to include *New Poems* has somewhat obscured the grimness of Yeats's last phase. *Last Poems and Two Plays* (and from here on *Last Poems* will refer to this work), framed as it is by 'Under Ben Bulben' and *Purgatory*, is a grim and desperately earnest book, recording Yeats's response to the mounting crisis in Western culture and asserting the values of that culture as opposed to all 'Asiatic vague immensities'. There are moments of relaxation, but the fun (as in 'High Talk') is usually highly ironic and it never lasts long. January 1938–January 1939 was truly an *annus mirabilis* for Yeats, for during it he not only composed or finished his *Last Poems*; he also wrote *On the Boiler*, *Purgatory*, and *The Death of Cuchulain*. There is a constant thematic and ideological interplay between these works; they reinforce and explain each other. And if we consider just the *Last Poems* themselves in Yeats's intended order, we will find that Yeats, as always, is guiding us with a sure hand. Again, poem reinforces and explains poem: Yeats's principal themes and ideas emerge more clearly and forcefully. Finally, he provides us, by carefully arranging a great variety of metrical forms and modes, with a musical experience both rich and intricate. Indeed the displacement of Yeats's intended order has perhaps done more damage to the musical aspect of *Last Poems* than to its other aspects.

## II: THE INTERPLAY OF THEMES

'Are You Content?', which echoes the *siete soddisfatto* spoken by
Shelley's ghost, is the last note heard in *New Poems*. It remarkably sets up, prepares the way for *Last Poems*, which opens
with 'Under Ben Bulben'. The discontented artist is now dead
and is speaking to us from the tomb, and what he speaks is his
poetic last will and testament. The effect is like that of an electric
shock, and the change of position of 'Under Ben Bulben' will
shock most of Yeats's readers who have never encountered the
poem anywhere but at the end of *Collected Poems* where it seemed
to belong. Yet, since we cannot doubt Yeats's intention nor his
skill in composing books, we should note the effect of the change:
Yeats speaks not only 'Under Ben Bulben' from the tomb, he
speaks all his *Last Poems* from the tomb. Taken together they
constitute his farewell to life and art. 'Under Ben Bulben' also
introduces the principal themes found in *Last Poems*: the need
for a new faith, however esoteric; the decline of the West, which
now involves even the bodies and minds of the various European
stocks; the artist's double duty in the face of this decline to

> Bring the soul of man to God,
> Make him fill the cradles right;

and the statement in the epitaph both of what our attitude should
be in the present time of troubles and of the burning necessity for
getting on with the job of re-creation. Yeats wanted the poem to
serve as an overture, not as a recapitulation of themes; certainly
it does this, and moved from the end to the onset it has a far
greater dramatic effect.

'Three Songs to the One Burden' is linked to 'Under Ben
Bulben' both by its theme and by its refrain, *'From mountain to
mountain ride the fierce horsemen.'* Yeats had invoked these
'ancient inhabitants of the country' at the opening of 'Under Ben
Bulben'. His theme, stated in the first song, is the decay of the
ancient Irish tradition; he then goes on to consider what should
be done about this decay. Should one simply withdraw from it,
however sympathetic, as his recluse cousin Henry Middleton

had withdrawn into his 'small demesne' at Rosses Point, or should one remind the Irish of the Easter Rebellion and then suggest that perhaps it is time to start a new rebellion? There are many links to *On the Boiler*, especially to section III of 'Private Thoughts'. The tone is lighter, easier than the tone of 'Under Ben Bulben', and in spite of, perhaps because of, the seriousness of Yeats's thought, he is notably funny when he has his Roaring Tinker invoke Crazy Jane and the ancient Irish god Manannan.

'The Black Tower', Yeats's last poem, finished during the week in which he died, goes over much the same ground but uses a different poetic method; it is a little allegory, an extended metaphor. Some oath-bound defenders of a bygone heroic tradition, no doubt exemplars of the 'indomitable Irishry', resist the present but refuse to believe their cook when he 'Swears that he hears the king's great horn'. The refrain hints at some sort of violent revival or renewal, but grows increasingly desperate. On its third recurrence the moon is dark, a time in Yeats's system when anything can happen.

In 'Cuchulain Comforted', another of Yeats's very late poems, he invokes for the last time his mythic example of heroic man. Cuchulain's situation is worse even than that of the soldiers manning the Black Tower; suffering from six mortal wounds received in his last battle he is not dispatched by the Blind Man as in *The Death of Cuchulain*, but finds himself wandering in some vague underworld. Here he is 'comforted' by the ghosts of convicted cowards who invite him to join them in sewing a shroud. Like 'The Black Tower' and many of Yeats's poems 'Cuchulain Comforted' was based on a dream vision, and perhaps this partly accounts for its curiously haunting quality. It picks up and completes with changed circumstances the action of *The Death of Cuchulain*, for at the end Cuchulain's reincarnation as a bird has taken place. The poem is retrospective. It looks back to Congal's reincarnation as a donkey at the end of *The Herne's Egg*, and back even further to the realm of *On Baile's Strand*. *Last Poems* grows increasingly retrospective until in 'The Man and the Echo' and 'The Circus Animals' Desertion' it becomes consciously retrospective.

'Three Marching Songs'. After Cuchulain has been so grimly comforted, Yeats invites us to recall the heroic Ireland he per- sonified, but the speaker of the refrain in the first song insists 'All that's finished, let it fade.' The first song reworks II of 'Three Songs to the Same Tune', and the revision of lines 15–16 links it to III of the present series. Song II is a nearly complete revision of III in the earlier versions, and the revision reflects Yeats's views, fully stated in *On the Boiler,* that the historical situation has grown increasingly desperate: 'What if there's nothing up there at the top?' reminds us of the mood and themes of *The Winding Stair,* of 'a time / Half dead at the top' from 'Blood and the Moon'. The refrain hints at 'tomorrow's revolution', but the young man who hints at it is restrained: 'No, no, my son not yet.' I of the earlier version becomes III and is supplied with a new refrain wherein the Irish resister of a former generation rattles out a tune on the moon before the rope strangles him. If he has taken down the moon, then again we are in the dark of the moon.

'In Tara's Halls' does something to relieve the by now almost unmitigated gloom, and after it we turn away from Yeats's invocation of the heroic Irish past. The poem raises the ghost, so to speak, of 'romantic Ireland', not yet quite 'dead and gone'; it reminds us of the realm of Yeats's earliest work. Perhaps he is writing a kind of counter-statement to Moore's 'The Harp That Once Through Tara's Halls'. Moore ends:

> Thus Freedom now so seldom wakes,
>   The only truth she gives,
> Is when some heart indignant breaks
>   To show that still she lives.

Yeats's old man behaves in a far more heroic fashion than does Moore's man with the breaking heart.

Here the first movement, so to speak, of *Last Poems* ends. Its theme, a re-examination of the heroic Irish past as Yeats has developed that in one of his many mythologies, is one of the themes stated in 'Under Ben Bulben'. The second movement is made up of a group of complex philosophical poems ('The Statues', 'News for the Delphic Oracle', 'Long-legged Fly', 'A Bronze Head', and 'A Stick of Incense') which form the very core of the book. From *The Tower* on, and especially in *The Winding Stair*, Yeats had tended to locate his most difficult poems in the middle of the book ('Two Songs from a Play', 'Byzantium', 'Vacillation') as he does in *Last Poems*. Here the displacement caused by the Macmillan arrangement has disastrous results, for the intellectual drive and thrust of this group of poems is destroyed when 'Three Marching Songs' is slipped in between 'News for the Delphic Oracle' and 'Long-legged Fly'. Yeats's principal theme is a concern with form in all its aspects: the form of a man or a woman and the relation of physical form to the sexual instinct, the form of a culture, the form of Paradise, form versus formlessness. There is some reduction of Irish allusion in 'The Statues', 'News for the Delphic Oracle', and 'Long-legged Fly'; Yeats's subjects involve the whole development of West European culture as he conceived it. As in his first movement his principal themes are either stated or restated in 'Under Ben Bulben', especially in section IV.

In 'The Statues' Yeats confronts Europe and Asia, a statue of a Greek athlete and a statue of Buddha. The form of the Buddha had its beginnings in European sculpture, since it grew out of the work of Greek sculptors who followed Alexander on his Asiatic conquests,[2] but by the Middle Ages had become symbolic of 'All Asiatic vague immensities'. Yeats in spite of his lifelong interest in Asiatic thought seems now definitely to prefer the 'form' of Europe to the 'formlessness' of Asia. He explores one of the themes he was to return to in 'Under Ben Bulben', that artists must give 'to the sexual instinct of Europe its goal, its fixed type', must make men 'fill the cradles right'. There is a constant interplay between the themes of 'The Statues' and the themes of *On the Boiler* on which Yeats was working when he sent the finished poem to Dorothy Wellesley on June 22, 1938. Section VII of 'Other Matters' in *On the Boiler* contains a prose version of the poem:

'Europe was not born when Greek galleys defeated the Persian hordes at Salamis, but when the Doric studios sent out those broad-backed marble statues against the multiform, vague, expressive Asiatic Sea'.

And in both the poem and the prose work Yeats's extravagant
desire somehow to join Greece and Ireland is at its height. The
poem is the most complex in the collection, perhaps the most
complex Yeats had written since 'Byzantium'. Its suggestivity
radiates in every direction, and the reader never comes to the end
of trying to understand it.

Knowing that Yeats intended 'News for the Delphic Oracle' to
follow 'The Statues' may help us to discover new areas of meaning in the poem without disturbing the expositions that Richard
Ellmann and others have made. No doubt the basis of Yeats's
arrangement was his desire utterly to shift his tone, indeed one
can hardly imagine a sharper contrast. Yet there is a definitive
imagistic and thematic relation: At line 14 in 'The Statues' Yeats
alludes to the Aegean Sea as 'The many-headed foam at Salamis'.
He picks this up at line 17 when he imagines a sculptor with the
image of a Greek athlete in his mind crossing the Aegean in the
wake of Alexander ('One image crossed the many-headed').
Then at line 29 he writes in contrast of 'this filthy modern tide'
whose 'formless spawning' wrecks the Irish . In 'News for the
Delphic Oracle' water is a principal image in each section: In
part I Plotinus, whom we saw swimming towards the Elysian
Fields in 'The Delphic Oracle upon Plotinus', has just arrived;
we know this because of 'The salt flakes on his breast'. In part II
the Innocents are borne across the sensual seas ('ecstatic waters')
on the backs of brute dolphins who pitch off their burdens as the
choir of love wades out to meet the arriving souls of the blessed.
We do not know at the outset of part III that the figures of Peleus
and Thetis (this allusion to them is unique in Yeats's poetry) are
projected against a seascape, for it is only at the end that Yeats
picks up the foam introduced in 'The Statues'. Perhaps Peleus
and Thetis are about to beget Achilles, Greek alter-ego of
Cuchulain, embodiment of the heroic ideal, and the outcome of
their sexual selection is intended to be contrasted with the
nymphs and satyrs unselectively copulating in the foam.
Poussin's picture which Yeats is remembering from the National
Gallery in Dublin is called 'The Marriage of Peleus and Thetis'.
(T. R. Henn first noticed this source.) If this is a right reading,

Yeats has stated or restated a central theme in 'The Statues', *On the Boiler*, and *Purgatory* (the exact dates of composition of 'News' are not known). As 'News' progresses, Yeats becomes more and more preoccupied with form, with form in art as that is illustrated by the picture he is recalling, but more directly with the glorious bodies of Peleus and Thetis. And again he has plunged us back into his earlier works: in part I to 'The Delphic Oracle upon Plotinus'; in part II to 'Byzantium'.

'Long-legged Fly' is closely related to 'News' by both meter and theme. The metrical link will have to wait for a while, but we note at the outset that both poems move toward a preoccupation with physical form. What Yeats does here is to juxtapose sharply three emblematic figures which constantly recur in his poetry: the conqueror or man of action, the beautiful woman, the artist. The refrain

*Like a long-legged fly upon the stream*
*His mind moves upon silence*

joins their activities and suggests that the conqueror by planning his conquest, the beautiful woman by merely being what she is, and the artist by creating what he creates is each performing what is ultimately an intellectual act. This is clear enough in stanzas 1 and 3; as for stanza 2 we should recall the statement in 'Adam's Curse' 'we must labour to be beautiful'. At the end of the poem we watch Michael Angelo at work on the figure of Adam in the Sistine Chapel frescos. This allusion recurs in 'Under Ben Bulben' and recalls again what Yeats says in *On the Boiler* that artists must give 'to the sexual instinct of Europe its goal, its fixed type'. Stanza 2 recalls another passage in *On the Boiler*: 'A woman's face . . . may foretell a transformation of the people, be a more dire or beneficent omen than those trumpets heard by Etruscan seers in middle air' (p. 25). The earlier poems of Yeats which 'Long-legged Fly' brings back to our minds are those poems found in *The Green Helmet* and elsewhere, usually addressed to Maud Gonne, which constantly allude to Helen of Troy, and part VI of 'Vacillation' concerned with the conqueror.

Yeats intended 'A Bronze Head' to follow 'Long-legged Fly',

and knowing this may help us with the þoem. I see two links to the preceding poem: stanza 2 of 'Long-legged Fly' may actually allude to Maud Gonne – the Helen reference would lead us to think so, though persons who knew Maud Gonne recall her immense dignity of bearing and cannot imagine her practising 'a tinker shuffle'. In any event the Helen allusion does remind us of many poems in which Yeats thinks of her as a re-embodiment of Helen, and this sets up, so to speak, 'A Bronze Head'. Also Yeats's preoccupation with form continues, and the word 'form', which has been hovering in the background from 'The Statues' on, now twice occurs. Yeats's exploration of the problem of form is given a new turn when he explores, as he had already done in 'Among School Children', the changing form of a human being from youth to age and sets the question: 'Which of her forms has shown her substance right?' Yeats speculates on this neo-Platonic question, but doesn't exactly answer it. He recalls, I think, certain events from his association with Maud Gonne in the nineties, visions that she had seen of her possible futures, which Yeats had used earlier in 'The Two Trees'.[3] He writes here that he had had a pre-vision of her present form and seems to conclude that her 'tomb-haunter' semblance is more appropriate to the 'foul world' of the present than would be her 'sleek and new' semblance in the nineties. The last stanza uses themes also used in *Purgatory*, *On the Boiler*, and 'Under Ben Bulben', the decline and fall of the West and that of families that must inevitably occur as the Christian era ends.

I think that by placing 'A Stick of Incense' immediately after 'A Bronze Head' Yeats intended to help us interpret his gnomic quatrain. It is a variation on a theme stated in this sentence from *On the Boiler*: 'Yet we must hold to what we have that the next civilization may be born, not from virgin's womb, nor a tomb without a body, not from a void, but of our own rich experience' (p. 27). Given its placing, 'A Stick of Incense' seems to comment on the final stanza of 'A Bronze Head'; the 'that' in 'Whence did all that fury come' in my reading is not a pronoun without an antecedent – a device which Yeats rarely used – but rather refers back to the final stanza of the preceding poem. Could the

violence that marks the end of the Christian era really come
'From empty tomb or virgin womb?' The question is unanswer-
able, though clearly it involves the problem of form and formlessness, so Yeats goes on to suggest that we should imitate St
Joseph, a bystander or acolyte at the onset of these ponderous
events, and concentrate on some immediate sensation. We look
back to earlier explorations of these themes in 'The Second
Coming', *The Resurrection*, and elsewhere. Yet the quatrain
separates, I am sure by intention, two poems concerned with the
women Yeats has loved.

Another movement of *Last Poems* begins, or is at least anticipated, in 'A Bronze Head'. Yeats is modulating from a general
consideration of form and the relation of the sexual instinct to
form, begun in 'The Statues', to a specific consideration of the
form or rather forms of a woman he has loved. The fact that 'A
Bronze Head' ended with a statement of the formlessness of
contemporary society led to the insertion after it of 'A Stick of
Incense', then with 'Hound Voice' Yeats returns to an aspect of
his personal life, the quality of voice which he has shared with all
the women he has picked. 'A Bronze Head' is connected to
'Hound Voice' not only by its autobiographical theme; the two
poems use the same stanza form, a form that does not elsewhere
occur in Yeats's poetry.

'Hound Voice' seems to me a rather artificial poem. Yeats kept
cats, not dogs, so was not for 'many years companioned by a
hound'. I agree with John Unterecker that the poem grew out of
Yeats's association with Dorothy Wellesley, who was for 'many
years companioned by a hound', as had been Maud Gonne. This
correspondence of events of youth with events of age no doubt
delighted Yeats as all correspondence did, and taken together
with the fact that his voice and the voices of the women he had
picked carried as does the baying of a hound led him to the writing of the poem. He moves on from this common quality to
another: many of the women he had picked had shared his
experiences of the supernatural – we know this certainly
of Maud Gonne, Olivia Shakespear, Florence Farr, and Mrs
Yeats.

> We picked each other from afar and knew
> What hour of terror comes to test the soul.

The terror associated with supernatural events is not unlike the terror one feels at the violence which marks the end of an era, and Yeats thinks of the women he has picked as experiencing along with him, all perhaps reincarnated, the violence present and to come but somehow transcending it, as living through and beyond it. To state this Yeats uses the figure of the hunt. There is a strong thematic link to the last line of 'A Bronze Head': 'And wondered what was left for massacre to save'. Yeats partly answers this question in 'Hound Voice'. Certain eternal human qualities which he has shared with the women he has picked must be saved. The moment of transcendence with which 'Hound Voice' ends is echoed in the two following poems, 'John Kinsella's Lament' and 'High Talk', even though the three poems are very unlike in other respects.

In 'John Kinsella's Lament' – and it simply has to come after 'Hound Voice', not before it – Yeats dons the mask of a 'strong farmer' to bid farewell to love. From 'The Statues' on the intellectual tension has been very great, as have been Yeats's demands on his readers. He now relaxes this tension by reinvoking the mode of the Crazy Jane poems. The 'Lament' is also the last poem in the collection wholly concerned with sexual love. Again the poem ends in transcendence as John Kinsella imagines himself in the Garden of Eden, where he will live eternally with his old bawd. Here Yeats's irony reminds us of 'News for the Delphic Oracle'.

'High Talk' follows, and for once Yeats's order is the order of composition – a rare event in the formation of his various collections. We know this because Yeats in his letter to Dorothy Wellesley inclosing 'Lament' wrote 'I have now begun on the stolen circus stilts'.[4] The rollicking tone of 'Lament' carries over into 'High Talk' with its punning title and colloquial diction – colloquially 'timber toes' is a man with a wooden leg – but the persona and the theme have changed. The mask of the strong farmer has been doffed and Yeats speaks to us more directly. His principal theme is that art must entertain, a concept which usually governed his practice. He stated this theme in a letter written to Dorothy Wellesley on April 20, 1936: 'These new men are goldsmiths working with a glass screwed into one eye, whereas we stride ahead of the crowd, its swordsmen, its jugglers.'[5] Malachi Stilt-Jack is an entertainer all right, but when he stalks out of the world of children and women into eternity we experienced a third moment of transcendence. Yeats's complete change of tone at line 11 prepares us for the poem which follows.

'The Apparitions' is based on a group of occult events which took place in 1933 and 1934. Yeats wrote in a manuscript book which he was using at the time: 'The first apparition was the passage of a coat upon a coat hanger slowly across room – it was extraordinarily terrifying.' As John Unterecker has observed, the worst apparition possible would be a vision of your own empty coat. The artist on his stilts can stalk on into eternity, but the artist is also a man, and the man is troubled by dreams of his death. He needs the support of his friends and the deep joy of his full heart. We are modulating back to the deeply felt personal tone with which *Last Poems* began.

After the direct address of 'The Apparitions' Yeats shifts momentarily to an impersonal tone in 'A Nativity', which recalls the riddling mode of certain 'Supernatural Songs', especially 'The Four Ages of Man' and 'Conjunctions', and which uses again the image which opened 'The Mother of God'. 'A Nativity' invokes one of Yeats's persistent themes, the woman with a god in her womb. Yeats gets help in constructing his nativity scene from certain nineteenth-century artists and actors whom he thought of as part of the tradition or school in which he himself worked.

'The Man and the Echo' returns to the direct address of 'The Apparitions'. The retrospective mood of many of the *Last Poems* is now expressed in Yeats's last treatment of the old-age theme which began to haunt his poetry in *The Wild Swans at Coole* and which thereafter has never been absent for long. The insomniac artist imagines himself in a symbolic landscape where he questions what the practical effect of his work has been. When 'Rocky Voice' echoes his 'lie down and die', he defends himself, but goes on to anticipate his own death and to wonder about the state of the soul after death:

> What do we know but that we face
> One another in this place?

The poem ends with the final image of violence found in this violent book.

The opening lines of 'The Man and the Echo' have prepared us for 'The Circus Animals' Desertion', wherein Yeats and his readers together look back over the long course of his work, back indeed to its very beginnings, and contemplate its sources in the events of his life and in the emotions which these events evoked. But Yeats never forgets nor lets us forget that these events became art only after they had become part of his 'phantasmagoria', only after they had been made permanent, intended, by the shaping spirit of his imagination. This long backward look is completely appropriate here near the very end of his poems.

These end as they should end on the mocking note of 'Politics'. This is the old man's gay goodnight, which we should have expected, but which has been hitherto denied him by the rearrangement of *Last Poems*:

> Never to have lived is best, ancient writers say ...
> The second best's a gay goodnight and quickly turn away.

Whereas in *New Poems* Yeats opened yet another door, the reflective and philosophical tone of *Last Poems* is more characteristic; it constitutes in a very deep sense a backward glance o'er travell'd roads. By echoing so many earlier motifs, themes, and allusions Yeats has quite remarkably brought all of his poetry together here at its close.


III: THE INTERPLAY OF METERS

The metrical or musical effect of *New Poems* is new, as it should be. This is largely a result of the preponderance of ballad meters.

Though Yeats as a young man had written many poems in ballad meter, his late ballads have a quite changed tone caused largely, I think, by his complete mastery of the refrain. His refrains can now only be described as marvels, and they are marvellously controlling. Though poems in ballad meter do occur in *Last Poems*, and though they are as fine as ever, they do not pre-dominate and thus set the tone. In *Last Poems* Yeats re-explores every realm of discourse and almost every metrical form which he had mastered during the long years of his work, so that metrically as well as thematically *Last Poems* is a summary work. Yeats does practise some new meters, and much of his diction is fresh; this we would expect from a writer who was always making new beginnings. He arranges poetic forms new and old with the hand of an absolute master; indeed the musical aspect of *Last Poems* is a sheer delight from beginning to end.

The first four poems move toward an increasingly strict metrical form: 'Under Ben Bulben' is in very loose tetrameter, the four-beat lines Yeats had explored in *The Herne's Egg* and perfected in *Purgatory*. The unit is a verse paragraph – not com-mon in Yeats's poetry – and he uses couplet rhyme. His diction produces that seemingly colloquial tone which he had per-fected in 'In Memory of Major Robert Gregory' and which he used with notable effect ever after on appropriate occasions. A line such as 'Can disturb globe-trotting Madam' gives this colloquial effect (especially when we remember that no Irishman would sound the 'g' in 'trotting'). This use of a seemingly col-loquial tone – actually it is not colloquial at all, but very carefully produced, as Richard Ellmann has shown – in a discourse of ultimate seriousness is a peculiarly Yeatsean effect.

'Three Songs to the One Burden' uses the ballad meter which Yeats had perfected in *New Poems*. The stanza has always eight lines, rhymed irregularly, and the beat of the lines is four against three. He introduces a notable metrical variation at the grave refrain line '*From mountain to mountain ride the fierce horsemen*', which is sometimes included in the rhyme scheme and some-times not. It was set off from the stanzas it concludes in *Last Poems and Two Plays*. Tune-wise we seem to be in a much

simpler world than the world of 'Under Ben Bulben', in a world
of folk poetry.

In 'The Black Tower' Yeats uses two of his carefully patterned
stanza forms; these recur regularly. The stanzas in roman are one
of many variants of Yeats's favourite stanza of six lines; the ever-
shifting refrain printed in italic uses a four-line stanza with a
rhyme scheme that regularly recurs until at its third repetition
Yeats omits the 'a' rhyme our ear has come to expect and
emphasizes 'blacker' by breaking his rhyme scheme; another
favoured device. Here the formal strictness is almost as great as
possible.

Yet this becomes greater still in 'Cuchulain Comforted',
which is in *terza rima*; apparently Yeats chose his meter before he
began work on the poem.[6] This is the unique occurrence of that
form in Yeats's poetry, and is an instance of his ability always to
surprise us. Here a five-beat line is first heard in *Last Poems*. The
complete formal strictness controls the rather eerie atmosphere
of the poem.

'Three Marching Songs' returns to the metrical lilt of 'Three
Songs to the Same Tune'. Though we seem to be in a realm of
folk poetry, the form is highly complex. As in 'The Black Tower'
a six-line stanza is followed by a four-line refrain. The opening
four lines of each stanza have usually four beats, though they all
have ten or more syllables, a result of the many anapaestic feet;
the fifth and sixth lines have three beats. The pattern of rhyme
shifts constantly, though the fifth and sixth lines of each stanza
always rhyme. In the refrain, lines one and four, which rhyme,
have four beats, lines two and three, which also rhyme, three
beats. In spite of this formal complexity, there has been a
definite shift in tone.

'In Tara's Halls' is Yeats's last poem in blank verse. Blank
verse is the staple meter of his verse plays, and he often used
it for narrative poems, but he has not used it in a lyric poem
since 'The Phases of the Moon'. Blank verse was a favoured
meter in *The Wild Swans at Coole*, but we have not heard it since
except in plays and in his last narrative poem, 'The Gift of
Harun Al-Rashid'. Frequent repetition of words at the ends of

lines here gives something of the effect of rhyme as it so often
does in Milton.

In 'The Statues' Yeats returns to his favourite form for
meditative and philosophical poems, an elaborate eight-line
stanza with lines usually of five beats, and rhymed in varying
patterns. This stanza is used in many of his greatest poems
and he seems to have reserved it for grave utterances. The rhyme
scheme here used (abababcc), that of *ottava rima*, is found also in
'Sailing to Byzantium', 'Ancestral Houses', 'Coole Park', 'Coole
Park and Ballylee', 'Her Vision', part I of 'Parnell's Funeral'
(except for the irregular first stanza), 'The Gyres', and 'The
Municipal Gallery Revisited'. The very titles of these poems will
indicate the immense distinction of this form in Yeats's work.
The form is in every way appropriate to his subject, and
here as in other poems using this form his rhetoric is noble.

The form of 'News for the Delphic Oracle' is the neatest trick
of the week and Yeats provides a complete contrast to 'The
Statues' in both form and tone. Here he devotes exactly
twelve lines to each section of the poem. Four-stress lines
alternate with three-stress lines, and the even-numbered lines are
rhymed in pairs. The form is nearly as complex as the form of
'The Statues', yet the mode is completely different, decidedly
jazzy. The diction is new as well as jazzy: 'codgers', 'man-
picker', 'straddling', 'belly', 'bum', 'fishlike', 'copulate' do not
occur elsewhere in Yeats's poetry. We here enter a new realm
of discourse.

The meter of 'Long-legged Fly' is a variation on the meter of
'News'. Again the poem is in three parts, now each ten lines long,
ending in a two-line refrain. The even-numbered lines before the
refrain rhyme in pairs, and the pattern of beats is usually four
against three though the pattern is less insistent than in 'News'.
The first line of the refrain is a five-beat line.

Yeats invented a new stanza for 'A Bronze Head' and used it
again in 'Hound Voice'. It is a variation on his favourite eight-
line stanza. The stanza here is seven lines long and rhymes
ababbcc; the lines usually have five beats. Seven-line stanzas are
rare in Yeats's verse as compared with six- and eight-line

stanzas, and no earlier example uses either the five-beat line or
this exact rhyme scheme. It is somehow very fitting that Yeats
should invent a new form for his last poem to Maud Gonne. We
return to the grave rhetorical mode of 'The Statues'. I think that
he was led to repeat this form in 'Hound Voice' partly at least
to indicate a similarity of themes; both poems are concerned with
women he has loved. (Mrs Yeats dates 'A Bronze Head' 1937–8;
'Hound Voice' June–August 1938.)

These two poems are separated by the last of Yeats's quatrains,
'A Stick of Incense'. He wrote quatrains all his life, a fact
somewhat obscured by his suppression of many of the early
ones[7] and by his refusal to print many of the later ones. I think
that writing quatrains usually provided a needed relaxation for
him, it was a kind of poetic doodling, though such gnomic
quatrains as 'There', 'A Needle's Eye', and 'A Stick of Incense'
are as far removed as possible from doodling.

'John Kinsella's Lament' can be dated exactly from the letters
to Dorothy Wellesley; Yeats finished it on July 27, 1938. It is
not, then, the last ballad he wrote, for he reworked 'Three
Marching Songs' in December 1938. (I do not know the date of
'Three Songs to the One Burden'.) But he intended it to be
the last poem in ballad meter heard in his poetry, and this is
fitting for it is among his finest. Formally it is very like 'News for
the Delphic Oracle' and 'Long-legged Fly', though the effect is
very different, largely because of the changed persona. Again as
in 'News' each section has twelve lines and the even-numbered
lines rhyme in pairs; the beat is four against three. The use of a
refrain links the poem to 'Long-legged Fly'. It should be noted
that the stanzas were numbered in roman in *Last Poems and Two
Plays*. Yeats used numbered stanzas when he wanted his readers
to make a longer pause between stanzas than they would make
when there were no numbers; it was with him an important
device of punctuation. The manuscript version he sent to
Dorothy Wellesley also had numbered stanzas.[8]

'High Talk' is a modification of the sonnet, in spite of Yeats's
fifteeners and his couplet rhyming. The poem has fourteen lines
and the division into octave and sestet is carefully observed. The

two parts of the poem develop in ways entirely in keeping with the sonnet tradition: the octave develops the extended metaphor, comparing the artist to a man walking on stilts; the sestet comments on the metaphor with ever-mounting intensity. There is a noticeable contrast between the colloquial diction, the rushing meter, and the formal strictness of the poem, and this contrast helps prepare the way for the quite changed tone at the end.

With 'The Apparitions' there is again a notable metrical change of pace. Yeats shifts to a four-beat line and uses couplet rhymes. Here a refrain occurs for the last time in his poems. He here anticipates the rhetorical mode of 'Under Ben Bulben'.

'A Nativity' is composed of six riddling couplets, made up of question and answer until in the sixth both lines are questions. (Not that the answers answer.) We are back in the realm of 'Supernatural Songs', especially that of 'The Four Ages of Man' and 'Conjunctions'.

We go on to 'The Man and the Echo', wherein Yeats practises the four-beat couplet he will shortly use in 'Under Ben Bulben'. The intimate confessional tone and the apparently easy language also remind us of the later poem. Again there has been a definite change of tone, and Yeats momentarily moves away from stanza forms. (Both in *Last Poems and Two Plays* and in the version of the poem given to Dorothy Wellesley[9] line 23 reads 'Nor can there be *a* work so great'.)

In 'The Circus Animals' Desertion' we listen for the last time to Yeats's stately *ottava rima*, the form used for 'The Statues' and for so many other great poems (listed above). Once more there has been a shift in tone.

Yeats shifts his tone again with 'Politics'. This has the exact form used for the three separate parts cf 'News for the Delphic Oracle': four-beat lines against three-beat lines, twelve lines, the even-numbered lines rhyming in pairs. Yeats's mocking voice is heard for the last time.

Joyce is reported to have said while at work on *Finnegans Wake* that he could do anything possible to be done with the English language. At the end of his life Yeats could do anything possible to be done with English metrics.

IV: RESULTS

When the poems of Yeats's last years are read in their proper order and under their proper headings we gain new insights into them. The suppression of the title *New Poems* in the collected editions was particularly unfortunate, for it has obscured a remarkable new beginning. This is not to say that all the *New Poems* are new: 'Lapis Lazuli' is a characteristic poem, and in 'The Municipal Gallery Revisited' he anticipates the retrospective tone of many of his *Last Poems*. This is as it should be for the identity of Yeats is now beyond dispute. Still the *New Poems* are usually new both in theme and meter, and Yeats begins them with 'The Gyres', in which he somewhat deflates his central emblem. That the recovery of his intended order for *Last Poems* has important results for their interpretation and enjoyment has been demonstrated above. No work of any English poet has been more carefully ordered than the poems of Yeats, and this ordering (broken in many places besides *Last Poems* but elsewhere recoverable from the Definitive Edition, 2 vols, 1949) needs to be reinstated.

NOTES ON THE TEXT AND CHRONOLOGY OF
COMPOSITION OF YEATS'S LAST POEMS

TEXT   During the summer of 1960, while working with the Yeats papers in Dublin, I found Yeats's MS table of contents for *Last Poems* – it had strayed into the file envelope containing the surviving MSS of *Responsibilities*. I printed this MS, with Mrs Yeats's permission, in *Modern Language Notes*, June 1961, pp. 515–16. The MS proves that Yeats was responsible for the order of the poems followed in the Cuala Press's *Last Poems and Two Plays*, and that the changed order of the poems found in *Last Poems and Plays* and later in the Definitive and other collected editions radically alters Yeats's intentions. The order of poems in the MS and in *Last Poems and Two Plays* is as follows:

1   'Under Ben Bulben'
2   'Three Songs to the One Burden'

3 'The Black Tower'
4 'Cuchulain Comforted'
5 'Three Marching Songs'
6 'In Tara's Halls'
7 'The Statues'
8 'News for the Delphic Oracle'
9 'Long-legged Fly'
10 'A Bronze Head'
11 'A Stick of Incense'
12 'Hound Voice'
13 'John Kinsella's Lament for Mrs Mary Moore'
14 'High Talk'
15 'The Apparitions'
16 'A Nativity'
17 'The Man and the Echo'
18 'The Circus Animals' Desertion'
19 'Politics'

(Yeats's MS also directed that his last two plays, *The Death of Cuchulain* and *Purgatory*, should follow the poems. This accounts for the fact that the Cuala Press printed *Purgatory* both in *Last Poems and Two Plays* and in *On the Boiler*.)

Not only do *Last Poems and Plays* and the various collected editions fail to follow the order in which Yeats wanted these poems printed, they also introduce textual changes which could not have had his sanction. I summarize the variant readings introduced into *Last Poems and Plays* as these are noted in the *Variorum Edition*: typographical or textual changes occur in 'Under Ben Bulben', 'Three Songs to the One Burden', 'Three Marching Songs', 'Long-legged Fly', 'John Kinsella's Lament', 'The Man and the Echo', and 'Politics'. There are changes in punctuation at the ends of lines in the poems numbered in Yeats's MS table of contents 1, 2, 3, 4, 5, 6, 7, 8, 10, 11, 13, 14, 17, 18, 19; and, a more serious matter since their effect is to introduce a caesura where Yeats may not have wanted one, new internal punctuation is introduced into the texts of poems 2, 4, 5, 6, 7, 8, 12, and 18.

These facts taken together lead me to the conclusion that the
received text of these poems is unreliable, and that until the
surviving MSS and TSS of these poems are examined with the
aim of establishing a text that will be faithful to Yeats's intentions,
readers of Yeats's poems should accept the text found in *Last
Poems and Two Plays*, easily reconstructed with the help of the
*Variorum* and Wade's table of contents for *Last Poems and Two
Plays*,[10] as the best available.

I can begin this process of correction by reporting the results
of comparing my transcripts of MSS or TSS of three poems with
the received text: A late TS of 'Under Ben Bulben' has at line 8
'That airs an immortality', the reading found in the *Irish
Independent*. (Here I would guess that Yeats explored two forms
of line 8, 'That airs an immortality', and 'That air in immortality'
and that this accounts for the unsatisfactory text of *Last Poems
and Two Plays* 'That airs in immortality'.) The TS of 'News for
the Delphic Oracle' into which Yeats inserted MS punctuation
shows that the commas introduced into *Last Poems and Plays*
at the ends of lines 3 and 14, and after 'Until' in line 21 do not
have his authority. Yeats's final draft of 'The Circus Animals'
Desertion' (mixed MS and TS) shows that the text found in *Last
Poems and Two Plays* follows the draft in the punctuation of
lines 9, 16, 21, 31, and 34 whereas the text found in *Last Poems
and Plays* does not. On the other hand, Yeats's MS supports the
reading 'sweepings of a street' in line 35 – the reading found in
*Last Poems and Plays* – not 'sweepings of the street' found in
*Last Poems and Two Plays*. In drafting line 35 Yeats first wrote
'the', then cancelled it and replaced it by 'a'.

CHRONOLOGY OF COMPOSITION   The dates given are derived from Yeats's letters, from Mrs Yeats's annotated copy of
Macmillan's *Last Poems and Plays*, from Richard Ellmann's chronology,[11] and from my own examination of the surviving MSS:
'Three Songs to the one Burden', unknown; 'A Nativity', August
1936; 'A Bronze Head', 1937–8; 'News for the Delphic Oracle',
1938; 'The Apparitions', March–April 1938; 'Long-legged Fly',
April 11, 1938; 'Politics', May 24, 1938; 'In Tara's Halls', June

1938; 'The Statues', April–June 1938; 'John Kinsella's Lament', July 21, 1938; 'A Stick of Incense', July 29, 1938; 'High Talk', begun July 29, 1938; 'Hound Voice', June–August 1938; 'Under Ben Bulben', September 4, 1938; 'The Circus Animals' Desertion', November 1937–September 1938; 'The Man and the Echo', July–October 1938; 'Three Marching Songs', December 1938; 'Cuchulain Comforted', January 13, 1939; 'The Black Tower', January 21, 1939.

## THE ORDER OF YEATS'S LAST POEMS[12]

Yeats always carefully planned the order of the poems which make up his various collections. Among the Yeats papers in Dublin are many manuscript drafts of tables of contents, going all the way back to *The Wind among the Reeds* and coming forward all the way to *Last Poems*. Since several writers have speculated whether the order in which *Last Poems* appear in the collected editions represents Yeats's intentions, I reproduce below his manuscript table of contents for *Last Poems*. The numbers as well as the titles are in Yeats's hand; the list has no title or heading:

1  Under Ben Bulben
2  Three Songs to One Burden
3  The Black Tower
4  Cuchulain Comforted
5  Three Marching Songs
6  In Tara's Halls
7  The Statues (Would like another copy if George takes this to Dublin)
8  News for the Delphic Oracle
9  The Long Legged Fly
10  A Bronze Head
11  A Stick of Incense
12  Hound Voice
13  John Kinsella's Lament etc.
14  High Talk

(Quoted with the permission of Mrs W. B. Yeats.)

It will be noticed at once that this list includes all of the poems in *Last Poems* except the three Yeats had put in *On the Boiler* ('Why should not Old Men be Mad?', 'Crazy Jane on the Mountain', and 'The Stateman's Holiday'), and that their order is that followed in the Cuala Press's *Last Poems and Two Plays*,[13] and not that found in the collected editions. Since this manuscript table of contents includes poems on which Yeats was working in January 1939, it must be one of the last things he ever wrote. It establishes the fact that Yeats himself was responsible for the order of *Last Poems and Two Plays* even though that book appeared after his death.

## NOTES

1. *Letters on Poetry from W. B. Yeats to Dorothy Wellesley* (reissued 1964) p. 40.
2. *The Letters of W. B. Yeats*, ed. Allan Wade (1954) p. 911.
3. See 'Yeats and Maud Gonne', in *Texas Studies in Literature*, III 456–7.
4. *Letters on Poetry*, p. 182.
5. Ibid. p. 58.
6. Ibid. p. 193.
7. See *Variorum Edition* (London and New York, 1957) pp. 734–5.
8. *Letters on Poetry*, pp. 182–3.
9. Ibid. p. 180.
10. Allan Wade, *A Bibliography of the Writings of W. B. Yeats* (1958) item 200.
11. *The Identity of Yeats* (1954), pp. 293–4.
12. Reprinted from *Modern Language Notes*, June 1961.
13. Wade, *Bibliography*, item 200.

D

# T. R. Henn

## THE MILL OF THE MIND (1965)*

> Neither loose imagination,
> Nor the mill of the mind
> Consuming its rag and bone,
> Can make the truth known.
>
> 'An Acre of Grass'

The mental world of Yeats's last poetry is like that of Renan in his old age, mischievous, volatile, passingly profound and secretly diverting in its sophistries.                    AUSTIN CLARKE[1]

... I am grateful for your letter. At my time of life a man wonders if the time has not come to cease from verse. Your letter makes me hope that if I have found a little wisdom to take the place of the passion I once had.                    (12 March 1938)[2]

### I

CRITICAL opinion has diverged sharply both as to the merits of *Last Poems and Plays* and its place in Yeats's poetic development. Some expressed a pained surprise at the obsession with lust and rage, the brutality and violence of an elderly and sex-ridden poet, who had lost sight of his original objective, or forgotten the synthesis achieved in 'Byzantium', and whose last writings were aimless and perverse, with something of the wilderness of senility. Others recognized the sense of excitement communicated in the poems, but gave no explanation of it; others, again, concentrated on the virtues of the ballad poetry, and the 'nobility' of the verses to Dorothy Wellesley. It seems desirable to attempt to view the collection in some sort of perspective: for I believe that the derogatory criticisms are based most often

* *Editor's Note.* This and the following essay are chapters from the 1965 edition of *The Lonely Tower*, first published in 1950.

upon a single quatrain, accepted at its face value, and, super-
ficially, a convenient salient for the reviewer:

> You think it horrible that lust and rage
> Should dance attention upon my old age;
> They were not such a plague when I was young;
> What else have I to spur me into song?[3]

I have argued previously that 'Byzantium' should not be considered as the final synthesis; that Yeats's prose, particularly that
of *On the Boiler* (in its original text), should be read in relation to
this period; and that the poems of *A Full Moon in March* are
closely related to *Last Poems*. I suggest that the whole can be
seen as a clearly defined pattern, a projection of previous thought
and technique; neither a regression nor a senile perversity, but a
reconsideration and readjustment (in the light of contemporary
events) of nearly everything that had gone before.

It seems to me that *Last Poems* falls into four main divisions.
There are first the 'cosmic' poems, projections or restatements of
Yeats's previous thought on the great mutations of the world.
These are 'The Gyres', 'Lapis Lazuli', 'An Acre of Grass', 'The
'Statues', 'A Bronze Head', and 'The Circus Animals' Desertion'.
They merge in one respect into the Cuchulain group, culminating
in the play on the hero's death; mystical, death-haunted, linked
to *The King of the Great Clock Tower* in *A Full Moon in March*.
They represent the last identification of the poet with the heroic
defeat of his hero, expressing the tragic exaltation of gaiety which
I find to be the dominant theme of the whole collection. And
since, through the Cuchulain image and the Statue in the Post
Office, Cuchulain is an emblem of the Easter Rising, there is a
link with the ballad poetry, both patriotic and dramatic; and this
itself is related to the first group (particularly through the
'Marching Songs') as a final aspect of the function and value of the
Rising in the processional cycles of history. The fourth group
concerns the so-called 'lust and rage' poems; related to the
'cosmic' poems of the first group, to the heroic love of the second,
and to the 'book of the people' in the third. This mood finds
expression in 'The Three Bushes' and the related songs, and in

'Hound Voice'. Finally, the four groups are, as it were, straddled or bracketed by three other central poems: 'The Municipal Gallery Revisited', 'The Man and the Echo', and 'Under Ben Bulben'.

II

The first poem, 'The Gyres', makes a double assertion. It is another view of the ending of a civilization, both in Ireland and in the world at large. Yeats's view, as always from the period of *Responsibilities* onwards, is that of Heraclitus and Plato rather than of Shelley. The threads are picked up from 'The Second Coming' — 'Irrational streams of blood are staining earth' – and from 'Coole Park and Ballylee' (remembering the pictures of the dead to be reviewed in 'The Municipal Gallery Revisited') – 'And ancient lineaments are blotted out'. Among those 'blotted out' is Lady Gregory, who died in 1932.

A year ago I found I had written no verse for two years: I had never been so long barren; I had nothing in my head, and there used to be more than I could write. Perhaps Coole Park, where I had escaped from politics, from all that Dublin talked of, when it was shut, shut me out from my theme; or did the subconscious drama that was my imaginative life end with its owner?[4]

His friends have gone; the Irish political scene has changed beyond recognition; but the oracle, Shelley's ancient philosopher in the shell-strewn cavern by the Mediterranean,[5] who might be Oedipus, or Ribh the heretic Hermit-Saint, or Yeats himself – an Irish Delphic oracle – in the 'Cleft that's christened Alt', near Sligo, accepts the mutability of things:

> Out of cavern comes a voice,
> And all it knows is that one word 'Rejoice!'

Conduct and work grow coarse, and coarse the soul. . . .

It was the complaint that he had made of the years of drudgery at the Abbey, when he half-doubted that his gift had been blunted; it is echoed from the passage on 'drudgery' in 'The Phases of the Moon'. But now the tone has changed. The comment is 'Rejoice!' and 'What matter?' There will be a new civilization, a new aristocracy, to take the place of the old. 'As we approach the phoenix nest the old classes, with their power of co-ordinating events, evaporate, the mere multitude is every-where with its empty photographic eyes. Yet we who have hated the age are joyous and happy. The new discipline wherever enforced or thought will recall forgotten beautiful faces. . . .'[6] The poem is shot through and through with memories of Shelley, and particularly of *Hellas*. 'Old Rocky Face' was 'Old Cavern Face' in the first draft.[7] A passage from the *Letters to 'A.E.'* is pertinent:

Had some young Greek found Shelley's 'Ahasuerus' in that shell-strewn cavern, the sage would not have talked mathe-matics or even 'those strong and secret thoughts . . . which others fear and know not', but given, I think, very simple advice, not indeed fitted to any momentary crisis but fitted perhaps for the next fifty years.[8]

But there is also a passage from Spengler which serves to tie this symbolism to the world-stream of events:

The second wave swelled up steeply in the Apocalyptic currents after 300. Here it was the Magian waking-consciousness that arose and built itself a metaphysic of Last Things, based already 'upon the prime symbol of the coming Culture, the Cavern'.[9]

The invocation may be addressed to Ahasuerus, or to the Sphinx, timeless and omnipresent, whether in the desert or on the Rock of Cashel; or heard as the 'Rocky Voice' as of the Delphic Oracle in 'The Man and the Echo', associated with the strange beast that stirs in the desert at the second coming. His civiliza-tion, and with it all civilization, is decaying.[10] Maud Gonne has lost her beauty, Lady Gregory of the 'ancient lineaments' is dead. The 'irrational streams of blood' that accompanied the rise of Christianity recur in the Easter Rising, and perhaps again (though I do not know when this poem was composed) in the events of Europe between 1934 and 1938. 'Empedocles has thrown all things about'; the allusion may have many sources. There is evidence that he read Cary's translation of Dante, and Shadwell's (which he preferred), and Lawrence Binyon's *Inferno*; and there is a note on the reference to Empedocles in Canto IV of Cary's *Inferno*:

> . . . [he] taught that the universe exists by reason of the discord of the elements, and that if harmony were to take the place of this discord, a state of chaos would ensue.[11]

Perhaps it is also a reference to the alternate cycles of movement.

Empedocles is cited as saying that 'of necessity Love and Strife control things and move them part of the time, and that they are at rest during the intervening time.'[12]

Or the proper reference may be to *A Vision*:

> 'When Discord,' writes Empedocles, 'has fallen into the lowest depths of the vortex' – the extreme bound, not the centre, Burnet points out – 'Concord has reached the centre, into it do all things come together so as to be only one, not all at once but gradually from different quarters, and as they come Discord retires to the extreme boundary . . . in proportion as it runs out Concord in a soft immortal boundless stream runs in.'          [(B) p. 67]

And so Yeats realizes and affirms his place in the cycle of events. 'Hector is dead and there's a light in Troy' – the image that recurs perpetually, whether of Maud Gonne's beauty, or Iseult's. This age is just such another, of violence and disintegration. Quiescent Being passes into active Becoming; the tragic joy is also the theme of 'Lapis Lazuli':

> Yet they, should the last scene be there,
> The great stage curtain about to drop,
> If worthy their prominent part in the play,
> Do not break up their lines to weep.          (*CP* 338)

The second stanza of 'The Gyres' is dispassionate. All is part of the cycle:

> What matter though numb nightmare ride on top,
> And blood and mire the sensitive body stain?
> What matter? Heave no sigh, let no tear drop,
> A greater, a more gracious time has gone;
> For painted forms or boxes of make-up
> In ancient tombs I sighed, but not again;

> What matter? Out of cavern comes a voice,
> And all it knows is that one word 'Rejoice!'

The 'numb nightmare' has been thought of before in relation to the Troubles: now it is world-wide. The sensitive body is stained – note the paradox – by its components, the mire and blood of the rescuing dolphin of 'Byzantium'. But there is to be no lamentation; the phrase 'A greater, a more gracious time has gone' picks up the thought of the first stanza. He has rejected Egyptian thaumaturgy, the pursuit of the dead into the labyrinth (compare 'no dark tomb-haunter once' of 'A Bronze Head' – *CP* 382). The voice out of the cavern is that of Sibyl or oracle: and the overtones of 'Rejoice!' set the mind wandering towards the Christian exhortation.

The third stanza opens with an allusion to the poet's own thought of himself in the last Phases of the Moon. The comment 'What matter?' is exactly right: in its arrogance comparable with 'And when that story's finished, what's the news?' of 'The Choice' (*CP* 278). The new gyre will begin:

> Conduct and work grow coarse, and coarse the soul,
> What matter? Those that Rocky Face holds dear,
> Lovers of horses and of women, shall,
> From marble of a broken sepulchre,
> Or dark betwixt the polecat and the owl,
> Or any rich, dark nothing disinter
> The workman, noble and saint, and all things run
> On that unfashionable gyre again.'

The tradition of aristocracy, of the great virile men, will return. The tone drops, labours with the complexity of its meaning, full of its allusions; *from marble* – the enduring thing – *of a broken sepulchre* – suggests the Second Coming ('I have a series of dramatic poems – very short – of Christ coming out of the tomb')[13] or the Second Resurrection, or a city rebuilt from the masonry of tombs; all this complexity is there, and more so in the next line, 'Or dark betwixt the polecat and the owl'. I doubt whether it is possible to fix the meaning precisely. The polecat and the owl, are, in the first place, associated with desolate places

and ruins;[14] the owl with wisdom and the supernatural, the polecat (as, in many poems, the weasel) with destruction. The resurrection or disinterment of the new age will take place *betwixt*
them (the ambiguity is obvious). It will be disinterred from *any
rich dark nothing*, and there is the thought of Donne again: both
in 'A Nocturnal upon St Lucies Day'

> But I am by her death (which word wrongs her)
> Of the first nothing, the Elixir grown –

and in 'The Relique'. The end will be the new gyre of an
hierarchy, an order, that is prophesied in 'Under Ben Bulben',
flaunted in the epitaph of 'Horseman, pass by!'

The same theme is developed in 'Lapis Lazuli' – 'almost the
best I have made of recent years'.[15] He is meditating over a
Chinese carving, and this is one more addition to the list of
poems in English literary history that have been stimulated by
such an object. 'Someone has sent me a present of a great piece
carved by some Chinese sculptor into the semblance of a mountain with temple, trees, paths and an ascetic or pupil about to
climb the mountain. Ascetic, pupil, hard stone, eternal theme of
the sensual east. The heroic cry in the midst of despair. But I am
wrong, the east has its solutions always, and therefore knows
nothing of tragedy. It is we, not the east, that must raise the
heroic cry.' There is expressed in it the exaltation in tragedy and
defeat which he had found in the Rising, and which is now to be
integrated with his own life, even though he hates the age. It is
the last knowledge that 'comes to turbulent men':

> They know that Hamlet and Lear are gay;
> Gaiety transfiguring all that dread.
> All men have aimed at, found and lost;
> Black out; Heaven blazing into the head:
> Tragedy wrought to its uttermost.

So in a significant passage in *On the Boiler*:

The arts are all the bridal chambers of joy. No tragedy is
legitimate unless it leads some great character to his final joy.
Polonius may go out wretchedly, but I can hear the dance music
in 'Absent thee from felicity awhile', or in Hamlet's speech over

the dead Ophelia, and what of Cleopatra's last farewells, Lear's rage under the lightning, Oedipus sinking down at the story's end into an earth 'riven' by love? Some Frenchman has said that farce is the struggle against a ridiculous object, comedy against a movable object, tragedy against an immovable; and because the will, or energy, is greatest in tragedy, tragedy is the more noble; but I add that 'will or energy is eternal delight,' and when its limit is reached it may become a pure, aimless joy, though the man, the shade, still mourns his lost object. (p. 35)

I suggest that this statement clarifies the whole issue. He himself may 'mourn his lost object'; he may see himself and his purpose defeated; he may suffer the decay of body and of desire. The 'pure, aimless joy' is that of the Fool, in the last of the Phases, who has all things from God. The other mask-figures support this: Timon for passion and rage at ingratitude, Blake for his energy, Lear for his progress through madness to peace: this last image fitting perfectly with Yeats's theory of purification through exhaustion of desire, and his image of himself as the dispassionate spectator of the political chaos of 1936:

> – so we'll live,
> And pray, and sing, and tell old tales, and laugh
> At gilded butterflies, and hear poor rogues
> Talk of court news –

(compare the poem 'Politics'),

> – and we'll talk with them too,
> Who loses and who wins; who's in, who's out;
> And take upon 's the mystery of things,
> As if we were God's spies; and we'll wear out,
> In a wall'd prison, packs and sets of great ones
> That ebb and flow by the moon.

'The Statues' picks up one of the threads of *A Vision*, which recurs again in 'Under Ben Bulben'. It is the old argument (repeated in *On the Boiler*) for the traditional sculpture, Greek deriving from Egyptian and its 'measurement'; and Alexander's conquest of the East by that achievement. (I believe that this apparent obsession with measurement is more profound than any mere numerology, and that it derives from Blake's engraving

D2                                                    S.Y.L.P.

'The Ancient of Days' that hung at Woburn Buildings,[16] in which God is measuring the world with compasses of lightning thrust down through the clouds. Compare 'Measurement began our might'.[17]) The artist's function in depicting the perfection of physical form 'to fill the cradles right', the guidance of sexual desire:

> But boys and girls, pale from the imagined love
> Of solitary beds, knew what they were,
> That passion could bring character enough,
> And pressed at midnight in some public place
> Live lips upon a plummet-measured face.    (CP 375)

This is perhaps the most difficult poem that Yeats wrote. Much light is thrown on it by Stallworthy's study of the drafts,[18] which supplements most admirably Vivienne Koch's essay in *The Tragic Phase*. The intensely difficult 'Grimalkin' of stanza 3 has been explained by Wilson;[19] I am not wholly convinced, but I do not know of a better exegesis. At the end, the poem is linked to the Easter Rising, and its mystical implications; a theme in one sense complementary to that of 'The Gyres'. 'Measurement' will bring about a Greek aristocratic stability as the myths converge:

> When Pearse summoned Cuchulain to his side,
> What stalked through the Post Office? What intellect,
> What calculation, number, measurement, replied?
> We Irish, born into that ancient sect
> But thrown upon this filthy modern tide
> And by its formless spawning fury wrecked,
> Climb to our proper dark, that we may trace
> The lineaments of a plummet-measured face.

There is, surely, no loss of control in this verse. The heroic arrogance of the two legendary figures, equated against each other, is linked mysteriously to the secrets of the ultimate philosophy, the perfection of form; which is in its turn the knowledge of God.

The strange 'Cuchulain Comforted' (CP 395) is a prophetic poem on his own entrance to the Kingdom of the Dead, with memories of Dante (and this is the only poem in which Yeats employs *terza rima*) cutting across Celtic legend. The hero is welcomed by the souls in the Country of the Blessed: 'They had changed their throats and had the throats of birds' – which I believe to be connected with the stage-direction at the end of *The Death of Cuchulain* following the dance of the Morrigu: 'Then she stands motionless. There is silence and in the silence a few faint bird notes.'[20] . . . I do not yet understand the full meaning of the play; though I am clear that it must be read side by side with *The King of the Great Clock Tower* and with 'Cuchulain Comforted', and that it is, in some sense, a projection of the theme of the former. The play is obscure because Yeats is trying to achieve a kind of desperate compression, working by juxtaposition of incidents in the hero's life which form a pattern at once too definite and too vague to be apprehended as a unity. The symbolism is not conceived as an integral part of the structure; the binding of Cuchulain by Aoife in the folds of her veil, the perception of Aoife as a Clytemnestra-figure, the Blind Man who kills him for twelve pennies, at the order of Queen Maeve – all these are set in a strained relationship to the Easter Rising and the Statue of Cuchulain in the Post Office. It is the not uncommon failing of the poet who has thought so deeply over a given theme that he moves among its intricacies with an ease which vitiates communication in the crude theatrical form.

III

The ballads of *Last Poems* appear at first to be in a class of their own, but are, I think, to be related closely to the other poems. There are four main themes; the glorification of the Easter Rising, and its establishment as part of the mythology, perhaps with the intention, however unconscious, of confirming in Yeats's own mind his organic part in the event. Such are 'The O'Rahilly', the Casement poems, 'Three Songs to the One Burden', and the much revised 'Three Marching Songs', of which an earlier variant is accessible in *A Full Moon in March*. They are a little strident, with whistle and concertina behind all of them, and not 'Colonel Martin' alone: the jerky excited rhythms reflect a feverish half-ecstatic mood, trying desperately to pull into the framework the characteristic relationships of his figures to the pattern of Love and War. The Steinach operation which he caused to be performed in 1934 resulted beyond doubt in a temporary recrudescence of vitality, but is insufficient of itself to account for the new excitement in the technique of 'Supernatural Songs', and the steady joyous contemplation of tragedy; which is, as I have suggested, a logical development of Yeats's thought. Nor can we attribute to it, as critics and 'the mirror of malicious eyes' have lately done, the alleged obsession with 'lust and rage'. Yeats was very much concerned with world events. 'Europe seems to be under a waning moon.' It was characteristic of him that the world disintegration should be reflected subjectively in terms of his personal experiences and theories. To Dorothy Wellesley he wrote: 'At this moment I am expressing my rage against the intelligentsia by writing about Oliver Cromwell who was the Lenin of his day – I speak through the mouth of some wandering peasant poet in Ireland.'[21]

The poem is 'The Curse of Cromwell' (*CP* 350), and is a lament for his decaying world:

All neighbourly content and easy talk are gone,
But there's no good complaining, for money's rant is on.
He that's mounting up must on his neighbour mount,
And we and all the Muses are things of no account.
They have schooling of their own, but I pass their schooling by,
What can they know that we know that know the time to die?
                    *O what of that, O what of that,*
                    *What is there left to say?*

At first the verse seems clumsy and the third and fourth lines strained, until we realize that it is written for a tune's sake: but (as so often in the ballads) the whole poem is softened and widened by the strange and shifting overtones of the refrain. It gains immeasurably by reading aloud. It is the theme of 'The Gyres' and 'The Statues', complicated by the preparation for death; and that finds an image in the poem 'In Tara's Halls'. 'The Pilgrim' is a return to the thought that the holy places of Ireland might effect a union of the two religions. It is a ballad that recalls, intensely, the world of some of Jack Yeats's paintings, the ritual of pilgrimage, and its ambivalent aspects.

The best of the other ballads is 'The O'Rahilly' (*CP* 354);[22] in which the effect depends on the tone, which varies from verse to verse, of the sea refrain (as at the changing of the watch) 'How goes the weather?' It is part questioning, part ironic, part a sort of chorus to move the action outside reality. It means in effect, *What of the Rising? What is going on in the day-to-day world of the farmer, the huntsman, or sailor?* – the background of the war; and perhaps, *What is the news of happenings in the world beyond these?* These overtones should be brought out by accent and tone of each verse[23] (all the ballads must be read aloud), the idiom being organic: for it seems to me that here, perhaps for the first time, Yeats achieves true colloquial speech:

> Sing of the O'Rahilly
> That had such little sense
> He told Pearse and Connolly
> He'd gone to great expense
>
> Keeping all the Kerry men
> Out of that crazy fight;
> That he might be there himself
> Had travelled half the night.
> *How goes the weather?*

By comparison with this, the Casement poems are forced, crude, factitiously violent – as if (and it may well have been so) they were the products of Yeats's pondering on an event which was mere political hearsay, of whose truth he was himself not wholly sure, but in which it was important to believe.

'Colonel Martin' (*CP* 361) is a special achievement in this technique. It is perfectly adapted to the narrative qualities of the Irish street-ballad: it allows for dramatic emphasis, for dialogue in character, even to the *tourneurs de phrase* suited to the social rank of each speaker; it has a little of the rapidity of movement, and of the artistic inconsequentiality of the true ballad. An irony that is uncommon in Yeats flickers over the poem, and, in the dénouement, shows a vivid knowledge of the ballad's prototype;

a tragic and cruel accentuation of the bathos of the events, which is entirely in keeping. If we examine these ballads side by side with those of *Crossways* – 'Moll Magee' and 'The Foxhunter' – there is no comparison for the vitality, the organic sense of rhythm (note, for example, the dramatic change in stanza VII), the delicate adjustment (even in such an apparently coarse medium) to tone and character in dialogue:

> 'And did you keep no gold, Tom?
> You had three kegs,' said he.
> 'I never thought of that, Sir.'
> 'Then want before you die.'
> And want he did; for my own grand-dad
> Saw the story's end,
> And Tom make out a living
> From the seaweed on the strand.
> *The Colonel went out sailing*

## IV

'The Three Bushes' grew out of a ballad by Dorothy Wellesley. It was continually modified and revised, and the account of its making is to be read in the *Letters on Poetry*. It is another handling of the old problem, whether love be of the body, or of the soul, or of both: the whole complicated, I believe, by the dramatic fantasy-solution which the poem offered. There are the two women, the 'daylight lady' and the chambermaid, soul and sense; the one tortured by sexual passion, yet inhibited: showing precisely the same conflict as the Queen in *A Full Moon in March*:

> I am in love
> And that is my shame.
> What hurts the soul
> My soul adores,
> No better than a beast
> Upon all fours.[24]

There are memories here of earlier work: the realism of woman in her attitude to this fulfilment, the Lear–Swift reduction to unaccommodated man, recalls

> And laughed upon his breast to think
> Beast gave beast as much.

By contrast, the Chambermaid is complete knowledge, complete objectivity. Her knowledge of the body is without amazement:

> How came this ranger
> Now sunk in rest,
> Stranger with stranger,
> On my cold breast?
> What's left to sigh for,
> Strange night has come;
> God's love has hidden him
> Out of all harm,
> Pleasure has made him
> Weak as a worm.

What may, perhaps, be missed at a first reading is the rightness of the word *ranger*; it is a common Anglo-Irish term, expressing at once admiration for manhood and virility, and a shadow of alarm. It is not a mere rhyme-word determined by the 'stranger' of the third line. So, too, the simile at the end; both are in character with the Chambermaid.

The Lady, in her second and third songs, struggles towards her own synthesis: dramatized by Yeats, mocked at as the cocotte who has not the courage of her love, and yet striving to justify her solution:

> He shall love my soul as though
> Body were not at all,
> He shall love your body
> Untroubled by the soul,
> Love cram love's two divisions
> Yet keep his substance whole.
> *The Lord have mercy upon us.*

It may not be immediately apparent that the liturgical refrain not only throws forward to the Chambermaid's final confession to the priest, but is a counterpointed gesture, as by some bystander, on the 'heresy' that the Lady propounds. In her third song she moves a step onwards towards a richly emblematic synthesis:

> That I may hear if we should kiss
> A contrapuntal serpent hiss,
> You, should hand explore a thigh,
> All the labouring heavens sigh.

*Contrapuntal* carries the long-drawn-out stress; the serpent as the emblem of the Fall, of the sex principle set against the neo-Platonism of, say, 'Hero and Leander'. (An ikon of the seventeenth century shows Eve in a posture as of crucifixion upon Adam's Tree, while the Serpent penetrates her.) Against these two are set the Lover with his single song: exquisitely modulated, picking up, in a different key, the theme of 'Beloved, may your sleep be sound'. I do not know of any short poem in which the workmanship is more perfect; with the virtue concentrated (as so often in Yeats's technique) on the single word *sighs* in the third line, with its depth and resonance:

> Bird sighs for the air,
> Thought for I know not where,
> For the womb the seed sighs.
> Now sinks the same rest
> On mind, on nest,
> On straining thighs.

For if our ear remembers the previous writings, there are in this the harmonies of all the Leda-imagery; the bird with its *straining* thighs; the symmetry of construction that draws *mind* and *nest* together, the sources of thought-in-action – the eggs of Love and War – the seed sighing, half-human but also remembering, I think, the passage in Hardy's *Woodlanders* where the low breathing of the newly planted trees is heard.

So 'The Wild Old Wicked Man' (*CP* 356), which bears upon the mask of Synge's brutality and violence; with its ending in a negation of purgatory, of the classic values of tragedy, and the modulation of the whole by the refrain. It is the theme of 'Must we part, Von Hügel', twisted ironically, and yet completely poised in knowledge:

> 'That some stream of lightning
> From the old man in the skies
> Can burn out that suffering

No right-taught man denies.
But a coarse old man am I,
I choose the second-best,
I forget it all awhile
Upon a woman's breast.'
                              *Daybreak and a candle-end.*

But there is one new aspect of the love-conflict; lifted, as it were,
to the plane of the Celtic hunting legends, and 'that wild
Tristram', and the whole archetypal image of the hound and the
deer. It is now all bare, stripped of the obscurities, the symbolism
of the earlier poems, simple and dignified:

The women that I picked spoke sweet and low
And yet gave tongue.

(He would choose them so, for Lear is the most strongly defined
of the latest masks, and Cordelia his dream.)

'Hound Voices' were they all.
We picked each other from afar and knew
What hour of terror comes to test the soul,
And in that terror's name obeyed the call,
And understood, what none have understood,
Those images that waken in the blood.[25]

## NOTES

1. *Dublin Magazine*, April–June 1939.
2. Letter from W. B. Y. to T. R. Henn.
3. 'The Spur', in *The Collected Poems of W. B. Yeats* (1950 ed.)
p. 359. The first draft has 'should dance attendance', which is a better
line (Allt). (Parenthetical *CP* page references hereafter are to this
edition.)
4. Preface to *The King of the Great Clock Tower* (Dublin, 1934).
5. See *Autobiographies* (1955) pp. 171 ff.
6. *On the Boiler* (Dublin, 1939) p. 25. Note the 'empty photographic eyes', as of the Roman statues.
7. I am indebted to A. N. Jeffares for this. But I do not know what
significance (if any) is to be found in the carved stone head, high in the
S.E. wall of Thoor Ballylee, and facing towards Coole.
8. *Dublin Magazine*, July–Sept. 1939.

9. *Decline of the West* (1926) II p. 249.

10. Consider (especially in view of what follows) Donne's 'Anniversarie': 'All other things, to their destruction draw'.

11. Dante (Everyman ed.) p. 17.

12. McNeile Dixon, *The Human Situation* (1937) p. 407. I am indebted for the allusion to E. M. M. Milne.

13. Joseph Hone, *W. B. Yeats, 1865–1939* (2nd ed. 1962) p. 402.

14. Compare Leonardo da Vinci's portrait of 'Lady Cecilia'; and (in Synge's *Deirdre* 'weasels and wild cats crying on a lonely wall'.

15. *Letters on Poetry from W. B. Yeats to Dorothy Wellesley* (1964) p. 83.

16. John Masefield, *Some Memories of W. B. Yeats* (Dublin, 1940) p. 6. It is the illustration to *Paradise Lost*, VII 225.

17. 'Under Ben Bulben'. But this concern with 'measurement' has many possible sources. He would have met it everywhere in his Cabalistic, Egyptian, Arabic and Renaissance studies.

18. *Review of English Studies*, I no. 3 (July 1963).

19. *Yeats's Iconography* (1960) p. 301.

20. But the mystery extends to the séance room: 'We sang, and then there was silence, and in the silence from somewhere close to the ceiling the clear song of a bird.' *Explorations* (1962) p. 365.

21. *Letters on Poetry*, p. 119. The spelling is Yeats's.

22. The raw material of the poem was provided by a newspaper account of The O'Rahilly's death.

23. T. R. Henn, 'The Accent of Yeats's *Last Poems*', pp. 122–37. It is possible that there is yet another overtone; for it was the weather that wrecked Casement's landing, and that contributed to the failure of the Rising.

24. 'The Lady's First Song', in *Collected Poems*, p. 343. The quotations that follow are from the same series of poems.

25. 'Hound Voice', in ibid. p. 385.

# T. R. Henn

## 'HORSEMAN, PASS BY!' (1965)

> *Martin.* There were horses – white horses rushing by, with white shining riders – there was a horse without a rider, and some one caught me up and put me upon him and we rode away, with the wind, like the wind –
> *Father John.* That is a common imagining.
>
> *The Unicorn from the Stars*

THE three final dated poems of *Last Poems* contain, perhaps, Yeats's *Grand Testament*. 'Under Ben Bulben' is the most intelligible of the three. In it, the six dominant themes are picked up, their essential threads run lightly and almost casually through the fingers. There is the magic of his Sligo childhood; the preternatural that he had pursued in Bloomsbury, Dublin, Paris or on Croagh Patrick; the Rebellion, and the forgiveness of the dead; the exaltation of war, of the Swordsman who was to repudiate – though with reluctance – the Saint;[1] the great traditions of art, the origins going far back into the mystical mathematics of Babylon and Egypt, linked to history by the returning movements of the gyres; the aristocratic hierarchy of the Ireland of the future. The verse swaggers, with its rough rhythms, across the pages with its characteristic Berkeleian boast:

> That we in coming day may be
> Still the indomitable Irishry

Then it sinks to a lower key, though still arrogant beneath its apparent restraint. He returns to the little churchyard of Drumcliffe, under the shadow of the enchanted mountain:

> No marble, no conventional phrase;
> On limestone quarried near the spot
> By his command these words are cut:

> *Cast a cold eye*
> *On life, on death,*
> *Horseman, pass by !*[2]

The Epitaph is not great poetry, but neither is Swift's, which in part it echoes; there are no grounds in history for supposing that poets do this sort of thing for themselves with any great success. We should see it as the climax of a long discursive meditative poem, in strong and sometimes violent clipped verse. It is typical of many aspects of Yeats: a desire to mystify, to suggest his own peculiar rhetoric of the ghost, to satisfy his dramatic nostalgia for a tradition of place and ancestry, and to emphasize two aspects of desired masks. It is said that he decided to be buried at Drumcliffe when he noted the crowd of 'A.E.''s enemies at 'A.E.''s funeral, but there were more cogent reasons than that.

The sense of the dramatic is held to the fall of the curtain, even to the rhythm of the galloping horses. Death must be seen with the cold dispassionateness of high breeding, with no sense of fear: for

> Death and life were not
> Till man made up the whole,
> Made lock, stock and barrel
> Out of his bitter soul . . .

It was, perhaps, as good a way as any, to dramatize that long-meditated experience so that it should reveal no trace of self-pity. The 'cold eye' – coldness is a favourite term for his own ideal of perfection in art – is this aristocratic dispassionateness and laughter that he spoke of; first in 'Upon a Dying Lady', of Mabel Beardsley, and then in 'Vacillation':

> And call those works extravagance of breath
> That are not suited for such men as come
> Proud, open-eyed and laughing to the tomb.[3]

But the phrase, 'Horseman, pass by!' has many meanings. In Irish idiom, the word 'horseman' has certain overtones that may be missed in ordinary speech. It carries a note of respect, even of awe; the rider has something of Hebraic strength and mystery,

or of the symbolic association of strength and wisdom that
produced the centaurs, 'the holy centaurs of the hills'.[4] The
horseman belongs to aristocracy,[5] he symbolizes possessions,
breeding, strength, virility, and a certain 'wildness of sorrow', as
in those figures of Jack Yeats's paintings of the horsemen at
Irish funerals. There is much of this suggestion throughout
Yeats's poetry. In his memories of the Ashmolean Museum he
recalled above all 'certain pots with strange half-supernatural
horses . . .'. His ancestry, with hard-riding country gentlemen
among them, was, he believed, famous on that account: Major
Robert Gregory, with all the virtues in Castiglione, was noted
too:

> Soldier, scholar, horseman, he,
> As 'twere all life's epitome.[6]

There is the remembered image of Countess Markiewicz:

> When long ago I saw her ride
> Under Ben Bulben to the meet,
> The beauty of her country-side
> With all youth's lonely wildness stirred. . . .[7]

Horsemanship becomes an emblem of an aristocracy that will yet
return:

> Those that Rocky Face holds dear,
> Lovers of horses and of women, shall,
> From marble of a broken sepulchre,
> Or dark betwixt the polecat and the owl,
> Or any rich, dark nothing disinter
> The workman, noble and saint, and all things run
> On that unfashionable gyre again.[8]

But the horseman, the images of the tomb, the memories of Sligo,
and Ben Bulben, are foreshortened against earlier memories. In
the prose tale of *Dhoya*, the Fomorian giant who is robbed of his
fairy bride, he leaps upon the leader of a herd of wild horses, and
on it gallops towards the North West along Ben Bulben 'down
that valley where Dermot hid his Grania in a deep cavern', and
finally plunges over a cliff into the western sea. The ghosts of
horse and rider go on: 'Sometimes the cotters on the mountains
of Donegal hear on windy nights a sudden sound of horses'

hoofs, and say to each other, "There goes Dhoya". And at the same hour if any be abroad in the valley they see a huge shadow rushing along the mountain.'[9] Dhoya himself, the angry passionate man, of enormous strength, is – with Oisin – an early dream-image of Yeats, just as Cuchulain is the last; and it is not altogether fantastic to see in this legend a kind of prophetic self-justification in the plea: 'Only the changing, and moody, and angry, can love.'

The phrase is linked to the Rosicrucians and the mountain tomb of their leader. The cataract that 'smokes upon the mountain side'[10] can be no other than that which falls from Ben Bulben into Glencar; the horsemen riding from Knocknarea to Ben Bulben are those in the 'Song for the Severed Head':

> Saddle and ride, I heard a man say,
> Out of Ben Bulben and Knocknarea,
> *What says the Clock in the Great Clock Tower?*
> All those tragic characters ride
> But turn from Rosses' crawling tide,
> The meet's upon the mountain side.
> *A slow low note and an iron bell.*[11]

To that procession of images come those that remain of the circus; Cuchulain, who had sought wisdom in battle, or in fighting the waves; Niamh, Aleel, Hanrahan; last and most sinister, a remembered character from *The Secret Rose*:

> The King that could make his people stare
> Because he had feathers instead of hair.[12]

There are, then, many images stored in those short lines. Death is to be confronted heroically and dramatically, for the two attitudes have become one. 'Cuchulain Comforted' is a vision-poem,[13] dictated near death, with its bird-like shrouds, and the strange overtones of Dante[14] and of Morris' 'Defence of Guenevere'. 'The Black Tower', the latest-dated poem of *Last Poems*, is also concerned with the two mountains, and it may well be that Yeats had in mind, not only the tower at Ballylee, but the round tower that stands beside Drumcliffe churchyard; and he celebrates the warrior Eoghan Bel buried near Maeve's cairn on the summit of Knocknarea:

> There in the tomb stand the dead upright,
> But winds come up from the shore:
> They shake when the winds roar,
> Old bones upon the mountain shake.        *(CP* 396)

But the poem itself is complex and obscure, as is the right of one written 'when the dark grows thicker'. Generally, the Black Tower, which has overtones perhaps from Browning, but which has its basic reference to Thoor Ballylee, becomes at the last the refuge and defence that once it was in the great period of his poetry. Now it helps to protect the King and his retainers, in their decrepitude, against the new generation. The conflict is political, philosophical, poetical, personal; perhaps all of these together. (One thinks of 'The New Faces'.) They come to bribe or threaten, to persuade the defenders to throw in their lot with the usurper; as the new government (which had rejected the Oath of Allegiance) had sought to induce Yeats to return to a more active part in affairs. At this point we may refer to the reference given by Wilson[15] to Plato's *Statesman*, where the ruler of the universe has withdrawn from active participation in it. Chaos has followed; the King waits till the return of the new order. This is the thought of 'The Gyres'; Arland Ussher has noted the Messianic yearnings of much Irish history.

So far so good. But W. J. Keith seems to have given depth to Yeats's poem by suggesting a possible reference to the Arthurian legend. For this he quotes from E. K. Chambers' *Arthur of Britain*:[16]

Beneath the Castle of Sewingshields, near the Roman Wall in Northumberland, are vaults where Arthur sleeps with Guinivere and all his court and a pack of hounds. He waits until one blows the horn which lies ready on a table, and cuts a garter placed beside it with a sword of stone. Once a farmer, knitting on the ruins, followed his clew of wool which had fallen into a crevice and found the vault. He cut the garter and Arthur woke, but as he sheathed the sword, fell asleep again, with the words –

> O woe betide that evil day
> On which the witless wight was born,

> Who drew the sword – the garter cut,
> But never blew the bugle horn.

The old cook of the Tower then, as Keith suggests, might be explained by the legend of Sir Beaumains and Sir Kay: who, degraded from his knighthood, became a cook in the buttery.

We can then see the poem as another instance of multiple or laminated meanings. The new order is defied by the 'right king' and his enfeebled retainers, in the Tower of old age, which is black because of approaching death. He defies the corruption of the new order –

> Those banners come to bribe or threaten
> Or whisper that a man's a fool –

though the old order seems bankrupt and feeble. The blowing of the horn will announce a rescue, the return of strength and order – is there an echo of Roncesvalles? – but the rumours of its distant sound are false. The whole is pointed by the refrain which suggests the growing blackness of approaching death, *and* the increasing darkness just before the dawn; the Mountain Tomb, not far from the sea (Ben Bulben or Knocknarea) so that the sea-winds are the heralds of change; and the shaking of the bones (in fear, excitement, anticipation – *The Dreaming of the Bones*) which will return to life when the Ezekiel-like prophecy is fulfilled; remembering that between Knocknarea and Sligo there are a number of ancient burial-mounds. And if, as I believe possible, he remembered Ricketts' 'Don Juan and the Statue', that strange, terrifying picture of the horseman with outstretched right arm and sunken corpse-face, there would be in the words a further symbol of Juan's lonely power on which he had meditated, and which had served to embody his contempt for 'those that hated *The Playboy of the Western World*'. It is a kind of evocation of the heroes that meet him, the dramatic assertion of his kinship with the supernatural. Perhaps in the thought of the traveller there is something of the finality of Swift's own epitaph;[17] Swift, who was 'always just round the corner', and by whose side, in St Patrick's, Yeats was to be offered a final burial:

> Imitate him if you dare,
> World-besotted traveller; he
> Served human liberty.

## NOTES

1. 'I have spent my life saying the same thing in many different ways. I denounced old age before I was twenty, and the Swordsman throughout repudiates the Saint – though with vacillation.' (MS note by W. B. Y. – Mrs Yeats.)

2. He dropped the original first line: 'Draw rein, draw breath': see p. 239.

3. 'Vacillation', III, in *Collected Poems* (1950 ed.) p. 283. (Parenthetical *CP* page references are to this edition.)

4. There is a magic gateway in the side of Ben Bulben through which the faery host emerges.

5. Sir Jonah Barrington gives the various categories of 'gentry': 'half-mounted', 'full-mounted', etc. (*Personal Sketches of His Own Times*, 3 vols. 1827–32).

6. 'In Memory of Major Robert Gregory', in *Collected Poems*, p. 151. But stanza VIII of this poem, which concerns the Galway foxhounds, was inserted to meet Mrs Gregory's wishes and against the poet's judgement.

7. 'On a Political Prisoner', in *Collected Poems*, p. 206.

8. 'The Gyres', in ibid. p. 337.

9. *John Sherman and Dhoya* (1891) p. 195.

10. 'The Mountain Tomb', in *Collected Poems*, p. 136.

11. *Collected Plays* (1952 ed.) p. 641. They turn from the tide, I suppose, because the ghost is reluctant to cross water.

12. 'The Wisdom of the King'.

13. The prose draft, the result of a dream, was dictated at 3 a.m. on 7 Jan. 1939: the poem was finished on 13 Jan. (Mrs Yeats).

14. e.g. *Inferno XV*, 20, 'come vecchio sartor fa nella cruna'.

15. *W. B. Yeats and Tradition* (1958) p. 224.

16. *Modern Language Notes*, LXXV (Feb. 1960): 'Yeats's Arthurian Black Tower'. But there was perhaps an additional strata of symbolism from the Golden Dawn and Rosicrucianism, and a strong case is made out for this by Virginia Moore in *The Unicorn* (1954) pp. 439 ff.

17. See *The Letters of W. B. Yeats*, ed. Allan Wade (1954) p. 525. It is perhaps worth noting that the Latin is poor, as it might be that of a stonemason.

# T. R. Henn

## THE ACCENT OF YEATS'S
## *LAST POEMS* (1956)

THE *Last Poems* of Yeats look as if they are on the way to
becoming an interesting problem in the criticism of his work, and
some recent conflicting views may offer a justification for glanc-
ing at them again.[1] It is possible to argue that they offer a typical
subject for *a priori* criticism, relying on two things: the fact of the
Steinach operation, and the quatrain called 'The Spur':

> You think it horrible that lust and rage
> Should dance attention upon my old age;
> They were not such a plague when I was young;
> What else have I to spur me into song?

It is worth while noting, for the moment, that the verses first
appear in a letter to Lady Dorothy Wellesley. But with this as
a sort of critical text Yeats appears to be in danger of suffering a
portraiture which would show him as something close to a sexual
psychopath, a loose imagination returning to the body in which
desire has outrun performance. In Miss Koch's words, 'The
sexual theme is of significance as the final symbolic statement of
that creative conflict which Yeats had early posited as the
dynamic of the universe.'[2] More justly, but not more elegantly,
she writes: 'In sexual experience, as I have suggested, Yeats
found the energy, the imagery and the basic antinomies of mortality organized into an intricate and tragic nexus.'[3] Other
evidence is adduced, mainly from *Letters on Poetry from W. B.
Yeats to Lady Dorothy Wellesley*. In these letters we see the
genesis, out of the rough drafts, of the poem 'The Three Bushes',
emerging in the first instance as a kind of contest in poetic
technique between master and pupil: admiration of the woman
becoming, perhaps inevitably, intertwined with an admiration of

the poetess' work. This poem, and what Miss Koch calls 'their terrifyingly frank songs' combine with 'The Spur' to produce a particular view of *Last Poems*. The object of this essay is to suggest a slightly different perspective.

To do so we must first glance at the road which Yeats had travelled since 'Easter, 1916'. Marriage, the slow forging and reforging of *A Vision*; the construction and abandoning of The Tower; the loosening of three[4] blood-dimmed tides; the Senator-ship and the 'sixty-year-old smiling public man'; the renewed conflict (noted in the Preface to *The Words upon the Window-pane*) between the One and the Many; the haunting by Swift; the miraculous peak of *The Winding Stair* giving place to *A Full Moon in March* and 'Supernatural Songs' as three religions seemed to converge, waveringly and uncertainly, under the influence of Purohit Swami. The Easter Rising had fallen into alignment (perceived a little too dramatically, but that was Yeats's way) with the Cuchulain myth; of which the violent complexities imaged, as it were mirror on mirror, his own multiple imagined personalities. Other myths he had transmuted to serve his art – Troy and its burning walls (so close, as a euphonious symbol, to the burning of Tara): Leda, and many swans: the patriotic legend that once had seemed fit to fire a smouldering and vulgar nationalism; but now a carven stone, a dancing girl, a metaphysical apprehension of Irish history against the great mutations of the world, are enough to serve him. And with old age it seems to me that his mind returned to an earlier cycle of his reading: Shakespeare, Blake and Dante: all three offering, as Miss Koch might have noted, *exempla* of the energy to be derived from sexual experience. But did it need a Freudian from across the Atlantic to tell us that? Let us suppose for a moment another text:

> Grant me an old man's frenzy,
> Myself must I remake
> Till I am Timon and Lear
> Or that William Blake
> Who beat upon the wall
> Till truth obeyed his call ...

Suppose, too, that the 'rage' of the 'Spur' quatrain is (as I believe) a memory of Swift's Epitaph, 'the greatest epitaph in history'; for Yeats speaks of his 'rage' as 'savage', and he had learnt both when Synge died. Let us then examine the 'lust' of *Last Poems*.

Setting aside 'The Three Bushes' and its songs, I find that no more than six out of the remaining forty-three titles in the book could be said, by any imagination, to be concerned with 'lust'. There is the theme of 'madness', 'wildness', but those who knew Yeats's idiom and language will recognize the overtones of those words as including, above all, energy, power, an arrogant rejection of authority, an assertion of youth, virility;[5] often in relation to horses, fishermen, the adventurous aristocracy of the great houses, of Lever's novels, or of Maxwell's West. The so-called patriotic poems, two on Roger Casement, 'The O'Rahilly', and 'Come gather round me, Parnellites', the two little Swiftian epigrams called 'The Great Day' and 'Parnell', seem to me machine-made, written from the teeth outwards, though not without a certain sincerity; for he was greatly moved by the Casement business. And while he recognized the poetic slightness of these ballads, he thought that young men might sing them after he was dead. (It is notable that 'The Curse of Cromwell' seems to have been written for two voices, a girl chanting the refrain; and it is effective when done thus.) Alone among the ballads 'Colonel Martin' has a peculiar quality of its own, its 'chorus almost without meaning, followed by concertina and whistle'.[6] Perhaps it is an artistic failure. 'It has a curious pathos which I cannot define. I have known from the start what I wanted to do, yet the idea seemed to lie below the threshold of consciousness, and still lies.'[7] There is a strange rhythmic beat, subtly checked, the tones rising and falling:

> – With Christian and with 'Infidel',
>     For all tongues he knew –

and at moments there emerges (as seldom in Yeats) the ironical characterization both of agent and narrator arising from the accent and intonation implicit in the rhythm:

> And he went in, and she went on
> And both climbed up the stair,
> *And O he was a clever man,*
> For he his slippers wore ...

or

> And there at all street-corners
> A man with a pistol stood,
> And the rich man had paid them well
> To shoot the Colonel dead;
> But they threw down their pistols
> And all men heard them swear
> That they could never shoot a man
> Did all *that* for the poor.

Yeats uses the words '*almost* meaningless' of the refrain. As usual, it changes slightly in function with each stanza, receiving its first charge of meaning from the opening verse 'The Colonel went out sailing'. It helps, perhaps, to remember two things: the habit of the peasantry of denoting each member of 'the family' by his rank or station, and the admiration for a violent, irrational, resourceful and eccentric aristocracy, which is yet half a satire upon itself: borne out by the ballad-maker's reverence for the 'travelled man', and the natural acceptance of murder (happily frustrated by Good Deeds) which is, simultaneously, fact and satire.[8] It is of a kind with the astringent rhetoric of

> And there is an old beggar wandering in his pride –
> His fathers served their fathers before Christ was crucified ...

in 'The Curse of Cromwell'.

There is yet another text that may throw light on our interpretation of *Last Poems*, the enigmatic stanzas from 'Those Images':

> Seek those images
> That constitute the wild,
> The lion and the virgin,
> The harlot and the child.

which in an earlier draft read:

> Seek majestic powers
> That constitute the Wild,
> The Lion and the Harlot
> The Virgin and the Child.

It is, I think, beyond dispute (as H. R. Bachchan has shown) that Yeats is thinking of the symbols in the personal seal of Madame Blavatsky; on which, enclosed in a serpent with its tail in mouth, there are the two interlaced triangles with which we are familiar from *A Vision*. At the top, on the left and right of the figure thus formed, are the two signs of the Zodiac, Leo and Virgo: at the bottom, left to right, there are the Hebrew letters *Shin* and the Greek *Omega*. If, as appears from the seal, these are intentionally in opposition, we have a Lion-Child, Virgin-Harlot balance: the Child and Omega being the beginning and the end: with the further intricacy of the Lion-Virgin-Christ in opposition to Harlot-Child-Man. Yeats follows Blake in using elsewhere the Lion-Child image[9] and that of the Harlot-Child.[10] It is unwise to press a poet too far when the rhyme may have gone some way to meet the thought; but it would be equally unfair not to do Yeats the courtesy of considering that he may have here meant what he said. If in old age these four images were to be perceived as dominants, or perhaps as type-images of mankind, I believe that a little light (though somewhat broken by the leaves) may be shed on *Last Poems*. The two poems on the Dancing Girl, the middle stanza of 'Long-Legged Fly', the whole theme of virginity and satisfied desire[11] in 'The Three Bushes', and the lesser poems on the theme, fall into place. Those to the two 'uncommon women' fall into place against the 'half-lion', 'half-child' of the early poem 'Against Unworthy Praise': to be picked up again, with the full weight of irony, in 'The Circus Animals' Desertion':

> I must be satisfied with my heart, although
> Winter and summer till old age began
> My circus animals were all on show,
> Those stilted boys,[12] that burnished chariot,[13]
> Lion and woman and the Lord knows what.[14]

I do not press this; I merely plead that, from what we know of
Yeats's mind, the fruits of the invocation to 'Those Images' can
be seen at least in part of *Last Poems*; the images begetting fresh
images, endued with their own peculiar archetypal mystery.
Dare one carry the last verse of the same poem a stage further?

> Those masterful images because complete
> Grew in pure mind, but out of what began?
> A mound of refuse or the sweepings of a street,
> Old kettles, old bottles, and a broken can,
> Old iron, old bones, old rags, that raving slut
> Who keeps the till. Now that my ladder's gone,
> I must lie down where all the ladders start
> In the foul rag-and-bone shop of the heart.

The *raving slut* I take to be the imagination, arbitrary, untidy,
that opens the coin-drawer when the whim takes her. The rags
and bones go back to many poems, to 'Every *tatter* in its mortal
dress' of 'Byzantium'; to 'Those Dancing Days Are Gone'; to
'A bone wave-whitened and dried on the strand.' Behind all are
the tinker-folk, the roaring, ranting Mannion, the world of
Synge's *Well of the Saints*: Yeats's own irrational miscellaneous
gatherings from sixty years of hasty retentive reading that had
snatched at and nourished the masterful images. Among them,
still returning, is the image of the Virgin, arrow, or star, tested by
reading, painting, dreams: as the severed singing head and its
revenge for woman's cruelty had taken his mind from Wilde's
*Salome*[15] to the Death of Cuchulain.

As to the remaining themes, I find them a poet's looking back
over a long  past, remembering his own injunction, 'Seek out
reality, leave things that seem', and the Heart's rejoinder, 'What?
be a singer born and lack a theme?' Now the 'reality' is that which
he perceived in Lear: gaiety (in his own peculiar sense) frenzy or
*hysterica passio* (as he uses the term in 'A Bronze Head') and the
stripping of things and humanity to their complex simplicity of
Blind Man, Beggar, Fool; for 'Unaccommodated man is but such
a poor bare forked animal as thou art'. As in Lear's world the
bawdy punctuates and counterparts the labouring mind, so in
*Last Poems* the body and its concerns punctuate the ancestral

night that now 'begins to split'. Like Timon he might say, in one mood,

> My long sickness
> Of health and living now begins to mend,
> And nothing brings me all things

as life moved towards the last station in 'The Phases of the Moon'. 'I must lay aside the pleasant paths I have built up for years and seek the honesty, the ill-breeding, the barbarism of truth.'[16] As in *Timon* the heroic reverie is mocked by clown and knave and harlot, and one must challenge that mockery:

> *What shall I do for pretty girls*
> *Now my old bawd is dead?*[17]

And as for Blake, did he not stand to Yeats for just this passionate man?

He cried again and again that everything that lives is holy, and that nothing is unholy except things that do not live – lethargies, and cruelties, and timidities, and that denial of imagination which is the root they grew from in old times. Passions, because most living are most holy – and this was a scandalous paradox in his time – and men shall enter eternity borne upon their wings.[18]

I would not suggest that Yeats's passion is always either 'pure' or 'holy'; like Donne, he ran his course between antinomies of soul and self. In one mood he might note (borrowing the image from Blake's *Jerusalem*) that

> Love has pitched his mansion in
> The place of excrement . . .

and in another (it is perhaps thus that all poets handle women)

> But when this soul, its body off,
> Naked to naked goes,
> He it has found shall find therein
> What none other knows . . .

I do not find either the Songs from 'The Three Bushes', or 'The Wild Old Wicked Man', 'terrifyingly frank'; only as a projection of the themes of a 'A Woman Old and Young', and with precedents for their images in Blake's Prophetic Books and, above all, in Blake's illustrations. Once a poet had edited the whole work of one such as Blake, it is reasonable to suppose that the whole burns itself into his mind.

And if, as in *Timon* and *Lear*, there were some measure of bawdry, if 'The Wild Old Wicked Man' should lament Mrs Kinsella, why should not an old man who was re-reading Donne, remember what he had once written to Grierson: 'His pedantry and his obscenity, the rock and loam of his Eden – but make me the more certain that one who is but a man like us all has seen God.'[19] There is, I believe, in *Last Poems*, a deliberately satirical component; a challenge to the ever-hardening censorship that had once stooped at 'Leda and the Swan', and sought to prove to its own amused citizens that the brothel depicted in *Ulysses* was a figment of a poet's imagination. There is throughout these poems a vein of malicious or passionate contempt for many things; for the new Ireland that might (in one mood in 'The Municipal Gallery') correspond to the poet's imagination, 'terrible and gay', and in another be thought to deserve that fierce indictment, the thought picked up from *Responsibilities* –

> We Irish, born into that ancient sect
> But thrown upon this filthy modern tide
> And by its aimless spawning fury wrecked,
> Climb to our proper dark, that we may trace
> The lineaments[20] of a plummet-measured face.

Berkeley and Swift, too, are behind the words; the pride of 'We Irish think this' (repeated in 'the indomitable Irishry' of 'Under Ben Bulben'); the bitter, spitting, weighted words of *aimless spawning fury* that might underlie the thought of *A Modest Proposal*. So, too, 'The Pilgrim'; a trivial gay poem that is yet of some complexity in satire and imagery. It is, I think, of no significance except as satire, in relation to that ascetic religious ceremony on Lough Derg that contrasts so strangely with other problems of conduct; the humour lies in the thought of Yeats's participation in it (remembering the projected pantisocratic colony on Lough Key). Yet my imagination persists in coupling the great black bird with that strange picture in the Municipal Gallery; where the black birds throng about the feet of St Patrick as he climbs the Holy Mountain of Crô-Patric.[21] The

E                                        S.Y.L.P.

satire extends through sex, religion, politics: to the Statesman who is an 'easy' man (the overtones of that word are impossible to define (it is often something like *eutrapelia*), but my ear recognizes some of its peculiar meanings here: 'slickness', superficiality, and a flavour of cynical irresponsibility are in it; the statesman on holiday with a monkey on a chain[22] – the fancy swoops and flits to the tune of fiddle or tambourine. We remember that other sentence from *On the Boiler*: 'Of late I have tried to understand in its practical details the falsehood that is in all knowledge, science more false than philosophy, but that, too, false.'[23]

Yeats was concerned always with what he called 'the book of the people', yet I do not think he had that happy gift of nature that would have enabled him to catch the very tone and accent of the countryside. Unlike the Scots, the Irish common thought has no quality that when set down does not easily become ridiculous. The mine that was opened in Aran and the Blaskets has one single shallow vein; once that had been worked by genius we can only grope among fragments of the slag.

In *Last Poems* we have, I believe, certain rhythms of the Dublin Street Ballad (but not its tones) opposed satirically to the Pre-Raphaelite rhythms and refrains of the earlier verse: checked and modulated, again satirically, to combine with the *mots bas* that seemed fitted to convey an old man's fancy, dispassionateness, aristocratic contempt. We can watch this counterpointing in progress:

> There all the golden *codgers* lay,
> There the silver dew –

– (*codgers* sugests agreeable speciousness with a suggestion of deliberate deceit, in relation to the 'ancient sages') –

> Whether man die in his bed
> Or the rifle knocks him dead –

where *knocks* is used less as a blow given than of a shot bird or rabbit; or that handling of the dominant symbol of the Sistine Chapel –

> Michael Angelo left a proof
> On the Sistine Chapel roof,
> Where but half-awakened Adam
> Can disturb globe-trotting Madam
> Till her bowels are in heat . . .

– changing suddenly in key to the next lines –

> Proof that there's a purpose set
> Before the secret working mind:
> Profane perfection of mankind.

and rising to the lyric passage on the pictures of the world, that brings us to Samuel Palmer's mysterious, hushed, serene land-scapes.

Indeed there is in *Last Poems* a preoccupation with statuary and painting, from the usual triple view; as significant expressions of men and times, as providing standards of human beauty for the choosing of a mate, and as serving to recall 'the images of forty years'. I have shown elsewhere how Yeats took a whole stanza of 'News for the Delphic Oracle' from the Poussin in the Dublin National Gallery; I think, but cannot prove, that the preceding verse is illuminated by one of Shannon's paintings[24] now in the Fogg Museum in Boston; and that the image repeated in the same poem, and previously used in 'Byzantium' of the cherub straddling the Dolphin, owes something to the Titian in the Isabella Stuart Gardner Museum at Boston, which Yeats haunted so much.[25] 'The Statues' recall his whole theory of Asia versus Greece, Phidias as the champion of the West; 'A Bronze Head' (I think, as sculpture, over-praised in the poem) in the entrance to the Municipal Gallery, a whole pattern of the earlier thought. In the poem on its revisiting we may pause to note what I take to be nostalgia overriding its ironically disposed layers. There are the portraits of the dead Ireland of Yeats's youth; Lady Gregory and Robert, the Irish Airman; the Laverys and the gracious women, with Mancini the erratic genius. Against these are set the Revolutionary Ireland that had begotten the Free State, and the Republicans; 'terrible and gay' in the patriotic painting, yet part of the 'numb nightmare' that had later murdered Kevin O'Higgins, and had left Coole desolate. And over the whole poem broods the ghost of Synge, with his ironic insight into the older Ireland; Synge pleading for 'an imagination that is fiery, and magnificent and tender', and dreaming of a poetry that had its roots among the clay and the worms: even to the 'stupidity / Of root, shoot, blossom or clay'.[26] There is something of fire and clay and worm in *Last Poems*: something, too, of Synge's and Swift's realism, like a tendril reaching to seek a hold upon reality.

I have left to the last two poems which are to me still mysterious and had, perhaps, better remain so. 'Cuchulain Comforted' and 'The Black Tower'. They are, both, I think, written between dream and waking; they are 'vision' poems, almost in Blake's sense: 'meaning by vision the intense realization of a state of ecstatic excitement, symbolized in a definite imagined region'.[27] They dissolve for the last time 'into a final unity that is beyond analysis'. Both, but particularly 'The Black Tower', suggest to me (as Yeats wrote to Ethel Mannin) 'peace and loneliness by some single object' (cf. 'Lapis Lazuli') or by some few strokes of a brush.[28] Neither (since we lack the thread wound on Hades' bobbin) is likely to be unravelled now. In the first the Hero, and the past dead, meet over the mummy cloth which is now become a shroud: the dead that comfort the hero are changed into birds. And then (without being able to connect them) I remember the stage direction to *The Death of Cuchulain*: '*There is silence and in the silence a few faint bird notes*'. For the spirits of the dead in Tir-nan-Oge (whether of *The Shadowy Waters* or of *The King of the Great Clock Tower*) are birds with the heads of men and women; and he describes a silence at the end of a séance when a few bird notes came from the ceiling of the room.[29] Behind all, that illustration of Blake's to the *Inferno* where, in the forest trees, the strange bird-spirits seem to crowd the branches.[30]

As to Cuchulain himself, and the stitching of the shroud, we may remember the letter dated twenty-four days before death: '... I know for certain that my time will not be long ... I am happy, and I think full of energy, of an energy I had despaired of.'[31]

'The Black Tower' is still more obscure; it was dictated in the small hours of the morning, shortly before death. I believe the refrain and place to be of Sligo and of the two mountains, Knocknarea and Ben Bulben, as in the song in *A Full Moon in March*; the old bones that shake may be in the Cairn of Queen Maeve, as the westerly gales sweep up the western slopes from the Atlantic, which might 'hear from the foam the beating of a bell'. The tomb (as I have suggested) may be that of the warrior buried upright to guard the strategic crossing: reinforced by that strange illustration for Wilde's *Salome* by Ricketts, 'Uprose the Painted Swathed Dead'.[32] Against this changing scene (for the refrain verse modulates through three stages to the proper dark) there is the old black tower with its garrison, oath-bound; to what? Do they stand for the poet in his last security, the last romantic, now about to be freed from 'the mirror of malicious eyes'? I cannot read in other sense the second verse

> Those banners come to bribe or threaten,
> Or whisper that a man's a fool
> Who, when his own right king's forgotten,
> Cares what king sets up his rule.
> If he died long ago
> Why do you dread us so?

– unless the new king is the new Ireland, the new men that it is breeding; the new government that had rejected the Oath of Allegiance. I believe that memories of Morris' ballads lie behind it; perhaps behind both poems, for the form of 'Cuchulain Comforted' – though most closely linked to Dante – is also that of *The Defence of Guinevere*, and we know that Morris was re-read in those last years.[33]

It is in something of this manner that I perceive what I have called the *accent* of *Last Poems*, a strange complexity of mire and blood; of old emotions recollected in a new dispassionate excitement, sometimes satirical, sometimes exalted. In this complexity the Easter Rebellion recedes into a new, and I believe, ambivalent perspective; modified by Yeats's pondering on the widening gyres of the new world. For in those last years his mind was much occupied with politics. *On the Boiler*, of which we have the first

number only, was to have been his *Fors Clavigera*. The tightening
coils of the Irish censorship roused him to fury, and below the
surface, sometimes apparent, sometimes veiled, is the attack on
obscurantism. 'An ignorant form of Catholicism is my enemy.'[34]
There were larger issues: 'For the first time I am saying what I
believe about Irish and European politics.'[35] And here, too, in
Yeats's manner, there was a convergence or mirror-effect at
work. 'I begin to see things double – doubled in history, world
history, personal history,'[36] and the masterful images, which had
so often been self-begetting, seemed (I believe) to be moving
towards a point in the mind in which the vaguer outlines of those
in the recessive planes would coincide with the harder lines of
those in the foreground of his thought. In the second movement of
'Parnell's Funeral' from *A Full Moon in March* a violent image
from anthropology foreshortens Irish history:

> Had Cosgrove eaten Parnell's heart, the land's
> Imagination had been satisfied,
> Or lacking that, government in such hands,
> O'Higgins its statesman had not died.

So Swift might have contemplated the filthy tide of politics that
had left him behind, and so he might have pondered on the fruits
of nationalism that had been harvested from *The Drapier's Letters*:

> I like awake night after night
> And never get the answers right.
> Did that play of mine send out
> Certain men the English shot?

For one dared not say that the shooting of the Sixteen Men had
paled before the executions by the Free State. And yet it seems
that events are being focused. The killing of the House – that
'capital offence' in *Purgatory* – now shown in blackened bones
over the Irish countryside; the stones of Coole were soon to be
torn down to build labourers' cottages in Galway. The very
mention of 'Yeats's tower' once provoked ignorant bewilder-
ment or laughter from the villagers around, before it and the
cottages were restored, and a sign-post set up on the main road
beside it.

In Yeats's calenture of memory there rises the thrice-vexed ghost of Cuchulain, symbol perhaps of Yeats's love and of his imagined or spiritual wars: the burning house seen in childhood, refracted through Troy and its shriek-pulsed towers, image of *Purgatory* and 'The Curse of Cromwell', the unforgettable fear of the fires which we knew, ruin and flame that merge.

> I came on a great house in the middle of the night,
> Its opened lighted doorway and its windows all alight,
> And all my friends were there and made me welcome too;
> But I woke in an old ruin that the winds howled through;
> And when I pay attention I must out and walk
> Among the dogs and horses that understand my talk.[37]
> > *O what of that, O what of that,*
> > *What is there left to say?*

And there is that shadow of violence, of Sato's ancient blade, that lived with Yeats as a desired mask, the fighting men of either mythology. (I mean the Cuchulain story, and the Easter Rising.)

> Know that when all words are said
> And a man is fighting mad,
> Something drops from eyes long blind,
> He completes his partial mind . . .

The wrack dislimns, a little. I have insisted elsewhere that all Yeats's work, verse, drama, prose, must be read as a unity. If we do this, *Last Poems* does, I believe, grow less heterogeneous as we see the past close in upon the poet like waves. This great and proud instinct for the dramatic, both in the moment and in the man, is still alive. There are the astonishing juxtapositions of 'Long-Legged Fly', the high gestures of the actor, the sudden metaphysical condensation of history, the Swiftian arrogance; the bitter dilemma, only to be resolved by irony, that he had half destroyed the civilization that he had half created by celebrating it in time of Civil War. Under the death-pressure Blake and Dante, Shakespeare and Swift and Morris return: virgin, harlot, lion, the children he had loved or pitied; chariot, beggar, fool; armed men in the tower that is the mind's last security; horses that speak, or are ridden at night between the mountains, or pass, with no rein drawn, the churchyard at Drumcliffe.

## NOTES

1. See, in particular, Curtis Bradford's 'On Yeats's *Last Poems*' (pp. 75–97) in which he proposes a return to the order of the poems in the Cuala Press edition of 1938.

2. Vivienne Koch, *W. B. Yeats: The Tragic Phase* (1951) p. 24.

3. Ibid. p. 21.

4. The Irish Civil War; the Spanish; the Night of the Long Knives; the 'irrational streams of blood' of 'The Gyres'.

5. Cf. the word in 'Mad as the Mist and Snow', the repeated use of 'run wild', and the implications of

> Why should not old men be mad?
> Some have known a likely lad
> That had a sound fly-fisher's wrist
> Turn to a drunken journalist.

6. *The Letters of W. B. Yeats*, ed. Allan Wade (1954) p. 896.

7. Ibid.

8. I have several examples in mind: both from 'The Troubles' and the Civil War. Cf. also *The Playboy of the Western World*.

9. e.g. in 'Against Unworthy Praise'.

10. 'Presences'.

11. cf. Blake's    'In a wife I would desire
>                  What in whores is always found –
>                  The lineaments of gratified desire.'

12. 'High Talk'.

13. 'Who will go drive with Fergus now?'; and, of course, Blake's Dante illustrations.

14. The Harlot? ('You might have rhymed').

15. The archetypal example in painting is perhaps Allori's 'Judith and Holofernes': where Judith is the painter's mistress, the head his own self-portrait.

16. *Letters*, ed. Wade, p. 903.

17. The irony lies, of course, in the character: Kinsella is a 'strong farmer'.

18. 'William Blake and the Imagination', in *Essays and Introductions* (1961) p. 112–13.

19. *Letters*, ed. Wade, p. 570.

20. Is there (remembering the lines from Blake quoted above) an overtone of composed satisfaction in the word?

21. By Margaret Clarke; formerly in the Municipal Gallery.

22. *On the Boiler* (Dublin, 1939) p. 37. 'Here in Monte Carlo, where I am writing, somebody talked of a man with a monkey

and some sort of stringed instrument, and it has pleased me to imagine him a great politician.'

23. Ibid. p. 36.

24. A grey sea, rose-strewn, with cherubs playing in it in ecstasy; one of the cherubs looks as if it were stained with blood.

25. Europa, balanced precariously on the back of a worried-looking bull, is emerging from the water. Beside her, a cherub rides a dolphin, holding it by the back fin. He is parodying, in poise and expression, Europa's position on the bull's back. It may be related to the 'Crazy Jane' verses:

> Great Europa played the fool
> That changed a lover for a bull.

26. 'The Spirit Medium'.

27. *Letters*, ed. Wade, p. 583. The imagined regions (if one dare speculate) I would take to be Dante's Purgatorio as seen by Blake, and a death-version of Thoor Ballylee perceived on a Sligo mountain; it might even be of Yeats's Lear, who comes with Edgar to the dark tower?

28. Ibid. p. 917.

29. Preface to *The Words upon the Window-pane*, in *Wheels and Butterflies* (1934) p. 33.

30. *Inferno*, canto 13. The Wood of the Self-Murderers.

31. *Letters*, ed. Wade, p. 922.

32. The *Letters* (ed. Wade) have confirmed my earlier guess as to Yeats's debt to Ricketts: the drawing of 'Don Juan'.

33. We may remember that he had written of Morris's 'astringent eloquence'.

34. *Letters*, ed. Wade, p. 873.

35. Ibid. p. 910.

36. Ibid. p. 887. Maybe there was a precedent for this in Blake?

37. Swift?

# J. R. Mulryne

## THE *LAST POEMS* (1965)

### I

NORTHROP FRYE, in an essay in the collection *An Honoured Guest*,[1] distinguishes what he calls the 'ultimate insight' in Yeats. In summary, this has to do with 'redemption' from the pressures of time and chance through the exercise of the poetic imagination. Redemption is secured by the poet's identifying with Man, who is also the metaphysical 'One', through the discovery of 'personal archetypes, daimons or moods', aspects of 'the greater form of himself'; 'in this perspective', Frye says, 'the whole cycle of nature, of life and death and rebirth which man has dreamed, becomes a single gigantic image', an image the imagining poet, its 'maker', has conquered. The poetic process, we might say, thrives on a conflation, or confusion, of the actual world and the world of imagination; the creation of an imaginary world becomes an act not only of artistic but of real worth; it empowers the poet and absolves from the pain of the actual. Yeats's prose confirms that at the time of writing *Last Poems* his view of the poet's craft and the poet's privilege was as Frye outlines it; in an essay published in 1937, two years before his death, Yeats wrote:

A poet writes always of his personal life, in his finest work out of its tragedy . . . [yet] even when the poet seems most himself . . . he is never the bundle of accident and incoherence that sits down to breakfast; he has been reborn as an idea, something intended, complete . . . he is more type than man, more passion than type. He is Lear, Romeo, Oedipus, Tiresias; he has stepped out of a play, and even the woman he loves is Rosalind, Cleopatra, never The Dark Lady . . . we adore him because nature has grown intelligible, and by so doing a part of our creative power.[2]

The hypnotic logic of this passage offers the poetic act as a true redemption of the Self; to write poetry is to be re-born, and to be so re-born, as to conquer 'accident', 'incoherence', 'tragedy'. The syntax brooks no argument: with this version of the 'personal archetypes', artistic remaking of the poet and his beloved, as type, passion, *dramatis personae*, can render nature no longer hostile, but enabling, 'part of our creative power'. The passage is interesting as theory; more immediately important, its language and its assumptions richly anticipate those of *Last Poems*. The *dramatis personae* of the prose reappear in the verse; 'tragedy' is much considered; 'creative power', under different guises, is frequently declared. The assumptions about actual and imagined reality, and about the poet's access to 'creative power', serve as an arena within which are drawn up the encountering dispositions and commitments of *Last Poems*.

The book opens with a transforming gesture of precisely the kind the prose envisages. The territory occupied by 'The Gyres' looks familiar: the end-of-an-era turbulence explored with sensitive resource by many a Yeats poem. But called on to 'look forth' over this tragic scene are unfamiliar lineaments: the im- periously invoked 'Old Rocky Face'. The confrontation is significant; over the time-dominated events of the poem broods the oracular, timeless Rocky Face. The things of time are not ignored: the 'numb nightmare' of verse two calls up the night- mare that rides upon sleep in 'Nineteen Hundred and Nineteen'; and the following phrase, masterfully condensed, envisages the terrible paradox of the 'sensitive body' 'stained' by its own very constituents, stained in Yeatsian language by 'mire and blood', the condition of body. Yet within the imaginative economy of the poem the Rocky Face dominates; exhorted to laugh in tragic joy, to rejoice in detachment, even if aware detachment, from the time-ridden events, this figure provokes our question. He is of course deliberately an enigma; the poem's strategy demands that he arrive abruptly and unexplained before our sensibilities. With the enigma sorts a claim to oracular status; we remember the 'Rocky Voice' of 'The Man and the Echo', where the voice proceeds from a chasm associated with the Delphic Oracle; and the suggestion that the figure recalls the sage Ahasuerus in Shelley, 'master of all human knowledge', is also plausible.[3] But Rocky Face is specifically one who 'holds dear, / Lovers of horses and of women', and who awaits the return of the antithetical gyre; as Yeats himself does. I think the alteration from the 'Cavern Face' of an earlier draft[4] might have been prompted by a reading of Ben Jonson's 'My Picture Left in Scotland'; in this beautifully deft piece of ironic self-pity a 'rockie face' is the poet's own pictured countenance seamed by time in contradistinction to his accomplished, ageless art. Yeats would have taken pleasure in such an oblique reference,[5] and in the varied conceits the poem suggests upon the relationship of Face with Mask and Time with Art – the face is aged and yet preserved through art. In any case the Rocky Face in Jonson's poem, as also evidently in 'The Gyres', is the poet's own – or a transformation of it. Nor do we need to go so far afield to discover its real significance; in 'Ego Dominus Tuus' Yeats ponders the 'hollow face' of Dante:

> I think he fashioned from his opposite
> An image that might have been a stony face.
>
> (*CP* 181)[6]

In the last verse of the same poem 'Ille' (as Pound remarked: 'Willie') indicates that he too 'seeks an image'. The Rocky Face of *Last Poems* is Yeats's symbolic discovery of an image that parallels the 'stony face' of Dante; for the 'antithetical' poet Will and Mask become one. The invocation of that mantic figure stands for a declaratory claim: the writing of poetry (and the completion of *A Vision*) liberates the poet from the world of cyclical nature; endowed with 'creative power' he may 'rejoice' in the midst of tragedy. 'The Gyres' declares the rewards the prose expected; the poet is re-born as an invulnerable 'stony face'.

An opening such as this is prescriptive for much that follows; transformation of the living to the condition of sculpted image everywhere brings its rewards in *Last Poems*. As the prose anticipated, the beloved is also re-born invulnerable, re-made as sculpted image; 'A Bronze Head' – Laurence Campbell's bust of Maud Gonne in the Municipal Gallery, – undergoes its apt consideration. The poem resumes themes familiar from earlier

work. The 'withered' appearance of the face recalls Eva Gore-
Booth, 'withered old and skeleton-gaunt',[7] the victim of just such
'abstract' politics as Maud herself had engaged in. Maud's own
'image' in 'Among School Children' had similar lineaments; its
'hollow of cheek as though it drank the wind' bespoke its taking
'a mess of shadows for its meat': the penalty of time's action and a
misuse of talents. There are further resemblances. Pondering on
Maud in that earlier poem, Yeats's 'heart is driven wild'; in 'A
Bronze Head' he records a sympathetic activity of imagination so
intense as to create virtual identity of experience; until

> I had grown wild
> And wandered murmuring everywhere, 'My child, my child!'

The 'wildness' is common to both occasions. But in the earlier
poem the disturbing reflection must be curtly dismissed; imagination brings together the 'living child' and the old woman, and the
implied knowledge of time's action is too painful to be tolerated
long:

> enough of that,
> Better to smile on all that smile, and show
> There is a comfortable kind of old scarecrow.
> *(CP* 243)

Now the pain is salved by the transformation of the human being
to the sculpted image, the bronze head. Appropriately, the
poem's gait is even-paced; the syntax is leisurely, and the connectives are the connectives of discussion, not of vehemence or
dismay: 'Or maybe', 'But even', 'Or else'. There is leisure even
to specify the actuality of the head by siting it precisely: 'at right
of the entrance'. Knowledge of the sculpted image offers and asks
such response; its dualities, 'human', 'superhuman', alive, dead,
reconcile the contraries of his knowledge of Maud: dark, light,
empty, full, human, possessed. Its imaginative redemption is
final; the pain of her ageing (and, by extension, of Yeats's own) is
salved by McTaggart's belief in the compositeness of substance,
that life and death are, like other manifestations of being, mere
terms in a single series – a reassurance that stands as philosophical
parallel to the most extensive poetic confusion of the real and
imaginary worlds, the imaginative transformation or redemption

of death. A deleted stanza[8] records, if slackly and with vacillation, the 'triumph' that comes with imaginative victory. Such is the characteristic response of *Last Poems* to what had seemed the endless fascination, and the endless despair, provoked by Maud's beauty; like Michael Angelo's sculpture, the Bronze Head 'can rule by supernatural right'.[9] Yeats's knowledge of Maud shares, by the intervention of a sculpted form, the invulnerability of the presiding Rocky Face.

Many among *Last Poems* adopt the strategy of 'A Bronze Head'. Behind major poems stand specific works of art: the statue of Cuchulain in the Post Office, the pictures in the Municipal Gallery, the sculpted piece of Lapis Lazuli, the Bronze Head itself: all openly and directly acknowledged now, not present, as in earlier books, merely by implication or oblique reference. Other poems, without summoning statue or picture, equally think of body willed, transformed, to the condition of the visual arts. Persons are arrested in typical gestures: Caesar, Helen, Michael Angelo caught in moments of silent expressiveness that declare their meaning in fixity ('Long-Legged Fly'); the 'beautiful lofty things', embalmed and apart like the Rocky Face, share the same condition of arrested posture: Yeats's father, Standish O'Grady, Lady Gregory, Maud. Margot Ruddock too is caught in a moment of ecstatic knowledge; in that momentary posture Yeats specifies her as a work of art: 'that girl I declare / A beautiful lofty thing,' (*CP* 349). Delacroix, Landor, Talma, Irving are presented in the immobility of cameo. Maud Gonne, 'Pallas Athene in that straight back and arrogant head', expects the sculptor's chisel. The book is peopled by a series of arrested figures, statue-like; but not inert; these are Yeats's 'personal archetypes' by imaginative knowledge of whom the poet becomes endowed with 'joy'. As will become explicit.

The Rocky Face of 'The Gyres', like the 'stony face' of Dante, implies the intervention of the sculptor's chisel. Some years ago, T. R. Henn suggested that the source of the Rocky Face might be a carving on the wall of Thoor Ballylee, Yeats's Tower; the conceit is attractive. Having climbed the winding stair to the roof of the tower, as Dante climbed the winding upward path on the mountain of Purgatory, the poet achieves apotheosis as the sculpted image. The Tower, Yeats tells us, symbolises the mind looking out upon men and events, the Cave the mind looking inward upon itself;[10] in 'The Gyres' the Rocky Face looks out – like a face on Thoor Ballylee – over the time-ridden world of cyclical change, while the voice from the cave (in a related significance, time considered as eternal recurrence[11]) bids him rejoice in achieved liberation from the pressures of mere transitoriness. Whether Yeats had that specific carved head in mind or not is of marginal importance; the defeat of the impersonal world is, whether or no, symbolised in *Last Poems* largely by reference to the sculptor's craft. The trend culminates naturally, and a whole significant aspect of *Last Poems* comes to focus, in 'The Statues', the poem which meditates sculpture.

The passage from *On the Boiler*[12] which lays the groundwork for interpreting the poem stresses that Greek Statues repudiate the accidental, the time-conscious detail, which draws the attention of 'our democratic painters'; on the contrary the sculptors accept 'those Greek proportions which carry into plastic art the Pythagorean numbers, those faces which are divine because all there is empty and measured'. The statues discover, that is to say, the ideal laws of form, the abstract definition that stands aloof from the particular, the norm that has no counterpart in the natural world of cyclical change. As a passage from *A Vision* (p. 291) explains, 'the human norm, discovered from the measurement of ancient statues, was God's first handiwork, that "perfectly proportioned human body", which had seemed to Dante Unity of Being symbolised'. To specify in sculpture the human norm, the perfect measurements, is to regain an imaginative Eden, whence one may look forth and rejoice at cyclical accident. This is the assumption underlying 'The Statues'; and the figure transformed, as in 'A Bronze Head', is Maud. As several critics note, her beauty had in the past prompted to sculptural metaphor: 'her face, like the face of some Greek statue, showed little thought, her whole body seemed a master-work of long-labouring thought, as though a Scopas had measured and calculated, consorted with Egyptian sages, and mathematicians

out of Babylon, that he might outface even Artemisia's sepulchral image with a living norm'.[13] Maud in her living beauty had
seemed a unique embodiment of the ideal laws of form. But that
unearthly beauty had been threatened by the transience of life
within nature. Now in 'The Statues' Yeats follows out the
provisional logic of his metaphor. To transform Maud's beauty
to the condition of sculpture, and to pare away altogether the
natural time-dominated woman, is to gather that beauty into the
appropriate imaginative idiom of *Last Poems*. 'Body' by espousal
of the sculpted image becomes 'soul'. The sculptor's art is one
which shares much with the poet's; in a late essay Yeats speaks of
'the sculptor toiling to set free the imprisoned image',[14] an artistic
endeavour answered by the 'union of theme and thought, fact
and idea, so complete that there is nothing more to do, nothing
left but statue and dream' (*E & I* 477). Just so in this sector of
*Last Poems* Yeats offers the statues as the embodiment of the
'dream'; to write them into the poetry is symbolically to declare
the discovery of their Unity of Being. Maud has become, along
with the other living statues we have mentioned, one of the
personal archetypes, contemplation of whom empowers the poet,
the Rocky Face, to rejoice.

The significance of 'The Statues' may become clearer if we
consider previous appearances of its peculiar language in Yeats's
verse; stone and statuary symbols had occurred earlier in more
equivocal guise. A half-mocking (and much less overt) epiphany
of the poet-as-statue occurs in 'A Living Beauty'; there the poet
is cast, not as a Rocky Face, but as a 'weather-worn marble triton
among the streams'. Worn out with making images, he suffers
from a divorce between the actual and the imagined; responsive
to the image, 'the pictured beauty', he is indifferent to the real,
the delicately and variously human. And the poem offers this as a
cause for dismay. Similarly the language of 'Easter, 1916' equates
the rebels' possession of their 'dream', their ideal image, with the
enchanting their hearts to a stone 'To trouble the living stream':
stone is inimical to the living tissue of experience. And on the one
occasion in Yeats's verse where the language richly predicts 'The
Statues', a disaffection for stone and sculpted stone persists. The

opening chorus of *The Only Jealousy of Emer* invokes ideal
beauty in terms that anticipate the 'calculation, number, measurement' of *Last Poems*:

> How many centuries spent
> The sedentary soul
> In toils of measurement
> Beyond eagle or mole,
> Beyond hearing or seeing,
> Or Archimedes' guess,
> To raise into being
> That loveliness?[15]

But the closing chorus interprets the play's action as a dismissal
of this ideal loveliness in favour of less exalted visions; the lure of
the ideal, as often in Yeats's plays and lyrics, is at odds with effective
living. 'A statue of solitude' endangers the distinctively human:

> He that has loved the best
> May turn from a statue
> His too human breast.[16]

Marble serves to specify the hostility of unearthly formal beauty.

The originality of 'The Statues', compared with these earlier
uses of its peculiar language, is that the fixity of marble becomes,
not the antagonist of living, but the potential locus of life-
enhancing knowledge. The release of this knowledge is accomplished by the exertion of imaginative energy, by the imaginative
possession of the archetype as discovered in the statue. The
tendency of the ideal image to 'keep a marble or a bronze repose'
('Among School Children'; the idiom persists) is cancelled by a
passion-generated act of imagination; the impressment of 'live
lips' upon a 'plummet-measured face' is the indicative act of
'imagined love' animating the ideal repose. The hour is 'midnight', always the moment of apocalypse in Yeats. 'Body' and
'soul' embrace in the act of imaginative apprehension, and solitary beds are exchanged for 'some public place'; the 'statue of
solitude' no longer enjoys its terrifying aloofness, the 'formality',
'abstraction' of the image becomes relevant for living. Later
verses extend the possibilities-for-living. The craft of the poet-
as-sculptor, acknowledged in verse two, performs an imaginative

function similar to that of the passion-driven boys and girls: 'dreams' are given their 'looking glass' in statues ('there is nothing left', one remembers, 'but statue and dream'), and the statues enjoy potential for swaying a nation's ideals. The 'intended, complete' image can, if recognised, subdue Asiatic variousness, formlessness, or the complexities of knowledge and appearance – the mere accidents of natural life – and establish the groundwork of an entire civilisation. At the poem's end Yeats answers his previous equivocal response to the 1916 rebels (see 'Easter 1916'); in summoning to imaginative presence the ideal image, the personal archetype, of Cuchulain, Pearse and his companions were enabled to 'climb to [their] proper dark' out of the accidental formlessness of contemporary living. The actual statue of Cuchulain in the Post Office, imaginatively realised, could serve as the locus for the establishment of a new and ennobling Irish civilisation – the long-cherished aim of Yeats's own dramatisation of the Cuchulain legend. Time and chance would be defeated and Rocky Face might properly rejoice.

If we wished to put this significance another way we might again turn to Northrop Frye. One weakness of Yeats's *A Vision*, he says, is the absence of an 'apocalyptic construct' to set against what the system conceives as 'the opposed and impossible ideals' of unity and individuality 'which only superhuman beings can reach'. 'The Statues', I think, offers specifically just such a construct; apocalypse becomes feasible, through imaginative exertion, within the framework of living. Frye draws attention to the sentence with which *A Vision* ends, contrasting the 'real Heracles' at the banquet of the immortal gods with 'Heracles the shadowy image bound to an endless cycle'; to 'mount' (the word is Yeats's own; it is at home among *Last Poems*) to that other Heracles – the real and the free – becomes a possibility for poet and nation. Imaginative knowledge of the personal archetypes carries its ultimate reward.

Knowledge of the sculpted image, 'The Statues' declares, bestows personal energy, power. Many of the *Last Poems* are occupied with the poet's desire to re-fashion himself (a variant on the rejoicing Rocky Face) into a figure of abundant energy. 'Grant me an old man's frenzy, / Myself must I remake. . . .' (*CP* 347); the unchristened heart exerts itself finally in this new context as 'The Wild Old Wicked Man' or John Kinsella; Crazy Jane momentarily returns; the images desired and invoked are those 'That constitute the wild' (*CP* 367);[17] figures of history, ancient and contemporary, are summoned to characterise some abundant energy of mind or person, Caesar, Helen, Irving, Talma, the O'Rahilly, Casement, Parnell: the last flourishes of the long-meditated delight in personality. Everywhere joy, gaiety, frenzy are invoked and declared; the vital rhythms of 'Three Songs' and some other ballad-like pieces contribute metric and syntactic energy.[18] 'An old man's eagle mind' is imaginatively discovered.

To write poetry is itself to know and to disclose imaginative energy. As John Holloway shows in another chapter of [*An Honoured Guest*], a common factor among many major poems is the giving incarnation to 'energised subjectivity . . . passionate and powerful self-possession'. In a manner characteristic of *Last Poems*, what had once been implicit in the reader's experience of the poem is now directly asserted. One among these poems allegorises the assumption of imaginative power. 'To Dorothy Wellesley' admits allegory because it is addressed to a fellow-poet; Lady Dorothy, with whom Yeats shared in these years 'intellectual sensuality', is a surrogate for the poet himself. The poetic experience is explicitly timed at midnight, the moment of visionary knowledge; at its conclusion the poetess climbs to the darkness of her book-lined chamber (the 'proper dark' of 'The Statues') and there gains knowledge of the Proud Furies 'each with her torch on high'.[19] The poem's action imitates the advance of an act of imaginative possession, the poetic process, and the assumption of the appropriate reward in personal energy. The first lines envisage the transmutation of external reality by (precisely) an apprehensive act: the poetess is bidden to grasp in her hand the 'moonless midnight of the trees' and to transform it to the condition of imagined reality: 'famous old upholsteries'[20] ('As though' is mere poetic tact.) She then possesses the artifice sensuously, recreates it within her own mind, becomes 'Rammed full with that most sensuous silence of the night'. Her reward consists in a visitation from the 'Proud Furies', instinct of energy, the very antithesis of 'Content' and 'satisfied Conscience'. The poet's dilemma at life's end is answered: 'My temptation', as he tells us, 'is quiet',[21] a temptation overcome by knowledge of 'frenzy', the gift of the Furies. And frenzy is known imaginatively in the poetic act; writing the poem involves a vicarious expenditure of imaginative energy: the verbs ('stretch', 'tighten', 'rammed', 'climb', 'bay') are notably indicative of the effortful nature of the experience. What it meant for Yeats is suggested by a passing note in *Autobiographies*, echoing the sixth and seventh lines of the present poem:

E—— himself, all muscular force and ardour, makes me think of that line written, as one believes, of Shakespeare by Ben Jonson – 'So rammed with life that he can but grow in life with being.'[22]

An alluring reward for the expenditure of imaginative energy by the ageing poet: to grow in life vicariously, as Time saps remaining physical strength. Shakespeare, ideally conceived, takes his place, though covertly, beside the other personal archetypes invoked and declared in *Last Poems*.

## II

Among the poems of *The Winding Stair* 'Vacillation' asks the question which precipitates the concerns and commitments of *Last Poems*:

> Between extremities
> Man runs his course;
> A brand, or flaming breath,
> Comes to destroy
> All those antinomies
> Of day and night;
> The body calls it death,
> The heart remorse.
> But if these be right
> What is joy?                          (*CP* 282)

'joy' turns out to be, as we have discovered, the imaginative possession of an image; reconciling or cancelling the antinomies, it makes joy possible. But so far the only antagonist has been 'remorse'; the second adversary remains. Yeats explains in a 1935 letter to Dorothy Wellesley: 'To me the supreme aim [of 'arranging' one's ideas and writing poetry] is an act of faith and reason to make one rejoice in the midst of tragedy.'[23] Yeats was at the date of writing 'still an invalid dreading fatigue'; other letters show him vividly conscious of approaching death. *Last Poems* are concerned to re-make the self and so win joy in the imminent presence of death; to go further: they seek to re-make death itself, to justify the taunt that 'Man has created death' (*CP* 264). Hence the emphasis, new in these poems, on tragedy – on the art form most preoccupied with man's response to his mortality.

Yeats's somewhat personal views of tragedy ask explanation. In common with other literary forms, tragedy is properly given over to 'action' not to 'thought': 'masterpieces, whether of the stage or study, excel in their action, their visibility; who can forget Odysseus, Don Quixote, Hamlet, Lear, Faust, all figures in a peep-show';[24] tragedy is, to put it simply, the locus of personality. Not of intricate psychology; the tragic heroes are a gallery of figures who exhibit, like the figures, the personal archetypes, of *Last Poems*, some abundant but uncomplicated personal energy. To identify with them, as author or spectator, is to discover joy, the familiar reward: 'Some Frenchman has said that farce is the struggle against a ridiculous object, comedy against a movable object, tragedy against an immovable; and because the will, or energy, is greatest in tragedy, tragedy is the more noble; but I add that "will or energy is eternal delight", and when its limit is reached it may become a pure aimless joy, though the man, the shade [the inferior Heracles?] still mourns his lost object.'[25] For the true tragic hero – the real Heracles – there will be no mourning: 'There may be in this or that detail painful tragedy, but in the whole work none. I have heard Lady Gregory say, rejecting some play in the modern manner sent to the Abbey Theatre, "Tragedy must be a joy to the man who dies!" ' (*E & I* 522). The implications of joy are specified: 'The heroes of Shakespeare convey to us through their looks, or through the metaphorical patterns of their speech, the sudden enlargement of their vision, their ecstasy at the approach of death.' (*E & I* 522–3) The metaphor is reversible: 'ecstasy is a kind of death' (*E & I* 71); to conflate, confuse, the two experiences is the outcome of Yeats's heady logic; death will be ecstasy, apocalypse – not an enemy – to the man who conceives of life as tragedy. Meditating on such a fittingly tragic death, that of Hamlet, Yeats tells us: 'This idea of death suggests to me Blake's design ... of the soul and body embracing.'[26] We are back at the language appropriate to 'The Statues', where body and soul embrace in knowledge of the sculptor's work. To re-make one's death in the tragic idiom is to discover an ecstasy closely allied to the joy attaching to imaginative possession of the sculpted figure, the joy known to Rocky Face. The writing of poetry, imaginative conquest, becomes subversive of the last reality.

The *personae* of tragedy, with whom the poet may identify, are frequent in *Last Poems*. Yeats elects to 're-make' himself as Timon and Lear ('An Acre of Grass'); Hamlet and Lear, Ophelia and Cordelia 'perform their tragic play' in 'Lapis Lazuli'; Hamlet is named in 'The Statues'. None of these characters had made previous appearances in the lyric verse. In 'Hound Voice' there is a reminiscence of *Lear*;[27] the madness of 'Why should not Old Men be Mad?' again remembers Lear.[28] Cuchulain, as tragic hero, is present in 'The Statues', 'Crazy Jane on the Mountain', 'The Circus Animals' Desertion', 'Cuchulain Comforted'; Parnell, hero of three poems, is described in prose as 'a tragedian';[29] Margot Ruddock, the unnamed heroine of 'A Crazed Girl', was 'a frustrated tragic genius' who found herself in the ecstasy of her frenzied dance upon the shore.[30] All serve within the economy of *Last Poems* as examples of tragic dying, or tragic ecstasy, by imaginative knowledge of whom Yeats may re-make his own death.

'Lapis Lazuli' is the considerable poem in which Yeats specifies the intimate connection between tragic joy and the poet's discovered power. The first two verses effect a redemption of the word 'gay'; contemptuously pronounced by the 'hysterical women' – bound as they are to the world of cyclical accident – it becomes in verse two synonymous with tragic joy, the joy of liberation. Unlike the despised actors of 'The Old Stone Cross', the actors of this poem understand 'what unearthly stuff / Rounds a mighty scene' (*CP* 366); by successful interpretation of their roles they achieve ecstasy and apocalyptic knowledge: 'Heaven blazing into the head.' The abrupt syntax, connectives altogether pared away, mimics the immediacy and the power of the dis-covered knowledge. 'Tragedy wrought to its uttermost' brings about the ecstatic confusion of death the prose describes. But the poet's especial craft has yet to be linked with this victory, his joy, 'gaiety', justified. Like 'A Bronze Head' and 'The Statues', 'Lapis Lazuli' took its origin from the contemplation of a sculpted image; a letter to Dorothy Wellesley speaks of 'a great piece [of lapis lazuli] carved by some Chinese sculptor. . . . Ascetic, pupil, hard stone, eternal theme of the sensual east. The heroic cry in the midst of despair. But no, I am wrong, the east has its solutions always and therefore knows nothing of tragedy. It is we, not the east, that must raise the heroic cry.'[31] The logic moves confi-dently between sculpted image, tragedy and the 'heroic cry' of poetry; 'Lapis Lazuli' offers an imaginative collocation of the same order. Section three contains properties that directly recall 'The Statues'; Callimachus 'handled marble as if it were bronze' (the characteristic materials), but his images that shaped the thought of a civilisation were destroyed by time's action; as in 'The Statues' each new 'gay' civilisation must rebuild its own focal images. The remaining sections recall 'A Bronze Head' and 'To Dorothy Wellesley'. They enact the imaginative possession of the sculpted image, to bring the poet 'gaiety', as Dorothy Wellesley possessed her environment to win her own apocalyptic vision. The short fourth section presents the lapis lazuli carving as it appears to an objective scrutiny; the final section mimics an encroaching act of imaginative possession. At first the stone of the carving remains actual; its 'Every discoloration . . . accidental crack or dent' merely 'seems' water-course or avalanche; but even here the process of re-making is incipient. Then details are added ('doubtless'), details not even registered on the stone by 'accidental' usage; plum and cherry-branch flower at the poet's command. The next phrase brings confession:

I
Delight to imagine them seated there;

The act of imaginative possession is complete. And on its completion the image is made to contradict its marble repose; the scene the last lines depict is one of animation, of request and compliance, music and glittering eyes. The outcome is inevitable; the poem comes to rest declaring the poet's achievement, through imaginative exertion, of his apocalyptic reward: the last word is 'gay'.

III

The emphatic stress in Yeats's view of tragedy falls on the hero's rejoicing at the moment of death; to experience tragedy is altogether life-enhancing, exhilarating, death-cancelling. The refrain of 'The Gyres' may therefore appropriately be 'What matter?'; a superb nonchalance invests many *Last Poems*. The other side of the tragic duality in common experience, the deeply painful sense of loss, of wasted potential, is barely noticed: 'there may be in this or that detail painful tragedy, but in the whole work none'. Towards such a position the brilliant logic of Yeats's career – or an important aspect of it – had tended; the writing of poetry and the whole elaborate structure of *A Vision* were to confer just such security, an invulnerable aloofness. A comparison between 'Lapis Lazuli' and 'Nineteen Hundred and Nineteen' will show the process at work: the earlier poem greets the inevitable breaking of 'many ingenious lovely things' with dismay, even despair; 'Lapis Lazuli' knows the same facts with the superb detachment Rocky Face is bidden to discover. But there is a sense in which Yeats as poet has been trapped by a remorseless logic of his own creating; the discovery of the sculpted image and the assumption of the poetic-become-real energy may indeed be the inevitably right outcome, the 'ultimate insight', of the dedicated career. But they may operate also to the impoverishment of the poet; to detach the poetic sensibility from painful circumstance makes for a poverty that cannot be compensated by any merely declaratory security. The real 'images' of the great poems are not the specifically summoned ones, tower and winding stair, golden bird or even chestnut-tree and dancer, but the infinite variousness of the poet's sensibility as he meditates, the varying deployments of allegiance and mistrust. There are signs of impoverishment in *Last Poems*; something of the assertive propagandist is felt, at his most unacceptable in the flat recommendation of violence for its own sake ('good strong blows are delights to the mind'); rhythm, though capable of niceties possible only to the aged virtuoso, is too often merely insistent. A certain thinness is bred; *Last Poems* almost wholly lacks the richly complex, brilliantly architected structure of many great poems. Yeats had claimed that his Church had an altar but no pulpit; the sheer assertiveness of some *Last Poems* would argue the prominent existence of pulpit at the end of life.

But to rest here would be to miss the opposed allegiances within the collection. Yeats is too intelligent a self-critic to have been blind to these new impoverishments; several poems consider explicitly the very dilemma we have noted. Some present, in contrast to the powerful aloofness of the Rocky Face, the natural man vividly conscious of time's injuries. Among these, 'The Municipal Gallery Revisited' looks at first glance a poem in the familiar idiom. The gallery pictures are the images to be possessed anew by the poet; they, like others, result from a work of imaginative re-making:

> [Not] The dead Ireland of my youth, but an Ireland
> The poets have imagined, terrible and gay.

The 'terrible beauty' of 'Easter 1916', to create which Pearse and the others had been 'transformed utterly', is here memorialised in art; 'terrible and gay' is the condition of tragic joy discovered in 'Lapis Lazuli'. And beside the poet's imagined Ireland hang portraits of his friends; the syntax demands that we take the 'permanent or impermanent images' to refer to such portraits; like the other characteristic poses of this collection, personal archetypes, his 'friends' take their place as fixed, 'sculpted' images to be imaginatively known. We seem about to have urged on us once more the advantages of powerful self-possession. But the idiom is largely distinct from others among *Last Poems*.[32] The syntax is one of colon and semi-colon; there is leisure to insert 'I say', 'certainly', leisure for repetition; long-suspended sentences may ignore even the break between verses (Yeats noted that complete coincidence between period and stanza brought 'energy'); rhythm is relaxed and diction plain, undemanding; the speaker's environment is generously, not to say superfluously, stocked. The general effect is one of easy gravity, an undesigning wandering amid memories; as against the telling compression, the abrupt energetic juxtapositions of 'The Statues' or 'Lapis Lazuli'. Where 'The Gyres' delights in enigma, 'The Municipal Gallery' seems anxious to lead us on, to explain as fully as possible. The distinction is absolute; it registers in an unaffected recording of personal emotion altogether foreign to the aloof detachment of those other poems:

> Heart-smitten with emotion I sink down,
> My heart recovering with covered eyes . . .

'What matter?' is replaced by a confession of despair at the loss of what was unique, irrecoverable:

> And I am in despair that time may bring
> Approved patterns of women or of men
> But not that self-same excellence again.

The 'approved patterns', the norm that was susceptible of becoming a sculpted pose, are rejected in favour of the variously human. Acknowledgement is made, not of the triumphant Rocky Face, but of the 'heart', the locus of natural feeling.

Other poems in the earlier part of the collection (the group closing with 'Are You Content?', first published as *New Poems* in 1938) betray something of the same commitment. Self-judging poems such as 'What Then?' view the poetic triumph, in refrain at least, with deflating irony:

> 'The work is done', grown old he thought . . .
> 'Let the fools rage, I swerved in naught,

> But something to perfection brought';
> *But louder sang that ghost, 'What then?'*    (*CP* 348)

The ambivalent refrain questions not only the value of the
achievement but the fate of the poet; the assurance of 'Heaven
blazing into the head' appears to recede. The power that attends
identification with the personal archetype is similarly undercut in
'Are You Content?' 'Infirm and aged' Yeats might

> demonstrate in my own life
> What Robert Browning meant
> By an old hunter talking with Gods;
> But I am not content.                    (*CP* 371)

Reference to the essays will disclose an association with Berkeley,
a recurrent hero, behind the lines (*E & I* 408–9); but even
imaginative identification with that 'angry unscrupulous solitary'
does not in this mood content the heart.

The mood incipient in the 1938 *New Poems* is developed in
those first published posthumously as *Last Poems* in 1939. In
this new group, the most terrifying of 'The Apparitions' becomes Yeats's own 'coat upon a coat-hanger'; death can no
longer be re-fashioned to ecstasy, but is regarded with the heart's
candour:

> His empty heart is full at length,
> But he has need of all that strength
> Because of the increasing Night
> That opens her mystery and fright.    (*CP* 387)

In a more considerable way 'High Talk' revalues the poet's craft,
the source of powerful self-possession in other poems. Yeats
casts himself as Malachi Stilt-Jack, the maker of metaphors, of
art in the grand manner. Already implicit in the chosen *dramatis
persona* is an ironic valuation: the walker upon stilts, though an
eye-catching figure, is inescapably an absurd posturing creature
on his 'timber toes'; the reaction he provokes from the onlookers
recalls only juvenile practical jokes: 'women shriek'. And the
activity he is committed to is a precarious one, carried out un-
naturally, under strain. The last few lines of the poem record
with desperate seriousness the human predicament from which

attention has been diverted by the stilted figure. Metaphor, the poet's craft, is explicitly abandoned. The setting registers apocalypse: 'night splits and the dawn breaks loose'; but it brings with it 'terrible novelty', not the welcome of a conquered territory. Under its brilliant light the natural man, no longer upon timber toes, 'stalks on', a hunted yet eager and vital being prompted and terrified by revelation. The apocalyptic grandeur is suggested by the 'great sea-horses' (symbolic, but by comparison with the stilt-walker part of the natural setting) 'laughing' at the dawn in ecstasy or terrifying superior knowledge; the poet's imaginings are seen as paltry contrivances beside such heart-recognised 'mystery and fright'.

The strategy of 'The Circus Animals' Desertion' parallels that of 'High Talk'; the circus phantasmagoria, the connection explicitly made by the '*stilted* boy', carries with it the same ironic valuation. The circus animals have merely been 'on show'; their triviality is gestured towards by the colloquial indifference of 'The Lord knows what'. In essence the poem is a direct espousal of the 'heart'; in the face of approaching death poetic triumph is not possible or not relevant; the 'masterful images', 'complete' and self-sufficient, have come to seem a showman's impertinence. 'Character isolated by a deed', the condition precisely of the powerful *dramatis personae* of earlier *Last Poems*, is set aside. The poet lies down in preference in 'the foul rag-and-bone shop of the heart'; the miscellaneous, chance, nature of the contents, their disorderly profusion, stands for the absence of identifiable meaning that attends direct on-the-pulses experience; the 'raving slut' indicates the kind of unmastered violence, the intoxicating vigour, Yeats commonly associates with such experience. In one of his latest essays Yeats speaks of his admiration for his 'brother's extreme book, "The Charmed Life" ', an admiration evoked by 'his pursuit of all that through its unpredictable, unarrangeable reality, least resembles knowledge'.[33] 'The Circus Animals' Desertion', whatever its negative aspects as a 'Dejection Ode', is equally a vote for such heart-reality against the belief in formality, 'calculation, number, measurement' of earlier poems.

'The Man and the Echo' answers 'The Gyres' directly. The

setting is again oracular; 'the cleft that's christened Alt' was
associated with the Delphic chasm. But where 'The Gyres' is
declaratory, assertive, this poem ends on a poignant note; its
temper is questioning, the poem's *raison d'être* being an inquest on
the self and the poetry. Nor has the poet been transformed to a
Rocky Face; his is the natural undefended sensibility con-
demned to 'lie awake night after night / And never get the
answers right'. The answers he receives from the Rocky Voice
are confessedly no more than an echo of his questions. To the
ultimate question,

> O Rocky Voice
> Shall we in that great night rejoice?

the oracle returns no answer. It is an effect of calculated restraint
to refuse even the token reassurance of an acoustic reply. In
place of the voice from the cavern with its confident knowledge
of one word, 'Rejoice', we have the anguish of not knowing. As
in 'High Talk', the poet's triumph seems trivial before the heart's
naked experience:

> But hush, for I have lost the theme,
> Its joy or night seem but a dream;
> Up there some hawk or owl has struck,
> Dropping out of sky or rock,
> A stricken rabbit is crying out,
> And its cry distracts my thought.

The anguish of death is overwhelmingly more vivid than poetry's
'theme'; 'joy', the familiar claim, and 'night', the threat, are both
impertinent rationalisations beside direct knowledge of death's
imminence.

'The Black Tower' was Yeats's last poem. Beside its disquiet-
ing uncertainty 'Under Ben Bulben', the 'official' tail-piece,
assertive, secure, looks almost brash. 'The Black Tower' in effect
makes over for the last time what remains Yeats's central symbol,
the tower. That proud image, with its winding stair conducting
to wisdom, is now a tower of refuge only, sombre, beleaguered,
suffering the exigencies of want. This poem, like 'The Gyres',
records the moment when the gyre changes direction; but not
now from a position of untouchable superiority – the poet is

deeply involved in the uncertainties the moment brings. Aware of distress, there exists also the possibility of release and new vigour when the dark of the moon comes round at last. The implied link with Yeats's own dying is barely escapable. The poised ambivalence with which the moment of apocalypse is awaited is characteristic of the temper of these latest poems. Terror is declared as well as joy, heart mysteries as well as heaven blazing into the head.

## NOTES

1. Ed. D. Donoghue and J. R. Mulryne (1965).

2. *Essays and Introductions* (1961) p. 599. Subsequent page references are to this edition.

3. See T. R. Henn, *The Lonely Tower* (1950) p. 303, and *Autobiographies* (1955) p. 171.

4. Henn, op. cit. p. 303.

5. For a reference to Jonson in Yeats's mind at this period see *Autobiographies*, p. 480, and p. 148 above.

6. Page references to the *Collected Poems* are to the 1950 edition.

7. 'In Memory of Eva Gore-Booth and Con Markiewicz', in *Collected Poems*, p. 263.

8. Printed in V. Koch, *W. B. Yeats: The Tragic Phase* (1951) p. 84. [*Editor's note.* This stanza was in fact deleted from 'The Circus Animals' Desertion', not from 'A Bronze Head.']

9. See 'Michael Robartes and the Dancer', in *Collected Poems*, p. 198.

10. *Essays* (1924) p. 107.

11. See *A Vision* (1937) p. 259.

12. (Dublin, 1939) p. 37.

13. *Autobiographies*, pp. 364–5.

14. A conceit associated with Michael Angelo, one of the important *dramatis personae* of *Last Poems*.

15. *Collected Plays* (1952 ed.) pp. 281–2.

16. Ibid. p. 295.

17. The images (of lion, virgin, harlot, child, eagle, and another, wind) are linked in the prose with Yeats's 'delight in active men', personal energy. *Essays and Introductions*, p. 530.

18. Contemporary letters to Dorothy Wellesley show a simplistic, almost childlike, delight in vigorous rhythms.

19. Compare 'Her Vision in the Wood', one of the few considerable poems in *Words For Music Perhaps* (*Collected Poems*, p. 312).

20. Does Yeats mean, perhaps, 'tapestries'?
21. In 'An Acre of Grass', in *Collected Poems*, p. 346.
22. *Autobiographies*, p. 480.
23. *Letters on Poetry from W. B. Yeats to Dorothy Wellesley* (1964) p. 12.
24. *On the Boiler*, p. 33.
25. Ibid. p. 35.
26. *The Letters of W. B. Yeats*, ed. Allan Wade (1954) p. 917.
27. Cf. 'The woman that I picked spoke sweet and low' with *Lear* v iii (of Cordelia): 'Her voice was ever soft / Gentle and low.'
28. Behind Lear stands that 'silent and fierce old man' William Pollexfen, another of the book's personal archetypes. See *Autobiographies*, p. 9.
29. See the *Variorum Edition* of the poems (ed. Allt and Alspach, 1957) p. 835; the contrast is with 'the great comedian' O'Connell.
30. See Yeats's introduction (p. ix) to her *The Lemon Tree* (1937).
31. *Letters on Poetry from W. B. Yeats to Dorothy Wellesley* (1964 ed.) p. 8.
32. An exception is 'A Bronze Head'; explaining, I think, Yeats's decision to cancel the original last stanza. [*Editor's note*. But see note 8 above.]
33. *On the Boiler*, p. 36.

# A. Norman Jeffares

## THE GENERAL AND PARTICULAR
## MEANINGS OF 'LAPIS LAZULI' (1967)

YEATS wrote 'Lapis Lazuli' in July 1936.[1] The subject of the
poem is the possible destruction of contemporary civilization, a
theme with which Yeats had long been occupied, and which he
treated in many of his later poems. The first stanza states that the
poet has heard that hysterical women are sick of painting, music,
and 'Of poets that are always gay', in view of the dangers of the
political situation and the threat of bombing raids. Edmund Dulac
had written to Yeats at the time he was writing the poem; he was
'terrified of what was going to happen if London was bombed
from the air'.[2] The statement develops into general tragedy:

> if nothing drastic is done
> Aeroplane and Zeppelin will come out,
> Pitch like King Billy bomb-balls in
> Until the town lie beaten flat.[3]

The Zeppelin, anachronistic for bombing purposes in 1936, is
probably due to the poet's memories of air raids on London in
the 1914–18 war. The 'bomb-balls', however, are of older origin,
for they seem to be derived from 'The Battle of the Boyne', a
ballad included in *Irish Minstrelsy*, an anthology edited by H.
Halliday Sparling:

> King James has pitched his tent between
> The lines for to retire;
> But King William threw his bomb-balls in
> And set them all on fire.[4]

The echo is stronger than the original. As well as calling King
William King Billy, a name more likely to stir up immediate
historical and political memories and associations in an Irishman,
Yeats took over the word 'pitch' and used it for the bomb-balls
instead of the tent. It is more suitable than the original's 'threw',

or, as might have been expected for an accurate description of the action of bombing from the air, 'dropped'; it has the necessary touch of violence that he required.

Frank O'Connor called on Yeats at the time he was writing the poem. After Yeats had discussed his pleasure at receiving the lapis lazuli, and told O'Connor of Dulac's letter, O'Connor then broached the subject of the production of Lady Gregory's *Dervorgillà* at the Abbey Theatre, which had been spoiled for him (he, like Yeats, was a Director of the Theatre) by the heroine weeping at the curtain. He asked Yeats 'Is it ever permissible for an actor to sob at the curtain of a play?' and he replied 'Never!'⁵

From the brief but effective picture of general tragedy in the first stanza the second moves to particular instances, to Hamlet, Lear, Cordelia, and Ophelia. Hysterical women had complained of poets who were always gay, but the word is taken up again in this stanza and the complaint answered; there is an implicit comparison of Cordelia and Ophelia with the modern hysterical women the poet had in his mind, to the disadvantage of the latter. Those who are worthy of their tragic roles 'Do not break up their lines to weep'.

The lines

> They know that Hamlet and Lear are gay;
> Gaiety transfiguring all that dread.

represent Yeats's own attitude to tragedy. A passage in 'A General Introduction for my Work' makes the point clear:

The heroes of Shakespeare convey to us through their looks, or through the metaphorical patterns of their speech, the sudden enlargement of their vision, their ecstasy at the approach of death: 'She should have died hereafter,' 'Of many thousand kisses, the poor last,' 'Absent thee from felicity awhile.' They have become God or Mother Goddess, the pelican, 'My baby at my breast,' but all must be cold; no actress has ever sobbed when she played Cleopatra, even the shallow brain of a producer has never thought of such a thing. The supernatural is present, cold winds blow across our hands, upon our faces, the thermometer falls, and because of that cold we are hated by journalists and groundlings. There may be in this or that detail painful tragedy,

F                                                S.Y.L.P.

but in the whole work none. I have heard Lady Gregory say, rejecting some play in the modern manner sent to the Abbey Theatre, 'Tragedy must be a joy to the man who dies.' Nor is it any different with lyrics, songs, narrative poems; neither scholars nor the populace have sung or read anything generation after generation because of its pain. The maid of honour whose tragedy they sing must be lifted out of history with timeless pattern, she is one of the four Maries, the rhythm is old and familiar, imagination must dance, must be carried beyond feeling into the aboriginal ice. Is ice the correct word? I once boasted, copying the phrase from a letter of my father's, that I would write a poem 'cold and passionate as the dawn.'[6]

He had in early youth imagined himself in the role of a Hamlet,[7] had developed the idea of Cuchulain as a suitable hero for his mythologizing processes in middle age, and later, in his obsession with the theory of history formulated in *A Vision*, he had returned to an old idea taken from Shelley of the man who had outlived 'Cycles of generation and of ruin',[8] and looked on at the vicissitudes of human civilization with detachment. These roles of Hamlet, Cuchulain, the old man were taken up by Yeats in order to face death unperturbed. The part of the somewhat inhuman spectator eventually arrived at has not a little in common with Yeats's desire, expressed in 'Sailing to Byzantium', to sing 'Of what is past, or passing, or to come'.[9] There it was to be achieved in the form of an artificial bird; in this poem as the spokesman of the hero:

> I think that the true poetic movement of our time is towards some heroic discipline. People much occupied with morality always lose heroic ecstasy. Those who have it most often are those Dowson has described (I cannot find the poem but the lines run like this or something like this)
>> Wine and women and song
>> To us they belong
>> To us the bitter and gay.

'Bitter and gay,' that is the heroic mood. When there is despair, public or private, when settled order seems lost, people look for strength within or without. Auden, Spender, all that seem the new movement *look* for strength in Marxian socialism, or in

Major Douglas; they want marching feet. The lasting expression of our time is not this obvious choice but in a sense of something steel-like and cold within the will, something passionate and cold.[10]

In 'Sailing to Byzantium' he wished to escape from 'that sensual music' of life; in 'Lapis Lazuli' he is making a gesture of defiance in the face of what seemed to him the inevitable coming of death upon our civilization; but he could also, towards the end of his life, come far nearer reality: 'I thought my problem was to face death with gaiety, now I have learned that it is to face life.'[11]

The third stanza of the poem links the personal and public tragedies together and reaffirms the need for gaiety:

> On their own feet they came, or on shipboard,
> Camel-back, horse-back, ass-back, mule-back,
> Old civilisations put to the sword . . .
> All things fall and are built again,
> And those that build them again are gay.

The reference to Callimachus in line 29 can be explained by reference to a passage in *A Vision*:

With Callimachus pure Ionic revives again, as Furtwängler has proved, and upon the only example of his work known to us, a marble chair, a Persian is represented, and may one not discover a Persian symbol in that bronze lamp, shaped like a palm, known to us by a description in Pausanias? But he was an archaistic workman, and those who set him to work brought back public life to an older form. One may see in masters and man a momentary dip into ebbing Asia.[12]

The fourth stanza, a description of a piece of lapis lazuli, appears to break the sequence of the poem abruptly, but a letter to Lady Gerald Wellesley illustrates its significance and relation to the theme:

Someone has sent me a present of a great piece carved by some Chinese sculptor into the semblance of a mountain with temple, trees, paths and an ascetic and pupil about to climb the mountain. Ascetic, pupil, hard stone, eternal theme of the sensual east. The heroic cry in the midst of despair. But no, I am wrong, the east has its solutions always and therefore knows nothing of tragedy. It is we, not the east, that must raise the heroic cry.[13]

In the last stanza Yeats pulls the poem together again; the bitter and gay are to meet despair and show forth the heroic mood. Gaiety predominates over bitterness, however, and the ending is more serene and less dramatic than might have been expected from what had gone before. The picture of the ascetic and pupil conveys serenity, and the poet allows his own thoughts to merge with those of the Chinamen, delighting

> to imagine them seated there;
> There, on the mountain and the sky,
> On all the tragic scene they stare.
> One asks for mournful melodies;
> Accomplished fingers begin to play.
> Their eyes mid many wrinkles, their eyes,
> Their ancient, glittering eyes, are gay.

## NOTES

1. Information from Mrs W. B. Yeats. Cf. *Letters on Poetry from W. B. Yeats to Dorothy Wellesley* (reissued 1964) p. 83, where he describes the poem as 'almost the best I have made of recent years'. He finished it on 25 July 1936, and it appeared in the *London Mercury*, March 1938, and in the *New Republic*, 13 April 1938. It was included in *New Poems* (Dublin, 1938), a Cuala Press edition of 450 copies, and then appeared in *Last Poems and Plays* (1940), a Macmillan edition of 2000 copies, subsequently in *Collected Poems*.

2. See Frank O'Connor, *The Backward Look* (1967) p. 174.

3. *Collected Poems* (1950 ed.) p. 338.

4. *Irish Minstrelsy*, ed. H. Halliday Sparling (1888) p. 319. There is a copy of this anthology, inscribed by the editor, in Yeats's library. It contained a poem by Yeats, who probably first met Sparling at the home of William Morris. Cf. a passage from Elizabeth Yeats's diary for 1888–9, quoted by Joseph Hone, 'A Scattered Fair', in *The Wind and the Rain*, Autumn 1946, p. 113.

5. Frank O'Connor, op. cit. p. 174. The lapis lazuli was a present from Harry Clifton, to whom the poem is dedicated.

6. *Essays and Introductions* (1961) pp. 522–3. Other comments can be found in *Essays and Introductions*, p. 322, in *On the Boiler* – see

*Explorations* (1962) p. 448 – and in *Letters on Poetry*, p. 12. See also 'Demon and Beast' and 'Tom O'Roughley', in *Collected Poems*, pp. 209, 158.

   7. *Autobiographies* (1955) p. 83.
   8. P. B. Shelley, *Hellas*, lines 137 ff.
   9. *Collected Poems*, p. 217.
   10. *Letters on Poetry*, p. 7.
   11. Ibid. p. 164.
   12. *A Vision* (1937) p. 270. See also 'The Cutting of an Agate', in *Essays and Introductions*, p. 225.
   13. *Letters on Poetry*, p. 8. R. Ellmann, *The Identity of Yeats*, pp. 185–6, remarks that Yeats justifies gaiety first in terms of the West and then of the East. The heroes of its tragedies represent the West. But the Asiatic defence is different. We move from staring at a high lighted stage, to stand upon a lofty mountain overlooking the world and the ages. From here the rise and fall of civilizations is no matter for pathos and female hysteria, but seems a necessary part of the scene. The Chinese find joy in recurrence.

# F. A. C. Wilson

## 'THE STATUES' (1957)

'THE STATUES' is a poem which one reads by the light of Vivienne Koch, whose reconstruction of the sources is perhaps her best piece of Yeats scholarship.[1] It is not for all this a final or even in the last resort an adequate analysis: it falls down in the third verse, where Miss Koch is simply not a good enough art-historian to follow the ramifications of Yeats's logic. My other objection to her work is that she over-rates her text aesthetically, a contention I would justify from the arguments of my *Emer* essay. I have spoken of the structure of the poem, how it begins from stasis and from the 'cold, hard' image of the Greek statues themselves, and proceeds by way of an extensive peregrination until the clinching image of Cuchulain presents itself and it can end in declamation. For my part the peregrination is too involved to make for perfection of form (it is possible to put too much material into a poem, and this is Yeats's error here); and the final peroration itself cannot be passed by without comment, for the apologist has to dispose of a criticism which has been voiced: that there is something immoral and 'sadistic' in the piled-up adjectives of Yeats's invective:

> We Irish, born into that ancient sect,
> But thrown upon this filthy modern tide
> And by its formless spawning fury wrecked . . .

Whatever one's attitude to this stanza, some rather careless technique in the second verse makes 'The Statues' an imperfect poem; but it remains, by sheer size, one of the most monumental of *Last Poems* and indeed of all Yeats's achievements.

It may be as well to begin from the imputation of 'inhumanity' (the word is Mr D. S. Savage's)[2] and I will say frankly that I began, like him, by being antagonised by what seems to be the intransigence and race-prejudice of the last period. The position Yeats had taken in his early verse and prose had been that spirit (*atma*), undifferentiated and incorruptible, is a constituent of 'every thing that lives'; that all human life is dignified and 'holy' and that art ought consequently to be 'forgiveness' and never 'accusation'; and how much his position changed can be seen by juxtaposing the early 'Paudeen' and the late 'A Bronze Head':

> There cannot be, confusion of our sound forgot,
> A single soul that lacks a sweet crystalline cry ...

> Or else I thought her supernatural,
> As though some sterner eye looked through her eye
> On this foul world in its decline and fall,
> On gangling stocks grown great, great stocks run dry,
> Ancestral pearls all pitched into a sty,
> Heroic reverie mocked by fool and knave,
> And wondered what was left for massacre to save.

Terrible as that sibilant last alexandrine may be, the transcendentalism of 'A Bronze Head' justifies the invective, as we shall see if we penetrate into the myth of the poem. It is in fact a last application of that theory of daemonic possession I have discussed in relation to *At the Hawk's Well*: Maud Gonne is possessed by an angel, which descants through her lips and with the terrible unsentimentality of heaven, on the degradation of spirit in the modern world. For spirit in the material world necessarily passes through what Blake calls 'states', as in the present century it seemed to Yeats to be passing through the state of extreme objectivity; and these states, when they are abject or degraded, one must concede to be a proper subject for invective. The 'modern tide', in 'The Statues' also, is judged transcendentally and therefore purely, and if it should be maintained that Yeats overlooks the essential sanctity of all spirit in his universal condemnation of humanity sunk in its present state, we have to allow that, from the point of view of the subjective tradition, he would have been much more seriously at fault (and would have courted sentimentality) if he had neglected to condemn the 'state' for the sake of the individual. The issue is complicated by the

terminology Yeats uses, as when he contrasts subjective or
'Aryan' culture (by 'Aryan' Yeats means 'Indo-European', the
Hindu as well as the Graeco-Roman civilisation) with the inferior and objective non-Aryan, or as he confusingly terms it
'Asiatic', ethos; terms which may seem to imply ugly racial
theories. And indeed I cannot dispute a fascist influence on his
*nomenclature*;[3] but his *meaning*, which is entirely pure, is simply
that the major subjective religions have owed their inception to
the Indo-European race, while his 'Asiatics' – the peoples of Asia
Minor and the steppe and desert country beyond – have normally
thought of God objectively, and have not been able to rise above
the 'many', 'the multiplicity of the generative universe', to a sense
of the 'One' or of the archetypal world.[4] Now in the twentieth
century and as the world cycle nears its end, Yeats tells us, the
'objective' or Asiatic impulse has won dominance over men's
minds everywhere in the world; and the ultimate intention of his
poem is to combat this inadequate intuition and to set up against
objective 'multiplicity' a great image of 'the One'; which seems
to me an entirely justifiable undertaking.

Before we can approach Yeats's text, a further digression is
needed into his theory of sculpture, on which all eventually
depends. The sculpture, like the poetry, which attracted Yeats
most was that which seemed to have been created from the
integrated Self. 'The end of art', for him as for Patmore, 'is
peace', and he loved best those artists who had experience of that
'peace which the world cannot give', or at least of that preliminary condition which he called Unity of Being and which
resembles the alchemical discipline of *perfectio* in demanding the
fusion of energy and spirituality, and the realisation and unifica-
tion of all the four faculties, emotion and intellect, spirit and
sense. *Perfectio* was the preliminary to *contemplatio*, Unity of
Being to visionary attainment, and the subjective artist who had
earned this inner harmony would produce works characterised
by spiritual fulfilment and affirmation, by the 'stillness' that
proceeds from an insight into the visionary world and the
'anonymity' which comes from the sense of oneness with all
created life. These qualities Yeats early found in archaic Greek

sculpture, as he tells us (in prose characteristically free from any false 'soulfulness') in his descriptions of those 'statues of Mausolus and Artemisia in the British Museum', 'private half-animal half-divine figures', 'images of an unpremeditated joyous energy that neither I nor any man racked by doubt and enquiry can achieve'; and he 'wanted to create once more an art where the artists' handiwork would hide as under those half-anonymous chisels'.[5] 'The Statues' represents the imaginative fulfilment of this ambition, for it presupposes that Irish sculptors of the coming era will probe the collective unconscious and resurrect the archetypal images of 'stillness' from its depths.

In sculpture, as in poetry, Yeats felt that there was a subjective tradition, and to this now unfashionable 'sect' he argues that the Irish sculptors of the next generation are the natural heirs. The earliest ascertainable traces of his sculptural tradition Yeats found in ancient Egypt, and in work which seemed to him indicative both of spiritual self-realisation in the artist, and of an elaborate metaphysical discipline imposed on him from without:

In Egypt that same age that saw the village headman carved [objectively] in wood, for burial in some tomb, with so complete a naturalism saw, set up in public places, statues full of an august formality, which implies traditional measurements, a philosophic defence.[6]

'Formality', or stylisation, seemed to Yeats the hallmark of his sculptural tradition, while the image of ideal human beauty that (by visionary insight) it achieved seemed to him its greatest glory; and from Egypt he saw penetrating into classical Europe a pure idea of physical pulchritude which combined 'immobility, dignity and power'; an archetypal 'face' that 'seems all the nobler for lacking curiosity, alert attention, all that we sum up under the famous word of the realists, "vitality" ', but which seemed instead to approximate to that pure 'being' which is possessed only by 'the mystic' and 'the dead'.[7] This sculptural archetype (in Yeats's lovely phrase 'like some phoenix at the end of its thousand wise years, awaiting in condescension the burning nest')[8] he saw as imported by Ionian artists, who had contact with Egypt, into the Greek world. Thus it pervaded archaic

Greek art; was combined by Pheidias and Scopas with their Doric technical accomplishment, for 'in Pheidias and Scopas Ionic and Doric unite . . . and all is transformed by the full moon (of their subcycle) . . . and all abounds and flows';[9] and is once more separated from Doric influence in Kallimachos, in whose 'stylistic management' of the 'falling folds of drapery' and 'lost masterpieces' 'known to us by a description of Pausanias' 'pure Ionic revives'; 'for Kallimachos was an archaistic workman and those who set him to work revived an older form'.[10] After this Yeats believed the Egyptian archetype to have been carried by Alexander's armies into India, where the authorities of his day thought, rightly or wrongly, that Greek influence could be detected on the Buddhas of Gandhara; and he supposed that in this way the 'traditional measurements' were imposed on the conventional image of the Buddha throughout the East.[11] They were by now well established in both branches of the Aryan consciousness and as such Yeats believed them to have remained accessible, through the collective unconscious, to later artists of East and West.

Yeats's sculptural tradition has not been taken seriously, but at least as far as Kallimachos he had authority for all his statements in the art-historian, Furtwängler, on whose work, and especially on his *Masterpieces of Greek Sculpture* he largely drew. Furtwängler supposed that a convention of stylisation originated in Egypt; was carried by Ionian traders to the Greek world; was handed down with the Ionian influence in archaic Greek art; and was fused with a Doric incisiveness and purposiveness in the works of Pheidias and especially of Scopas.[12] In Kallimachos, Furtwängler says, Ionic was clearly dominant, as we may judge from 'Pausanias' descriptions' of his 'tightly archaic manner combined with great elegance and a free treatment of the draperies', and especially from 'the most valuable objects kept in the Erechtheon, . . . the golden lamp of Kallimachos surmounted by the palm-tree of brass'.[13] The lamp according to tradition 'passed through the roof', while the palm symbolised 'the east vanquished by the Greek militia';[14] and how thoroughly Yeats remembered this and the preceding matter may be seen from his poem 'Lapis Lazuli', where much of the detail is pure Furtwängler:

> No handiwork of Callimachus
> Who handled marble as if it were bronze,
> Made draperies that seemed to rise
> When sea-wind swept the corner, stands;
> His long lamp chimney shaped like the stem
> Of a slender palm, stood but a day . . .

And in the previous lines Yeats describes the coming, on 'camel-back' or on 'ship-board', of the Aryan tribes to Europe, and tells how they evolved a sculptural tradition, a 'wisdom', that – as he reiterates in 'The Statues' – now has gone 'to rack'.

Whatever the intellectual basis of Yeats's theory of Greek sculpture, we ought not to overlook the personal element in his assertion that the subjective artists penetrated to the Idea of beauty itself. There is always in the background that strange passage that compares Maud Gonne, through whom Yeats himself penetrated to the Idea of beauty, to a sculptural figure; and more especially to those statues of Mausolus and Artemisia which I have mentioned 'standing in the middle of the crowd's applause or sitting above it measuring out unpersuadable justice':[15]

Her face, like the face of some Greek statue, showed little thought, as though a Scopas had measured and long calculated, consorted with Egyptian sages and mathematicians out of Babylon, that he might face even Artemisia's sepulchral image with a living norm. But in that ancient civilisation abstract [*sc.* 'objective'] thought scarce existed, while she rose but partially and for a moment out of raging abstraction.[16]

This passage ends with a variant image for Yeats's 'filthy modern tide', and another occurs (together perhaps with a further reminiscence of Maud Gonne's beauty) in a passage from *On the Boiler* whose immediate relevance to 'The Statues' was first pointed out by MacNeice. Yeats's intention is now to show how the European sculptural tradition was born and why it is necessary that artists should return to it, and he suggests that the Pythagorean theory of number (which Pythagoras, he believed, derived from Egyptian metaphysics and Egypt in turn derived from Babylon) gave the calculation and mensuration of the Doric studios its philosophical justification:

There are moments when I am certain that art must once again accept those Greek proportions which carry into plastic art the Pythagorean numbers, those faces which are divine because all there is empty and measured. Europe was not born when Greek galleys defeated the Persian hordes at Salamis, but when the Doric studios sent out those broad backed marble statues against the multiform, vague, expressive Asiatic sea, they gave to the sexual instinct its goal, its fixed type.[17]

The Aryan sculptors were the real conquerors of objective Asia simply because they opposed to Asiatic formlessness that beauty whose origin is in the divine world, and which the subjective is able to discern by means of contemplation. It should by now be clear that the symbolism of 'The Statues' is precisely that of *Emer*; the 'marbles' and 'bronzes' of the poem symbolise that perfect and demanding loveliness which Yeats's Platonism made him worship,[18] and which it was the business of the subjective sculptural tradition to delineate.

Yeats's poem, like the last passage given, presumes that the Pythagorean theory of qualitative number gave the Greek sculptors a mathematical basis on which to work. In this sense Pythagoras is the 'onlie true begetter' of the statue so dramatically set before us in the first few lines:

> Pythagoras planned it. Why did the people stare?
> His numbers, though they moved or seemed to move
> In marble or in bronze, lacked character.

Classical statuary is philosophy in action, but though the metaphysics of harmony and right proportion have enabled the artists to penetrate to the ideal beauty, to that Galatea-image which is the likeness of the divine Aphrodite herself, they do this at the apparent expense of 'character'. 'Character' was of course a term charged in Yeats's vocabulary with a certain contempt, one of those 'famous words of the realists' we have seen him attacking; it seemed to him a function of 'becoming' as opposed to 'pure being'; an expression of the isolated individuality of the ego as against that passionate 'anonymity' that goes with the discovered Self. In his poem, he says that the common people may require such vulgar individuality, but that adolescence, with its

intuitive insight into the ideal world, will understand that
'character' is irrelevant to passion; for love can infuse an ideal
personality into the object of desire:

> But boys and girls, pale from the imagined love
> Of solitary beds, knew what they were,
> That passion could bring character enough,
> And pressed at midnight in some public place
> Live lips upon a plummet-measured face.

Here Vivienne Koch is right to see reminiscence of Blake, and of
some lines in *Visions of the Daughters of Albion* which tell us that
'desire', once it is divorced from living flesh and blood and
becomes desire for an image, is a form of 'religion'. Yeats, of
course, is concerned with the visionary propensity of adolescence
at its highest and noblest reach, while Blake's business is merely
with the impure 'image' generated by simple lust, so that there is
matter for contrast as well as for comparison in the relevant
passage:

The moment of desire! The moment of desire! The virgin
That pines for man shall awaken her womb to enormous joys
In the secret shadows of her chamber: the youth shut up from
The lustful joy shall forget to generate and create an amorous
      image
In the shadows of his curtains and in the folds of his silent pillow.
Are not these the places of religion, the rewards of continence
The self-enjoyings of self-denial?[19]

Yeats's adolescents are less fallen than these; 'imagined love' has
led them beyond the sexual into the archetypal world and they
are therefore able to understand the true religious significance
of Pythagoras' statues; and they go out 'at midnight to some
public place' to pay homage to that beauty whose spiritual depth
has required such niceties of scientific measurement. We may
compare that profound insight into adolescence communicated in
*On the Boiler*, where Yeats says that a young man choosing a
lover seeks always some image 'opposite' to his own vitality: he
needs to 'take his own death into his arms' and beget upon pure
being 'a stronger life'.[20]

   This verse seems to me great poetry and the second is of

almost the same stature, but I find in the development of Yeats's poem a certain coarseness of rhythmical texture. This was an inevitable expense, for 'The Statues' stands at the end of a long sequence of poems in *ottava rima* and its variants, and Yeats's self-delight in his form had diminished by a process of habituation; after the unselfconscious artistry of 'A Prayer for my Daughter' and the deeper resonances of 'The Tower' and 'Sailing to Byzantium' the keen edge of the verse becomes blunted, and some of the rhythms of 'Parnell's Funeral' for example ('An age is the reversal of an age . . .') are merely mechanical. In his last period, his Steinach operation could give him new energy, but it could not bring back his first refinement of ear: the *ottava rima* is now characterised by rhythmical crudities, of which the worst is perhaps in 'The Municipal Gallery Revisited':

> . . . all that we said or sang
> Must come from contact with the soil, *from that*
> *Contact everything Antaeus-like grew strong . . .*

Yeats's most consummate rhythms, in *Last Poems*, come when he is working in the smaller, more ephemeral, forms, and the *ottava rima* of 'The Statues' can be as grating as elsewhere:

> No, greater than Pythagoras, for the men
> *That with a mallet or a chisel modelled these*
> *Calculations that look but casual flesh*, put down
> All Asiatic vague immensities . . .

The *logic* of this verse is perfectly simple, and corresponds exactly with what is said in *On the Boiler*: Pheidias and Scopas, or whatever Greek sculptors made the marbles and bronzes of the poem, are in retrospect 'greater' than Pythagoras, and more deserving of the credit which the first verse gives to him. They are creators where he was a mere theoretician, and they excavated from the collective unconscious, in its purest and most developed form, that archetype of ideal beauty which has been the fixed type of European sexual-religious contemplation ever since. They, consequently, and not 'the banks of oars' that fought at Salamis, set a limit on Asiatic formlessness by realising that hard definite image of which the oriental imagination was in-

capable. After them, subjective man could 'put off' the 'foam' of
the 'many-headed' objective tide ('many-headed' is Aeschylus's
term for the sea and is thus appropriate, but it also stigmatises
Yeats's Asiatics as the worshippers of multiplicity):

> Europe put off that foam when Phidias
> Gave women dreams and dreams their looking-glass.

Woman had not been able to evolve, out of the shifting, in-
definite, 'multiform' sea of the Asiatic consciousness, an 'image'
towards which to adapt herself, but after Pheidias she could. His
masculine archetype could give her 'dreams' and provide those
dreams of the ideal manhood with their concrete 'objective
correlative'; while his feminine archetype, the lines may also
imply, would provide her with the idea of a new and perfect
femininity, towards which (by a conscious process of endeavour
and between incarnations by the process explained in my *Emer*
essay) she could evolve. In this way Greek art bridged the gap
between the ideal and the real and canalised desire into desire for
the heavenly beauty.

One reason for the rhythmic constriction of Yeats's second
verse is that he quite simply had too much to say in it, and this is
transparently the case in his continuation. We have been shown
the process by which the European consciousness broke free
from Asiatic domination, and now Yeats proposes to show us
how his 'resolute European image' eventually conquered the
East. This involves him at once in a vast historical panorama,
which he presents as follows:

> One image crossed the many-headed, sat
> Under the tropic shade, grew round and slow,
> No Hamlet thin from eating flies, a fat
> Dreamer of the middle ages. Empty eyeballs knew
> That knowledge increases unreality, that
> Mirror on mirror mirrored is all the show.
> When gong and conch declare the hour to bless
> Grimalkin crawls to Buddha's emptiness.

Vivienne Koch's analysis of this verse becomes a shambles
because she does not understand (though Yeats explains it in a
letter to Edith Shackleton Heald)[21] that these lines describe the

importation of Greek statuary into India by Alexander's armies
and the influence that (it was believed) such statuary had exerted
on 'the figure of the great seated Buddha'. Yeats describes how
this variant form of Pheidias' archetype became the central
image of Eastern religion, and explains how the Buddha was
envisaged sitting under his bo-tree like some contemplative
Hamlet; not, he says, like the lean and hungry 'intellectualised'
Hamlets of modern stage convention, but like Hamlet as Shakespeare saw him, 'fat and scant of breath', 'a dreamer of the Middle
Ages'. And together with the Indian image went spiritual values
much like those which Pythagorean religion had independently
evolved: the Buddha did not stand for the merely rational intellectualism and 'unreality' of 'abstract' modern thought, but for
the spiritual condition of the religious, whose mind is made a
'purified vacancy' by the discovery of the Self: he stood for
*contemplatio* and *perfectio* and for that state of 'pure being' where
the external world ceases to exist. In this sense, Yeats concludes,
the Buddha is still worshipped, even though modern India may
be in process of abandoning its traditions and falling victim, like
all the world, to objectivity (so that the modern worshipper may
be materialist, ego-centred, misshapen like the witch's cat). If we
are connoisseurs in Eastern art we shall connect with his last line
those illustrations where the material world is symbolised by
dragonish monsters and misshapen beasts, who prostrate themselves before an empty space symbolic of the Buddha's holiness,
itself too sacred for pictorial delineation.[22] In such a way the
'multiform' objective consciousness of degenerate modern India
abases itself before the image imported by Alexander 'where all is
divine because all is empty and measured'.

In case this reading is thought conjectural, I had better confirm
it by cross-references to Yeats's prose, and to do this is to establish a connection between 'The Statues' and *At the Hawk's Well*.
Morris is a dominant influence on Yeats's play, as a writer who
had achieved the Self and whose 'heroes and heroines' are 'always
in the likeness of Artemisia and her man';[23] and a memory of
Morris informs the present stanza. Here, from *Autobiographies*, is
the description of his portrait painted by Watts, and it is clear

that the detail of the prose constituted an image-cluster of great importance to Yeats himself:

Its grave wide-open eyes, like the eyes of some dreaming beast, remind me of the open eyes of Titian's Ariosto, while the broad vigorous body suggests a mind that has no need of the intellect to remain sane, though it give itself to every fantasy: the dreamer of the Middle Ages. It is the 'fool of faery, wide and wild as a hill', the resolute European image that yet half remembers Buddha's motionless meditation, and has no trait in common with the wavering lean image of hungry speculation, that cannot but because of certain famous Hamlets of our stage fill the mind's eye.[24]

Here Yeats establishes a connection between what he clearly saw as several variant forms of the one archetype (or 'resolute European image'): Titian's Ariosto, Shakespeare's Hamlet, and Watts's 'William Morris'; and calls into question also the symbols of the Buddha, the medieval court-fool, and the Irish Amadan or fool of faery, who is said to sit 'wild and wide as a hill' cupping in his hands his magical vessel or emblematic grail. All these, it is probable that Yeats supposed, are at one level conscious or unconscious reminiscences of the sculptural archetype delineated by Pheidias, and all would no doubt have found a way into Yeats's poem had there been room for them: Hamlet and the fool of the Middle Ages in fact do so, and are contrasted with the objective Hamlet of the modern theatre, abstracted, unheroic and 'thin from eating flies', an antipathy Yeats elaborates elsewhere.[25] In this rather confusing way the antithesis between subjective *contemplatio* and objective intellectualism is introduced, and it is reinforced by the contrast between the Buddha's 'empty eyeballs' (Yeats speaks in *A Vision* of the eyes of Greek statues 'staring at nothing')[26] and what he calls elsewhere the 'photographic' vision of objective man, who is preoccupied with that wilderness of reflecting mirrors which is the physical world. This image of reflecting mirrors is also one developed in Yeats's prose, and especially in the preface to 'Fighting The Waves', where it is used to typify the objective mentality of Stendhal and the nineteenth century.[27] Finally, the image of Grimalkin is one

coined in an essay of this period on 'Parnell', where Yeats
contrasts the Goddess Astraea as the symbol of pure subjectivity
and the coming cycle, and her antithesis in 'the brindled cat'.[28]
The witch's cat of the poem connects with this passage as the
symbol of absolute objectivity, the 'dark of the moon', and it
humbles itself before Gautama as primitive and inept intuition
must before what is tranquil and achieved.

On the Boiler contains a strong attack on modern egalitarian
India, and this bears me out in enforcing on the final couplet
above the interpretation I have done: 'the modern Indian worshipper, who has been caught up in the materialist "tide" and
has become almost wholly objective, so that his true gods are the
witch's cat and the dragon-monster of Eastern art, even today at
the hour of prayer is ironically compelled to pay homage to
subjective religion'. The contrast of Yeats's two religious types
and the contemporaneity of his allusion thus pave the way for his
last stanza, where the decadent modern world becomes the theme:

When Pearse summoned Cuchulain to his side
What stalked through the Post Office? What intellect,
What calculation, number, measurement, replied?
We Irish, born into that ancient sect
But thrown upon this filthy modern tide
And by its formless spawning fury wrecked,
Climb to our proper dark, that we may trace
The lineaments of a plummet-measured face.

Here Yeats's immense peregrination rights itself, as if by miracle,
on the image of Cuchulain, and on the episode of the Easter
Rebellion that so often inspired him to great art. We are shown
Pearse, during that last stand, invoking the ancient hero of his
race – Yeats tells us elsewhere that Pearse 'had a cult of Cuchulain',[29] which explains why he should have done so – and asked
whether the image that materialised to his imagination will not
have had the lineaments of some Greek statue, its every feature
precisely calculated and numbered according to the Pythagorean
laws. Yeats then takes this particular heroic defeat as an index to
the state of the world and tells us that the many-headed sea of
Asia has now everywhere reasserted itself against the European

consciousness. The Irish, he says, are the rightful heirs of the 'ancient sect' of subjectivity – the word 'sect' here may suggest to us the Pythagorean community at Crotona – and, while the words may mean no more than that the Celtic peoples have kept alive their original traditions, we may if we like read them as a reference to the origin in Egypt of the Milesian race who were the first colonists of his country.[30] For this reason the heredity of the Irish especially equips them to resuscitate the laws of intellectual beauty; they preserve an unconscious knowledge of the great Indo-European archetype; and they will climb proudly to their proper eminence in that 'darkness' from which the new cycle must emanate, until the time comes for them to emulate Pheidias and bestow the laws they guard upon a new world.

'The Statues', as Vivienne Koch has said,[31] is in the last resort an *oracular* poem: out of the sheer drama of his beginning, and by means of an 'almost primitive' 'machinery of questions' 'in the style of the ancient oracles in the Greek anthology', Yeats manufactures a prophecy of the nearness of the moment of cyclical change, when humanity will revert to the religion of Platonic beauty and ideal love. As such, the poem both completes and compensates for the underlying logic of *Emer*, which is perhaps that aspect of Yeats's metaphysics most central to the present book.* *Emer*, one has always tore member, is in many way as negative statement, for though it is Yeats's fullest investigation of the philosophy of physical beauty, it concludes by saying that the demands of the ideal world are such that we cannot measure up to them, and that the end of the discipline of love is the abandonment of the quest.

> He that has loved the best
> May turn from a statue
> His too human breast.

'A Prayer for My Daughter' takes this argument a stage further in that it is a deliberate rejection of the archetype of ideal beauty; Yeats prays specifically that his daughter may *not* be given 'beauty to make a stranger's eye distraught', lest she lose 'natural

* *Yeat's Iconography* (1960).

kindness' and 'heart-revealing intimacy' and 'never find a friend': and he asks for her instead Unity of Being and the discovery of the Self, which can convert her into a living image of the Tree of Life:

> May she become a flourishing hidden tree . . .

In *The Bridegroom*, finally, whose metaphysic of love is for me Yeats's profoundest statement on the subject, he says that the physical personality is irrelevant to the act of loving; that the secret Self of the man will divine the secret Self of the woman; and that love is the act of adoration of that aspect of the human personality where the beloved is identical with Christ.

Beyond this sequence of poems lies Yeats's disaffection for Maud Gonne: for there is of course no reason, save that the poet himself in private life had found it necessary to do so, why he should have divorced the adoration of ideal beauty from the love of the Self. Yeats's attempt to reintegrate beauty and the Self begins, as I have already suggested, with 'Among School Children'; continues during many of the last poems and completes itself with 'The Statues', which ought I think to be read against *The Bridegroom*, and perhaps 'Solomon and the Witch' also, for the understanding of his philosophy of intersexual love in its totality. 'The Statues' is thus at the deepest level a poem of inner reconciliation, and suggests that Yeats's personal suffering may eventually have resolved in peace.

## NOTES

1. *W. B. Yeats: The Tragic Phase* (1951) pp. 59–75.
2. *The Permanence of Yeats*, J. Hall and M. Steinmann (1950) pp. 202, 213.
3. It is interesting to recall that Nietzsche influenced this side of Yeats's thought.
4. This makes Islam objective. But I have no space to dissect Yeats's sweeping generalisation.
5. *Autobiographies* (1955) p. 150.
6. *Essays* (1924) p. 278.
7. Ibid. p. 280.
8. Ibid.

9. *A Vision* (1925) p. 182.

10. Ibid.

11. Coomaraswamy would not accept this, and I believe that modern scholarship would assert that the two branches of the Indo-European race discovered the traditional measurements in mutual independence. But the 'myth' of Yeats's poem largely depends on the theory of direct cultural influence and it has therefore to be borne in mind.

12. See *Masterpieces of Greek Sculpture* (*passim*).

13. Ibid. pp. 437–50.

14. Ibid.

15. *Autobiographies*, p. 150.

16. Ibid. pp. 364–5.

17. *On the Boiler* (Dublin, 1939) p. 37.

18. Equally (of course) they symbolise ideal masculinity.

19. *Visions of the Daughters of Albion*, 7, 3, *The Complete Writings of William Blake*, ed. G. Keynes (1957) p. 194.

20. *On the Boiler*, p. 22.

21. *The Letters of W. B. Yeats*, ed. Allan Wade (1954) p. 911.

22. Yeats's own misshapen beast, his Grimalkin, ought not to be connected with Minnaloushe, so much as with the 'objective' Sphinx that contends with the Buddha in 'The Double Vision of Michael Robartes'.

23. *Autobiographies*, p. 152.

24. Ibid. pp. 141–2.

25. See *Plays And Controversies* (1923) p. 215.

26. *A Vision* (1937) p. 277.

27. *Wheels And Butterflies* (1934) p. 73.

28. *Essays 1931–1936* (1937) p. 3.

29. See *Letters*, ed. Wade, p. 911.

30. See, for instance, Standish O'Grady, *History of Ireland* (1881) I 164.

31. Op. cit. pp. 63–5.

## Arra M. Garab

## TIMES OF GLORY: YEATS'S 'THE MUNICIPAL GALLERY REVISITED' (1965)

THE old order, gone or passing away, the aged Yeats was determined not to let go uncelebrated. Many times before, he had meditated on the uncommon men and women who had shaped Ireland's turbulent history, and at the age of seventy-two he wrote one of his most memorable tributes to the immoderate past he loved so well. A testimonial banquet of the Irish Academy of Letters moved him to revisit Dublin's Municipal Gallery, where amid familiar faces he found fresh images of vanished times. Privately printed for presentation to the friends and patrons who had gathered to honor him, 'The Municipal Gallery Revisited' now adorns the impressive canon of a long life's work. Though we need not accept Yeats's judgment that it is 'perhaps the best poem I have written for some years',[1] it deserves more serious attention than critics have granted it. Never singled out for intensive study, this poem merits scrutiny not only because of Yeats's feeling for it, but, more importantly, because the weight of its theme and the subtlety of its form mark it as one of his most formidable accomplishments.

Though in one sense an enumeration of old themes, through a brilliant series of sharp images demonstrating how 'things both can and cannot be' (to quote from 'The Curse of Cromwell', a contemporary poem sung at the Academy banquet) this poem proves nevertheless that there was much 'left to say' of Ireland's irreplaceable 'tall men' now gone 'underground'. Clearly 'still their servant', Yeats becomes a pilgrim before their pictured presence. Sacramental, their portraits (outward signs of 'a greater, a more gracious time' – see 'The Gyres') become instruments for the miraculous transformation to which the poem moves. Though in the fourth and fifth stanzas these ghostly images bring him to his knees and to simultaneous states of devotion and despair, by the end of the poem, as the motif of rootedness takes firmer hold, they enable him to rejoice. These powerfully associative images, not only limning his friends and Ireland's history but symbolizing his career as well, become so heavily charged and intertwined that they lead him ultimately to an even more overpowering realization – the awareness that the 'glory' he senses in the gallery is the greater glory of all. Like the 'great-rooted blossomer', proud nation, noble friends, and inspired labor grow into one.

Immediately after the formal opening of the first line, anonymous 'ambush' (John Keating's painting 'The Men of the West') and anonymous 'pilgrims at the water-side' (John Lavery's 'Saint Patrick's Purgatory') metaphorically define and establish opposing states which we discover more concretely in each of the specific persons mentioned thereafter. From the very beginning the connotations presented constitute the type for all that is yet to come, for informing this antithetical pair of images (with its overtones of dusty roads and still waters, abrupt death and life eternal) are hints of outward movement and inward gaze, uprooting and deep-rootedness, chaos and tradition, war and peace, guilt and redemption, pride and humility, and perhaps even many-facing power and glory, the dominant note on which the poem comes to a measured but triumphant close.

Roger Casement, Arthur Griffith, and Kevin O'Higgins (recalled in three paintings by John Lavery), three strong-willed and tough-minded figures emblematic of the turbulent public life of Yeats's time, in the name of high principle, stirred troubled waters in their revolutionary pursuit of violent political ends. Their secular pilgrimage, full of sound and fury, was either frustrated or only partially completed; for two of them, it led the way to cruel and dusty death.

Casement, a man of divided loyalties, who stubbornly remained loyal to his conception of right, nobly served imperial Britain; yet, after he was knighted, he came to conspire against that land whose dominion over Ireland and himself he decried and denied. The nobility of his famous speech from the dock and the dignity of his bearing on the gallows contrast violently with the baseness of the infamous writings attributed to him and the even more appalling possibility of their genuineness.[2] Though as British consul he brought to light outrage after outrage and freed Congolese and Putamayan natives from inhuman treatment, his portrait and its setting ('The Court of Criminal Appeal') must show the inhuman circumstances of a man ambushed by fate, 'upon trial, half hidden by the bars, / Guarded'.

Arthur Griffith, whose stare of 'hysterical pride' is compounded of contrasting elements, in Yeats's eyes sometimes worked for opposing ends. Though in 1899 he defended *The Countess Cathleen,* offering to bring 'a lot of men from the Quays' who would 'applaud anything the Church did not like', eight years later this Sinn Fein leader sent 'the little clubs' out to jeer Synge's *Playboy.*[3] Without culture, Yeats told Lady Gregory, 'men like Griffith ... can renounce external things ... but no envy, revenge, jealousy and so on. I wrote a note a couple of years ago in which I compared Griffith and his like to the eunuchs in Ricketts' picture watching Don Juan ride through Hell'.[4] Though he indirectly pleaded Yeats's cause by urging his friend John MacBride not to marry Maud Gonne, this influential editor angered Yeats by his attacks on Synge, Hugh Lane, the Abbey Theatre, and Yeats's work. Because he held that 'literature should be subordinate to nationalism', it is not surprising that Yeats long deplored his influence on the Irish mind; convinced that literature 'must have its own ideal', he wanted to challenge Griffith to a debate on 'our two policies'.[5] 'Yeats could never forgive Griffith ... or think of him as other than a fanatic', we are told.[6] Yet this same man, imprisoned by the British, could tell the Governor of Gloucester Jail that the Irishmen there 'would require special facilities on June 13th, as it was the birthday of their national poet'.[7] In this poem his nationalistic 'hysterical pride' stands in antithesis to the solid, earthy pride of Lady Gregory and John Synge, who, searching for a nation's roots, labored to shape its national identity.

Kevin O'Higgins, Vice-President of the Executive Council of the Dail and according to Yeats 'the finest intellect in Irish public life', was ambushed outside his home by gunmen.[8] 'A great man in his pride / Confronting murderous men', Yeats wrote ('Death') of the man whom he looked upon as 'Parnell's successor'.[9] Yet, as the stark contrast between the 'gentle questioning look' of his countenance and his soul's incapacity for 'remorse or rest' indicates, O'Higgins was a violently divided man. A sensitive intellectual, in a speech to the Dail he called for the blood of Erskine Childers, a scapegoat executed on the sole charge of possessing a toy pistol (ironically, one given him by Michael Collins, the enemy leader) fastened to his braces by a safety pin.[10] (Convicted late in the evening of 23 November 1922 after a trial remarkably similar to Casement's, Childers was shot at dawn the following day before an appeal could be made. 'Even in England this execution was held by jurists to be a judicial murder. . . . His execution excited grief, anger and shame.'[11]) In the name of authority and the establishment of the rule of law, O'Higgins actively promoted the shooting of jailed prisoners. Tugged to extremes, this strange figure, while attempting in a speech before the Dail to justify the reprisal execution of his close friend Rory O'Connor and three other political prisoners, wept in public for the only time in his life.[12]

The impersonal but concrete images of the 'revolutionary soldier kneeling to be blessed' and the priest 'with an upraised hand / Blessing the Tricolour', recalling and extending further the images in the second line ('ambush', 'pilgrims at the water-side'), frame the first stanza of the poem and develop its theme more fully. We have here not only antithetically constructed analogues for the divided lives of the public men mentioned previously, but a metaphorical expression of Ireland's recent public character, where Church and State, revolutionary power and vested authority, form an unholy but popular alliance.[13] And looking ahead to the fourth, fifth, and sixth stanzas, we see here also the two dominant elements which, when yoked together, within Yeats's lifetime toppled the Anglo-Irish Ascendancy.

Each of these two figures (inspired by John Lavery's 'The Blessing of the Colours') is basically antithetical: we note a soldier, perhaps on his way to or from an ambush, 'surrendering';

and a representative of ecclesiastical authority, perhaps confusing
Caesar and Christ, blessing the green, white, and orange flag
presented to the Young Ireland Movement a century earlier by
republican, anticlerical Frenchmen.[14] Juxtaposed, the two figures
ironically form a paradoxical image: we note antitheses of 'down'
(genuflection) and 'up' (blessing), guerrilla and hierarch, new
and old.

Much of the theme and technique of this section is reminiscent
of 'Easter 1916', another evocation of men who with tragically
'enchanted' hearts 'troubled the living stream' of history. Casement, Griffith, and O'Higgins, they too are now numbered in
Yeats's memory as men who brought 'excess of love' to the
terrible and bewildering pursuit of imagined ideals.[15] 'This is
not the dead Ireland of my youth,' Yeats says of their trans-
figured times, 'but an Ireland / The poets have imagined, terrible
and gay.' 'Imagined', suggesting at once the poet's ordered
re-creation of experience (such as this poem itself), the practical
results of impractical art ('Did that play of mine send out /
Certain men the English shot?'), and the quixotic possibility that
bitter actuality may have been but a dream of life, performs an
important function here.

The third stanza focuses on Major Robert Gregory, Hugh
Lane, and Hazel Lavery, who in company with the political
figures just seen are emblematic of frustrated ends, only
partially fulfilled destinies. Like the above political men, these
figures are all associated with controversies of various sorts. On
the other hand, though incomplete, they are to be esteemed for
their gracious natures and magnanimous acts. In this sense they
anticipate Lady Gregory, the grandest of them all. Two of them,
we observe, are denoted in terms of their relationship to Yeats's
patroness: 'son', 'her sister's son'. The third, Hazel Lavery,
figures here not only because her painter-husband's work is
amply represented in the gallery, two of them ('Hazel Lavery at
Her Easel' and 'It Is Finished', a death-bed scene) providing
Yeats with the 'living and dying' image, but also because of her
friendship with Lady Gregory and the common cause they made
in trying to recover the Lane paintings. The branches of the

Gregory tree, we note, embracing Synge and Yeats, are evident in this poem as well.

Abortively ended, the relatively short but finely balanced life of Robert Gregory is marked by the tragic contrast between all he embodied and all he could never do. (A talented painter himself, he is recalled in the gallery by Charles Shannon's portrait.) And his cousin Hugh Lane, who 'joined the profession of a picture-dealer with the magnanimity of a Medici',[16] by the ironical fact of an unwitnessed codicil to his will was prevented from donating his paintings to a city whose Biddys and Paudeens had scorned them while the paintings were still in Dublin.[17] 'There is something heroic and pathetic in this old importunate widow begging at this doorstep and that,' says Lennox Robinson of Lady Gregory's fifteen-year struggle to reclaim her nephew's paintings.[18]

It is evident, then, that the first three stanzas, though divided into two groups, share a common antithetical understructure: the contrast between what the figures dreamed and expected, and what they had to settle for. Surely this is one of the reasons why Yeats, 'Heart-smitten with emotion', had to 'sink down, / My heart recovering with covered eyes'. As in 'Easter 1916', however, 'We know their dream; enough / To know they dreamed and are dead.' Because each of them, like Casement, 'did what he had to do', their 'living and dying' is lifted to epic stature. In the gallery portraits, in Yeats's consciousness, and in the poem before us, their 'tale' is now offered to all 'As though some ballad-singer had sung it all'.

If it is meet that a ballad simile should close the first movement, it is equally right that it should anticipate the next group of stanzas, for it is here that Yeats turns to his own work and to the ground from which it arose. The strong tensions and sharp juxtapositions characteristic of balladry not only underscore what he has just finished setting forth, but, along with other ballad techniques, characterize much of his best verse, especially that of his last years when 'with impediments plain to all' he learned to sing 'with the ancient simplicity'.[19] 'Ancient simplicity' he found, too, in John Synge, who (after a sojourn in the Aran

Islands) made it a specialty; and in proud and humble Lady
Gregory, who collected old tales and young poets. From now to
the end of the poem they stand on either side of Yeats, as they
literally do in the second line of stanza six ('John Synge, I and
Augusta Gregory') and as they did on the occasion of his lecture
to the Swedish Royal Academy when he won the Nobel Prize for
1923:

'When your King gave me medal and diploma, two forms should
have stood, one at either side of me, an old woman sinking into
the infirmity of age and a young man's ghost. I think when Lady
Gregory's name and John Synge's name are spoken by future
generations, my name, if remembered, will come up in the talk,
and that if my name is spoken first their names will come in their
turn because of the years we worked together. I think that both
had been well pleased to have stood beside me at the great
reception at your Palace, for their work and mine has delighted
in history and tradition.' I think as I speak these words of how
deep down we have gone, below all that is individual, modern
and restless, seeking foundations for an Ireland that can only
come into existence in a Europe that is still but a dream.[20]

   The fifth stanza, lacking a line, looks back to times of wholeness and health:

> My mediaeval knees lack health until they bend,
> But in that woman, in that household where
> Honour had lived so long, all lacking found.
> Childless, I thought, 'My children may find here
> Deep-rooted things,' but never foresaw its end,
> And now that end has come I have not wept;
> No fox can foul the lair the badger swept –

Now, Yeats's 'mediaeval knees' must 'bend' because he is old
and – especially without Lady Gregory's sustaining presence –
weak; and also because he is 'in despair' that we will never again
see her type of 'pride' and 'humility', seemingly antithetical
attributes actually complementary, and descriptive of her unique
'excellence'.[21] Echoing the image of genuflection in the first two
stanzas, this rich metaphor also suggests Yeats's 'pilgrim soul'
(in the context of his early poems) as well as his posture of feudal
devotion.[22]

It suggests filial piety, too, for while Lady Gregory flourished, those lacking wholeness could achieve it in her 'household', a metaphor not only for 'honour', but all else that makes for unity of being. If, reconciling opposites, Coole fostered wholeness (Yeats tells us that 'childless' he once foresaw there 'deep-rooted' experience for his 'children'), so too its passing now reduces everything to vulgar incoherence. In the fifth stanza this condition is expressed in the counterbalancing of 'all lacking found' by 'its end'. However, just as the first two conjunctions ('but', lines two and five) abruptly shifted the mood of his meditation (in both instances the clauses coming before and after thus standing in antithesis), so too the third: '*And* now that end has come', developing 'never foresaw its end', is completed by the counterstatement of 'I have not wept'. Thus, the chiasmus of lines five and six in which opposing elements are balanced is followed by the terse affirmation of the concluding line, 'No fox can foul the lair the badger swept', which in itself perfectly effects a balance of strongly opposing elements. Hence we may note that 'lair', the fulcrum of this crucial line, not only functions as a metaphorical echo of ravaged Coole, but also establishes it firmly as the courtly 'household' of abiding 'traditional sanctity and loveliness'.[23]

'Traditional sanctity and loveliness', the chosen theme of 'last romantics' such as Synge, Yeats, and Lady Gregory, are the essential features of 'the book of the people' praised in 'Coole Park and Ballylee, 1931' and in the sixth stanza of this poem. These values, inherent in the 'deep-rooted things' of Coole, must be native to poetry as well. Like that giant wrestler Antaeus (who, as son of Terra, remained invincible so long as he touched the earth), poets who would create vital art must draw their sustenance from 'contact with the soil'. Just as Antaeus was strangled when held aloft by Hercules, so too – the suggestion follows – the artist who loses this vital contact is made sterile by the technological values of our Herculean machine age. Poetry is made profound and lovely, invincible and proud, only when its roots grow from the 'deep down' depths of nourishing tradition, 'below all that is ... modern and restless'. This, Yeats tells us, is the 'sole test' of value.[24] 'The noble and the beggar-man' for whom such verses are written properly preside over the close of the stanza and the second major movement of the poem, for these images, recalling Antaeus (giant, earth), also recall Lady Gregory and Coole ('pride' and 'humility').

Antithetical to the last, Yeats's 'dream' does not acknowledge middle ground. 'The noble and the beggar-man' is significant also in the sense that, excluding the middle class and its de-racinated values, it relegates the nationalist heroes of modern Ireland to a less gigantic level. The context of the sixth stanza, we must remember, is not restricted to poetry; Yeats says 'All that we did, all that we said' as well as merely 'sang'. Thus, 'We three alone in modern times', he suggests, have served the highest interests of the nation. Not that Yeats wanted to lord it over Casement and Griffith, O'Higgins and others. Far from it. Rather, the point here in this stanza and throughout the poem as well is that just as art imitates 'life', so too must life imitate 'art'.

As we might expect from a meditation on the meaning of friendship, devotion forms the all-embracing and unifying theme of the entire poem. The nationalist heroes, the revolutionary soldier, and the clergyman are devoted to abstractions; Augusta Gregory's son, nephew, and friend are devoted to noble deeds; while Lady Gregory herself, quintessentially aristocratic, is nobly devoted to Irish culture and two of its most brilliant ornaments; finally, Synge, Yeats, and Lady Gregory, devoted to each other and adorning everything, are sworn to the gigantic task of defining and achieving the truest type of life and art. Surely, Yeats suggests, this type of devotion makes terrible beauties of us all.

'Ireland not as she is displayed in guide book or history, but, Ireland seen because of the magnificent vitality of her painters, in the glory of her passions', was to be the subject of a poem, Yeats announced on 17 August 1937 to guests at his testimonial banquet.[25] The terrible gaiety of 'that great pictured song'[26] not only reveals an Ireland 'imagined' only by artists and poets, but shows as well the norm and the means for achieving such an imaginative revelation. For conclusive evidence we have the final stanza, which, integrating and raising all to mythic dimensions, also illustrates this metamorphic process.

Yeats's conception is clear: just as the political destiny of a nation is (for good or for ill) hammered out in the forge of energetic dedication, so too is the cultural and ideological unity of that nation moulded by strenuous devotion to timeless patterns. Likewise, Yeats tells us, does the whole of a man's life rest on an organic arrangement of devoted relationships. Therefore, 'You that would judge me, do not judge alone / This book or that. . . .' Rather, judge in the larger context of this complexity of allegiances, this 'deep-rooted' tangle of relationships whereby a man's country, his co-workers, and his craft cohere gloriously, like the components of some impressive feudal structure.

Moreover, just as the history that these dead men and women of the gallery once made now makes them holy to our remembrance, so too their holy aspect transforms the gallery into a temple, a 'hallowed place' for their ghostly and abiding presence.[27] Their story, the story of Yeats's participation in their common enterprise, and the literature created out of both, must be seen and judged as one. In old age, a time to judge and to be judged, Yeats senses that the judgment may be glorious. In its ambiguity, however, the line 'Think where man's glory most *begins and ends*' precludes an easy victory or a facile judgment. While 'begins and ends' refers primarily to the totality and wholeness of man's glory (its 'framed' state, according to the portrait context), it also – echoing the 'despair' of stanza four ('I am in despair that time may bring / Approved patterns of women or of men / But not that selfsame excellence again') and the end of Coole – hints that the times of glory are ended. Nevertheless – and herein rests the triumph – it is clear that the 'history' of which Yeats is now an integral part is a glorious one indeed, for the 'lineaments' of its 'permanent or impermanent images' embody everything that rooted men esteem and must emulate for ever.

## NOTES

1. *The Letters of W. B. Yeats*, ed. Allan Wade (1954) p. 897. Dated 5 Sept. 1937.

2. The reader of Peter Singleton-Gates and Maurice Girodias' *The Black Diaries of Roger Casement* (London and New York, 1959) is struck by this ironical antithesis all the more as he sees Casement's official reports on the left-hand pages and his alleged secret writings on the right.

3. Quoted in Joseph Hone, *W. B. Yeats, 1865–1939*, 2nd ed. (1962) p. 161.

4. *Letters*, ed. Wade, p. 525. Dated 8 March 1909. See 'On those that Hated *The Playboy of the Western World*, 1907'.

5. Ibid. p. 422. Dated 2 Jan. 1904.

6. Hone, p. 344.

7. Ibid.

8. Note appended to 'Death'.

9. See Hone, p. 382, and Hone's essay, 'Yeats as Political Philosopher', in *London Mercury*, XXXIX (March 1939) 494.

10. See Frank O'Connor's autobiography, *An Only Child* (London and New York, 1961) pp. 213–14, 237.

11. Dorothy Macardle, *The Irish Republic* (Dublin, 1951) p. 814. A.E., for one, tried to save Childers; see *Lady Gregory's Journals, 1916–1930*, ed. Lennox Robinson (1946) p. 184. O'Connor, who knew Childers well, writes (pp. 237–8): '. . . again and again in my own imagination, I have had to go through these last few moments with him almost as though I were there: see the slight figure of the little grey-haired Englishman emerge for the last time into the Irish daylight, apparently cheerful and confident but incapable of grandiose gestures, concerned only lest inadvertently he might do or say something that would distress some poor fool of an Irish boy who was about to level an English rifle at his heart.'

12. Edgar Holt, *Protest in Arms* (1960) p. 305.

13. '. . . what we were bringing about', O'Connor says (p. 210) of the Civil War, 'was a new Establishment of Church and State in which imagination would play no part, and young men and women would emigrate to the ends of the earth, not because the country was poor, but because it was mediocre'.

14. See Macardle, p. 47.

15. Hone (p. 349) says that Griffith (1872–1922) died from 'sheer exhaustion'.

16. Charles Ricketts, quoted in Hone, pp. 225–6.

17. See 'To a Wealthy Man, who Promised a Second Subscription to the Dublin Municipal Gallery if it were Proved the People Wanted Pictures'.

18. *Journals*, p. 286. Robinson adds: 'There are two portraits of Lane in our Municipal Gallery, one by Mancini showing him sitting on a sofa, febrile with exciting background, the Lane that was a friend of Royalty and of the Peerage, the flashy Lane. The other is the Sargent portrait, the "dreamer of dreams".'

19. *Essays and Introductions* (1961) p. 278.

20. *Autobiographies* (1955) pp. 553–4.

21. At Coole, Yeats says in 'Coole Park, 1929', Synge and others 'found pride established in humility'.

22. 'In later years he was the born servant, even though it was of a phantom court . . . the Roman prelate, the secretary, the go-between; adept in courtesies and ready to serve any great man.' – Frank O'Connor, 'The Old Age of a Poet', in *The Bell*, 1 (Feb. 1941) 17–18.

23. See 'Coole Park and Ballylee, 1931'. In 'Edmund Spenser' (1902), noting Spenser's devotion to the Earl of Leicester, Yeats observes: 'At the end of a long beautiful passage he laments that unworthy men should be in the dead Earl's place, and compares them to the fox – an unclean feeder– hiding in the lair "the badger swept".' – *Essays and Introductions*, pp. 359–60.

24. Yvor Winters writes that the transition from stanza five to six is 'awkward' because 'Yeats apparently thought that the line at the end of five needed a footnote, and I dare say it does; but he puts this footnote in parentheses at the beginning of six, and it is unimpressive as poetry, and it detracts from the unity of six.' – 'The Poetry of W. B. Yeats', in *Twentieth Century Literature*, VI (April 1960) 18. I would say that the fox/lair/badger metaphor does not *require* a footnote because it is comprehensible and effective without any special information as to its source, and that the parenthetical opening line of stanza six does not detract from the unity of the poem. Winters misunderstands the function of the line. The line is, I would urge, eminently successful because it serves a two-fold *unifying* function: (1) it points back in the poem to courtly Spenser, whose 'tongue' (as we have just seen in the homey metaphor) is laudably 'common' and whose inimitable poetry is rooted in the common heritage of our tongue; and (2) it looks ahead to the substance of the stanza, where we learn that the 'common tongue' flourishes only in rooted sources, something uncommon in our uncourtly and tawdry day.

25. *The Variorum Edition of the Poems of W. B. Yeats*, ed. Peter Allt and Russell K. Alspach (London and New York, 1957) p. 839.

26. Ibid. pp. 839–40.

27. I read *hallowed place* both as 'consecrated' ('holy') and as 'sainted', 'full of saints' ('inhabited by hallows').

# Jon Stallworthy

## 'THE BLACK TOWER' (1963)*

IN January 1939 Yeats lay on his death-bed in the south of France. From the sick-room window at Cap Martin he looked out towards Roquebrune with its graveyard-covered slopes rising to the church of Saint Pancras at its summit. He must have been reminded of that other Saint Pancras in London, in whose shadow he had lived at Woburn Buildings. Now dying on the Riviera he found, I suspect, in this view the stimulus for his last poem. 'The Black Tower' is dated 21 January, and on the 28th the poet died.

There are in Mrs Yeats's possession ten loose-leaf sheets of manuscript and a single corrected typescript. There is in the National Library, Dublin, one further page of manuscript among the drafts of *The Death of Cuchulain*, a play on which Yeats was also working at the time of his death. The hand-writing throughout is that of an old, myopic, and dying man.

F. 1r is a prose draft:

*1*

*of the black tower*
*I speak for the ~~gyres~~ gyres*

~~*Of the black tower (*~~————)*~~go.~~*

~~*We form no alliance*~~

*You are not of our kin ~~so begone~~*

~~*We form no alliance we need no help*~~

* This essay is a revised chapter from *Between the Lines: W. B. Yeats's Poetry in the Making*, first published in 1963.

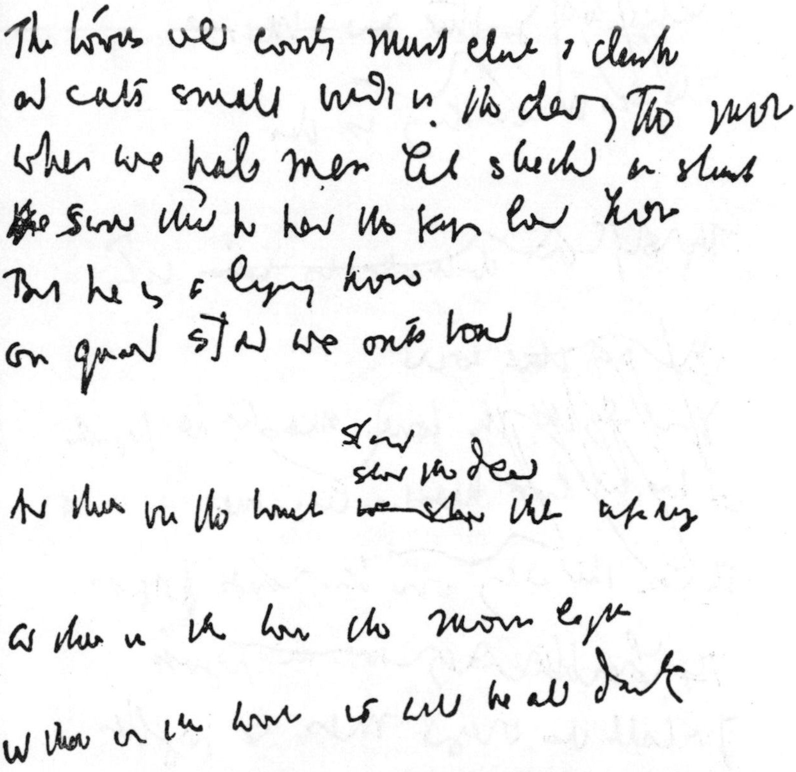

F. 4v of 'The Black Tower': see page 212 for transcription.

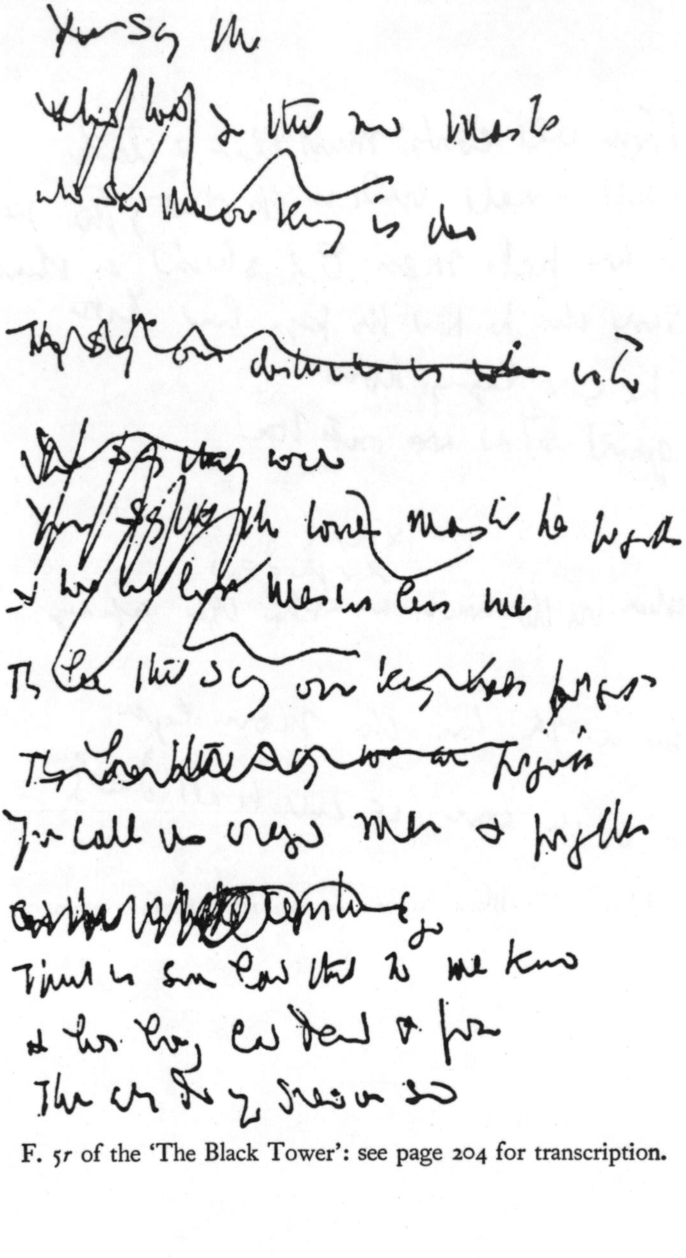

F. 5r of the 'The Black Tower': see page 204 for transcription.

*The Gods have brought us milk & flesh*

*Nothing remains to us but this*

*But this high lonely place*

*Begone you are not oath bound*

*The old tower*

2

*He we that we await will come*

*You say that he died long ago*

*Say what you will*

~~sworn~~ *sworn*

*We have ~~sworn~~ & we wait.*

*We need no help, we seek no allies*

*We love this barren spot*

*Old tower*

3

The poem's basic situation begins to emerge. The inmates of a black tower prefer their present independence to a proffered, and it may be profitable, alliance to another power not of their kin. They await the return of someone who died long ago. P. Diskin and W. J. Keith have shed light on the origins of the poem's narrative structure; Diskin showing it to be

based essentially on [Yeats's] recollections of an episode in Standish O'Grady's *Finn and his Companions*, published in 1892, with illustrations by Jack B. Yeats.[1] O'Grady's work consists of a popular rendering of sections of various Ossianic tales, but he treats the material with marked freedom and in some places elaborates considerably on the original story. This is true particularly of the first chapter of Part ıv of the book, entitled 'Noble

Ancients in Adversity', for which the Irish story, 'The Youthful
Exploits of Finn', provided hardly more than a hint. It is from
this chapter that the underlying structure of Yeats's poem is
derived, though it appears unlikely that he was conscious of the
source at the time of its composition.

The story, in O'Grady's version, describes how one wild
December evening, half a dozen old men are found in a booth
situated in a deep forest in the heart of Connacht, 'nourishing
here in poverty and famine some unconquerable resolution'.
They are a last remnant of the followers of the rightful leader of
the Fenians, Cool, father of Finn, who had been killed in battle
and his army defeated by the sons of Morna, one of whom,
Gaul, assumed the leadership. Nearly all Cool's followers 'were
obliged to make terms with the new tyranny'. A very few did not,
these being the remaining old men, who oppose to the sons of
Morna 'a resolution which hunger and death shall never break'.
They are eventually oppressed by years and hardship and try to
obtain food for themselves by setting traps and springes near
their cabin by means of which they sometimes catch a few birds
and small game. On the evening in question nothing has been
caught except a small thrush which when roasted is divided
among them by their leader who informs them that 'the youth of
many prophecies', who was to overthrow the sons of Morna, has
appeared.[2]

Keith suggests an Arthurian source and supports this convincingly
with a quotation from E. K. Chambers's *Arthur of Britain*:

Beneath the Castle of Sewingshields, near the Roman wall in
Northumberland, are vaults where Arthur sleeps with Guinevere
and all his court and a pack of hounds. He waits until one blows
the horn which lies ready on a table, and cuts a garter placed
beside it with a sword of stone.[3]

It seems probable that Yeats was here drawing, consciously or
unconsciously, on these separate but similar legends.

To return to his first prose draft, the figure 3 at the foot of F.
1r shows that Yeats had a further stanza in his head at this stage,
but there is no prose draft of it that I have seen. On F. 1r he
makes no attempt to disguise his voice. 'I speak for the gyres of
the black tower'. By 'gyres' he means primarily, I think, the

'winding, gyring, spiring treadmill of a stair'. On behalf of the inmates of the tower – 'we' – he addresses the alien forces: 'You are not of our kin'. This is expanded on F. 1*v*:

*We thank your king in the name of the tower*

~~*We men that would have all that we need*~~
   *it has*
~~*But we have all that soldiers need*~~

~~*We make no hard bargain*~~ ,
~~*But make no*~~

*But it has all that we soldiers need*

*It makes no bargain – great its power*

*Although we feed as the goatherds feed*

←————————————————→

*And this a*

       ~~*and the oath b*~~      *And we outlaws are few*
*And seems (   ) a desolate home,*     *We laugh because we knew*
~~*Though we that the secret knew*~~

*And the oath (   ) bound are few*

~~*Our fathers stand among the rocks*~~
~~*Winds make an old bone shake shake*~~
~~*It blow from the black pigs*~~

~~*Our fathers stand among the rocks*~~
~~*But winds can an old bone shake*~~
~~*When it old blows from the black pig's dike*~~

Mrs Yeats's statement that this is a poem 'on the subject of political propaganda'[4] already begins to make sense. The tower symbol has gathered associations like a snowball, until it is here only Thoor Ballylee in so far as Thoor Ballylee is a microcosm of Ireland. 'In the name of the tower' the poet thanks a second king for his offer of assistance, and declines it. On the political plane this can only be the king of England. The Irish are soldiers: Yeats could never forget the heroic ideal. They are outlaws that 'feed as the goatherd feeds', but they have a secret that enables them to reject the overtures of England. This, I take it, is the knowledge that their king will return. On a literal plane this could mean one of the high kings of Cashel, ancient rulers of Ireland, who might come back like Arthur from Avalon to release his people from bondage. On a more simple and figurative plane it could mean that the dormant spirit of Ireland will awake and inspire the people to attain their former dignity and power.

This is made clearer by the reference to 'the black pig's dike'. On this allusion to folk-lore, Yeats himself supplies us with the relevant gloss in connection with a poem written before the turn of the century, and entitled 'The Valley of the Black Pig'. His note I quote in full:

The Irish peasantry have for generations comforted themselves, in their misfortunes, with visions of a great battle, to be fought in a mysterious valley called 'The Valley of the Black Pig', and to break at last the power of their enemies. A few years ago, in the barony of Lisadell, in county Sligo, an old man would fall entranced upon the ground from time to time, and rave out a description of the battle; and I have myself heard said that the girths shall rot from the bellies of the horses, because of the few men that shall come alive out of the valley.[5]

Again, he writes in one of the tales in *The Celtic Twilight*:

Presently our talk of war shifted, as it had a way of doing, to the battle of the Black Pig, which seems to her a battle between Ireland and England, but to me an Armageddon which shall quench all things in the Ancestral Darkness again.[6]

What were at first 'old bones . . . among the rocks' are now more specifically 'Our fathers': these are the ancient heroic dead. They do not lie in their graves, but stand. It has been suggested that Yeats was thinking of the old Irish warrior, Eoghan Bel, who after the battle of Sligo in 537 was buried in an upright position, with his red javelin in hand and pointing out to sea. This is, I think, too specific. He had in mind a common Irish practice, that he may have heard of for the first time in *Ancient*

*Cures, Charms & Usages of Ireland*[7] by Lady Wilde. I have seen the poet's own marked and annotated copy of this book. There are pencil marks on the last page (p. 256), which make it certain that he read the last paragraph. This I give in full:

There was also another mode of burial for warriors. The dead were placed in a standing position, their arms and shield beside them, and a great circular cairn of earth and stones was raised over them. Thus the heroic king of Munster slain in battle, was placed in his grave. 'Mogha-Neid lies in his sepulchre, with his javelin by his shoulder, with his club which was strong in battle, with his helmet, with his sword; long shall he be lamented with deep love, and his absence be the cause of darkest sorrow.'

A reader new to Yeats and new to Irish folk-lore might be forgiven for wondering how the wind can make bones shake, which are presumably underground. Yeats again supplies the answer in his note to an earlier poem, this time 'The Hosting of the Sidhe':

The powerful and wealthy called the gods of ancient Ireland the Tuatha De Danaan, or the tribes of the goddess Danu, but the poor called them, and still sometimes call them, the Sidhe, from Aes Sidhe or Sluagh Sidhe, the people of the Faery Hills, as these words are usually explained. Sidhe is also Gaelic for wind, and certainly the Sidhe have much to do with the wind. They journey in whirling winds, the winds that were called the dance of the daughters of Herodias in the Middle Ages, Herodias doubtless taking the place of some old goddess. When the country people see the leaves whirling on the road they bless themselves, because they believe the Sidhe to be passing by.[8]

The Gods of ancient Ireland then inspire the bones of the heroic dead, reminding them of the valley or dyke of the black pig, where their ultimate victorious battle is to be fought.

The manuscript leaves being now detached from the original notebook, it is impossible to order them with any certainty; to say whether stanza I was written before stanza II, or the refrain before either. Mrs Yeats says that he worked to no definite pattern, but passed haphazardly from stanza to stanza and back again, as the spirit moved him. The best I can do is to assume that he wrote the stanzas in their final order. There are in all four

drafts of the first stanza. One I have given already. F. 2r is still
very rough:

       *Say that the men in this old*
~~goat~~     *Lack nothing that a soldier*
       ~~*Say that the men that keep this*~~

       ~~*Go Towns men & say that the*~~ *men of the tower*
              *have got all that*
       ~~*Have Lack that*~~ *a soldier needs*

       ~~*That they lack (      ), & their wine gone sour*~~

       *That their (      ) is scarce & their wine gone sour*

       *And they but feed as the goat herd feed s*

       *Old tower* ~~*This desolate spot their home*~~

       ~~*Here on this spot we stay*~~ *Oath bound men & we stay*

       *Not of our kin are they* ~~*Go for your work is*~~
               ~~*Go for your*~~ *task is done*    *our*
       ~~*Go You are not our kin Was*~~ *& They say they are not* ~~*your*~~ *kin*

\*     *You are not of our kin*

\*     *That banner comes not in*

              *stand*
       *Our fathers* ~~*are buried*~~ *up right in* ~~*the tomb*~~ *their tomb*
        *But*
       ~~*Wind*~~ *Wind comes from the shore*

       *And they shake when the winds roar*

       ~~*Among the mountain rocks they shake*~~

       *Old bones upon the mountain shake*

       *Old bones shake upon the mountain*

              ~~*or among*~~ *the*

     \* Denotes a line inserted from the top of the page.

F. 3r is as follows:[9]

> We thank the towns men in the name of the Tower
>           it has
> Say ~~we have~~ all that soldiers need
>
> Why should it bargain great its power
>
> Although we feed as the goatherds feed
>
> ~~Say to~~
>
> Say
>
> Go to the men of the black pig's banner
>           That
> ~~Say~~ we have all that a soldier needs
>           Though is spent & the wine is bitter
> ~~Though the wine is sour bitter & the bran spent~~
>
> And we but feed as the goat herds feed
>
> This desolate shore is our home
>
> No talk can make us come
>
>
>           The     ⟨————————⟩ our fathers stand up right in the
> ~~Old bones upon the mountain~~
>           Which     ~~the~~ wind comes from the shore
> But ~~shake when the wind roars~~
>
> ~~Up from the sea shore~~
>
> They shake with the winds' roar
>
>                                                       mountain
> ~~The old bones shake upon the mountain among the rocks~~
> The old bones upon the mountain shake

On F. 4r the 'towns men' have disappeared, but there is still reference to 'the black pig's dyke':

~~Who stands~~

~~Begone from this by the old black tower~~
                        ~~this ancient (        ) this dark~~ wall
I thank you in name of ~~the black tower~~
                        *the ancient tower*
                *is not a thing*
But there is ~~nothing~~ that we need

~~You that you who~~ We know that your king (      ) & proud

And we but feed as the goat herds feed

Our fathers stand in the tomb up right

But wind makes an old bone shake

When it blows from the black pig's dyke

Our fathers stand in the tomb up right

The next time that this stanza appears is in the first composite draft. There are two further drafts of the second stanza before the poem is put together as a whole. F. 5r shows the poet thinking on paper:

~~You~~ say that

~~You We & this no master~~

~~Who say that our king is dead~~
        ~~that~~

~~They say our destruction is when~~ (      )

~~You say that we're~~

~~You say that the tower's master be forgotten~~

~~& we but left master less men~~

~~They lie that say our king has forgot~~

~~They lie that say we are forgotten~~

You call us crazed men & forgotten

~~And (                              )~~

> *That is some law that no men know*
>
> *He has long laid dead & (       )*
>
> *Then why do you dread us so*

On F. 2*v* the stanza begins to take shape, and the alien power is no longer addressed as 'you' but 'they':

> *They think that they can buy us*
> > *And*
> *~~Yet~~ say that our dead*

Then after five lines of chaotic scribbling Yeats continues:

> *They send a messenger to buy us*
> > *They (                )*
> *~~Say we were lost & our king dead~~*
>
> *That all we need is an alliance*
> > *~~That~~*
> *Offer us those great affairs*
>
> *Should we accept that law instead*
>
> *If he died long ago*
>
> *Why do they hate us so*

At this point we are forced to ask ourselves who is the messenger. Subjectively, he might represent the temptation of atheistic rationalism that denies the God in which Old Tom (see stanza III below) believes. On the England–Ireland level the messenger may simply represent the British Government. There is a further area of interpretation which must have been in Yeats's mind in 1939: the wider international one. The shadows of the Nazi banners were extending over Europe, and on this plane the messenger comes from Hitler.

Prior to the first full draft there are three sheets of working on stanza III whose precise order of composition is difficult to fix, but it is not important. F. 5*v* is brief:

*There is an old man that goes out clambering*
*      ⟨————⟩ snaring small birds for his cooking pot*
*While all ⟨————⟩ all sound men lie slumbering*

*That say he's a lying hound*

*~~Who stand here the oath bound~~*

*He stand the oath bound*

Fs. 6r and 7r are more revealing. F. 6r, which has workings from
*The Death of Cuchulain* on its verso, reads:

*The old bones shake among the rocks*

*They stand up right there*

*And the wind roars up from the shore*

*The old bones shake among the rocks*

————————————

### 3

*Old Tom said he has*
*                    he has heard upon the hill*
*He has heard it before dawn*

*But is crazy because of his age*

*And (          ) with nothing*

*But we are oath bound & we (          )*

*        that*
*Our cook goes out to climb & clamber*

*And catch small birds in the dew of the morn*

*When ~~decent men prefer their slumber~~/better men lie stretched in*

*Says that he heard the king's low horn*

*But he is a lying hound*

F. 7r is similar:

*Old Tom ~~our cook~~ upon the rock must clamber*

*~~To snare small birds for our cooking pot~~*

*~~When young men when we hale men are stretched in slumber~~*

*~~And sets his snare & catches a bird~~*

            *the rough rock*
*Old Tom that over ~~rocks must~~ clamber s*
         ,
*To ~~snare his birds between night & morn~~*

*~~Snare small birds between night & morn~~*

*~~From For~~ For birds & eggs before night & morn*

*When all hale men prefer their slumber*
            *king's great horn*
*Swears he ~~has heard our master's~~ horn*
    *I think he's*
*But ~~he is~~ a lying hound*
    *But*
*~~He stands~~ Here stand we the oath bound*

*But here*

These drafts show the inmates of the tower to be waiting for a king whose horn the cook claims to have heard. The poet's counter-assertion 'But he is a lying hound' is for some reason not wholly convincing: we are secretly inclined to believe the cook, and, I submit, it is intended that we should. Another character, who eventually merges with the cook, is Old Tom who has heard something upon the hill, and before dawn. That something is clearly the horn; yet again we hear the sceptical voice of the poet: 'But [he] is crazy because of his age'.

Who is Old Tom? I think it not improbable that Yeats had been impressed by the dramatic possibilities in Shakespeare's Poor Tom, the sane man aping the fool upon the heath. The mask of Old Tom is one of the many through which the poet speaks. Tom the Lunatic had said in an earlier poem:

> Whatever stands in field or flood,
> Bird, beast, fish or man,
> Mare or stallion, cock or hen,
> Stands in God's unchanging eye
> In all the vigour of its blood;
> In that faith I live or die.

Number xxiii of the 'Words for Music Perhaps' is entitled 'Tom at Cruachan', and number xxi, 'The Dancer at Cruachan and Cro-Patrick'. Although Tom is not mentioned in the latter, clearly he it is who says:

> I, proclaiming that there is
> Among birds or beasts or men
> One that is perfect or at peace,
> Danced on Cruachan's windy plain,
> Upon Cro-Patrick sang aloud;
> All that could run or leap or swim
> Whether in wood, water or cloud,
> Acclaiming, proclaiming, declaiming Him.

This Tom is the wise fool, and more Christian than lunatic, or it may be that Yeats is deliberately equating the two. I believe myself that Tom represents the Christian in Yeats, whom he could never entirely suppress, and struggled with particularly, Mrs Yeats told me, when he was ill.[10] If Tom is waiting for the horn of somebody, a king, who died long ago, the king may be Christ and the horn related to the trumpets that sound on the other side. A symbolic poem such as 'The Black Tower' does not have one meaning but several. I would not press this subjective interpretation too strongly, since a more objective meaning is quite clearly the dominant one; but their co-existence is not only possible but desirable if the poem is to make its 'full, perfect and sufficient' impact on the reader.

I come now to the first composite draft of the poem on Fs. 7*v*, 8*r*, and 9*r*. Arrows show quite clearly that in the original notebook 7*v* and 8*r* faced each other; 8*r* being on the right. It reads as follows:

                    The watch men
          Say that the men in the old Tower
                        the
          Lack nothing that ~~a~~ soldier needs
                Their
          ~~Though~~ money is spent & ~~the bread~~ their wine gone sour

          ~~That~~ And they but feed as the goat herd feeds

          But this banner comes not in

          Because not of our kin


          Our fathers stand upright in the tomb

          But wind comes up from the shore

          They shake when the winds roar
                        upon
          Old bones ~~on~~ the mountain shake


          They have sent their messenger to buy us
                ~~And leave        men swear that~~
          And ~~some that have sworn~~ our king is dead

          Their leave proof that our king is dead

          That we lack is their alliance

          Their messenger has come to buy us

          ~~To proof that our king is dead~~

          ~~To bring some proof~~
Prove|                              rightful
          ~~And prove~~ by ~~the book~~ that our king is dead
                        that
          That all we lack is alliance
                    this alien blood
          And ~~to accept their rule instead~~ With their alien blood instead

          If he died long ago

          Why do you dread us so

~~The moon is out & a light~~   still throws its beam on
~~A crumbling crescent has lit the tomb~~

    (    ) &c.

On F. 8r both stanzas I and II are crossed out, and arrows indicate that the following stanzas on F. 7v are to be inserted here:

*Say the men of this black Tower*

*Though they but feed as the goat herd feeds*

*Their money spent & their wine gone sour*

*Lack nothing that a soldier needs*

~~*And this And that*~~ *That banner shall not in*

                  *Because not of our kin*


~~*The*~~ *This messenger that comes to buy*

*Swears that our own king is dead*

*That all we lack is their alliance*

*Their better law all that we need*

*If he died long ago*

*Why do they dread us so*


      *The moon still moves its beam in the tomb*

On F. 9r we hear the last of Old Tom:

                *climb &*

~~*Old Tom the cook delights to clamber*~~

    *snare*        *in the chill of*

~~*And snare small birds between night & morn*~~

~~*When all hale men better*~~

            *lie warm in*

~~*When better men are in their slumbers*~~

~~Then an old man that goes out to —~~

~~Old clown Tom the cock cook is proud if he clambers~~

The tower's old cook rambles and clambers

After small birds in the chill of the morn

When all hale men are deep in their slumber

He swears that he hears our king's great horn

But he is a lying hound

We stand ~~at~~ on the wall oath bound


                                    *is*
The moon has gone and dark the tomb

~~The~~ But now comes up from the shore

      They shake when the winds roar

Old bones upon the mountain shake

With reference to the subjective and religious level of interpretation, one should notice in this draft the bread and wine in stanza I, and an oblique mention of what can only be the Bible in the line: 'And prove by the book that our rightful king is dead'. Old Tom's connection with *King Lear* would seem to be strengthened by the reference to 'Old clown Tom'.

   This poem approaches its final shape in a second manuscript draft covering three pages. F. 10r gives all but stanza III and the last refrain: the title makes its first appearance:

The Black Tower

Say that the men of this black Tower

Though they but feed as the goat herd feeds

Their money spent, their wine gone sour

Lack nothing that a soldier needs

That all are oath bound men
    ~~Those that~~
Those|  ~~That banner s~~ come not in.        That banner|

There in the tomb stand the dead upright
But wind comes up from the shore
They shake when the winds roar
Old bones upon the mountain shake

        Those
~~Their~~ banners come to bribe or threaten
Or whisper that a man's a fool
Who when his own right king's forgotten
Cares what king sets up his rule
If he died long ago
Why do you dread us so

There in the tomb drops the faint moonlight
But wind comes up from the shore
They shake when the winds roar
Old bones upon the mountain shake

Stanza III is on F. 4v:

The tower's old cook must climb & clamber
And catch small birds in the dew of the morn
When we hale men lie stretched in slumber
~~He~~ Swears that he hears the king's loud horn
But he is a lying hound
On guard stand we oath bound

>                         *stand*
>                     *stand the dead*
> *And there in the tomb ~~we stand~~ there upright*
>
> *And there in the tomb the moon's light*
>
> *but there in the tomb it will be all dark*

In this draft of the refrain Yeats cannot escape from his own predicament. See the emendation of what was clearly to have been 'we stand', to 'stand the dead there upright'. The dying poet is not only thinking of his heroic 'fathers', but of himself, as he writes: 'but there in the tomb it will be all dark'. F. 11r shows the crystallization of the final stanza and refrain:

>                     *that           clamber*
> *The tower's old cook must climb & ~~ramble~~*
>         *Catching*
> *~~And catch~~ small birds in the dew of the morn*
>
> *When we hale men lie stretched in ~~slumb~~ slumber*
>     *~~He swears~~ Swears*
> *~~Swore~~ that he heard the king's great horn*
>
> *But he's a lying hound*
>
> *Stand we on guard oath bound*
>
>
> *There in the tomb the black grows blacker*
>
> *But wind comes up from the shore*
>
> *They shake when the winds roar*
>
> *Old bones upon the mountain shake.*

Except for punctuation and a few minor one-word alterations[11] 'The Black Tower' is now complete. The poet has so distanced himself that he appears to be narrator rather than participator. Indeed, he sounds in the opening stanza almost as if he were himself outside the black tower. The references in lines 23 and 26 to 'we hale men' and 'Stand we on guard' alone correct this impression. All superfluous and over-specific details have been winnowed away. But for the manuscript drafts we would not have heard of an 'alliance', a 'bargain', 'outlaws', the 'black pig', or even of the 'old clown Tom' who 'is crazy because of his age'. So skilful is Yeats's verbal masonry that though the reader may admire the height and proportions of 'The Black Tower', he can never hope to break into it and ransack its meaning. The stones are fitted too closely for any foothold to remain, but the manuscript drafts allow us, as it were, to look in at the lowest loophole. Our view, because it is confined, is the more fascinating: we return to the tower over and over again in the hope that we may see further. If we were to succeed, perhaps we should not come again. Everest certainly lost something of its mystery and fascination for being climbed. It is enough that we perceive that the Tower can be Yeats himself, Ireland, and a world threatened by the Third Reich. These several interpretations are complementary rather than mutually exclusive; and what of the message – in so far as such a poem has a message?

Though 'in the tomb the dark grows blacker', and the shaking of the bones can only be an evil omen, the cook, who is the one man in the tower not 'stretched in slumber', 'Swears that he hears the great king's horn'. If we were not to believe him he would not be there. Unlike us, he stands at the top of the tower, to catch the birds of heaven 'in the dew of the morn'. Can this be other than a symbol of natural regeneration? After the midnight terrors of 1939, day would break on Yeats, on Ireland, and on the world.

## NOTES

1. That Yeats had read the book seems evident from his note to 'The Secret Rose': cf. *Collected Poems* (1950 ed.) p. 528.

2. Patrick Diskin, 'A Source for Yeats's "The Black Tower" ', in *Notes and Queries* (March 1961).

3. See W. J. Keith, 'Yeats's Arthurian Black Tower', in *Modern Language Notes*, LXXV (Feb. 1960).

4. G. B. Saul, *Prolegomena to the Study of Yeats's Poems* (1957) p. 176.

5. *The Variorum Edition of the Poems of W. B. Yeats*, ed. Peter Allt and Russell K. Alspach (New York and London, 1957) p. 161.

6. *Collected Works* (1908) V 154.

7. 1890 ed.

8. *Variorum Edition*, p. 800.

9. F 3v contains an early draft, written previously, of the refrain to the second of the 'Three Marching Songs'.

10. 'I am gradually becoming healthier & well – when I am ill I am a Christian & that is abominable.' *Letters on Poetry from W. B. Yeats to Dorothy Wellesley* (1964) p. 130.

11. On the single sheet of typescript Yeats makes the following changes:

> Line 1. ... the old black tower
>
> 8. But winds come up ...
>
> 24. Swears that he hears ...
>
> 27. ... the dark grows blacker

# Jon Stallworthy

## 'UNDER BEN BULBEN' (1966)

In 1938 Yeats was seventy-three and increasingly aware that he had months rather than years to live.

> 'The work is done,' grown old he thought,
> 'According to my boyish plan;
> Let the fools rage, I swerved in nought,
> Something to perfection brought ...'

'Something to perfection brought' – the elegy for example. 'In Memory of Major Robert Gregory', 'Upon a Dying Lady', 'Easter 1916', 'In Memory of Eva Gore-Booth and Con Markie-wicz', and 'Coole Park 1929' had established him as one of the greatest elegists in the English language. At seventy-three he had only one elegy left to write: his own.

Hone says that a prose draft of 'Under Ben Bulben' was written in August 1938 and the final version read to F. R. Higgins on the night before Yeats left Ireland for the last time. Higgins, in fact, would not have heard the *final* version, as Hone tells us that on Thursday, 26 January 1939 Yeats 'rallied towards night-fall and gave Mrs Yeats corrections for "Under Ben Bulben" '. On Saturday, 28 January he died at two in the afternoon.[1]

It is possible to date the conception of the poem yet more closely, since on 15 August 1938 Yeats wrote to Dorothy Wellesley from Riversdale:

... I have found a book of essays about Rilke waiting me; one on Rilke's ideas about death annoyed me. I wrote on the margin:

> Draw rein; draw breath.
> Cast a cold eye
> On life, on death.
> Horseman pass by.[2]

Mrs Yeats's recollection of this incident is somewhat different. One morning when, as was his habit, he was working in bed, she heard him call, and entered his room to see him hurl to the floor in disgust the book of essays on Rilke. He did not then write in the book's margin, she tells me, the quatrain that was to become his epitaph, but on a scrap of paper. This first draft I believe to have been lost, though there does remain a quarto sheet of typing-paper on which is written, in ink:

> *Horse man*
>
> *Draw rein; draw breath.*
>
> *Cast a cold eye*
>
> *On life, on death.*
>
> *Horse man pass by.*

The title suggests that, at this stage at least, it was considered as a separate poem. Another version of these lines on F. 7*r* of the 'Under Ben Bulben' drafts (see below, p. 226), in which 'Turn that indifferent eye' is corrected to 'Cast a cold eye', would seem to indicate that by 15 August when he wrote to Dorothy Wellesley Yeats had already begun 'Under Ben Bulben'. The last line of his quatrain suggests the influence – whether conscious or unconscious it is impossible to say – of the words '*Abi viator*' in Swift's epitaph. We know that Yeats considered this 'the greatest ... in history'.

There remain twenty-six folios of manuscript and typescript working, not counting the draft of the epitaph cited above: these show that the composition of 'Under Ben Bulben' fell into four phases. First, on nine folios of a small loose-leaf notebook Yeats made three very rough prose drafts. Then on two more folios in the same notebook his poem starts to stumble into rhyme. Phase three is a complete, but rough, verse draft on six folios of a large loose-leaf notebook. Finally there are three typescripts, each of three quarto sheets. The prose drafts are very rough indeed: many words are – to me, at any rate – illegible. The problem of transcription is further complicated by the fact that Yeats at this

stage was thinking on paper. His sentences are often unfinished,
left in the air, as his mind changes direction. In my transcription,
brackets indicate a passage I cannot read and dots within
brackets the actual number of illegible words.

F. 1r is entitled 'Creed' and begins, not surprisingly, 'I
believe':

*Creed*

*I*

*I believe what the old saints*

*a thousand years before Christ, sitting under*

*the palms, like the old saints about*

*the Mareotic sea.* ~~*that*~~ *From eternity*

*through eternity to eternity man moves.*

*I believe with the men upon the road*

*& the common men that there are*

*(  .  . ) play (  .  .  .  . )*

*the newly dead show themselves*

*here & there, or sport there above*

*(  .  . )*

\* *I have desired what the proffets*

\* *know or sages that (  . )*

\* *among old women & beggar men*

*II*

*I believe that there is nothing to fear*

*that* ~~*death & pain are dreadful*~~

~~*Yet I shake to hear the word when*~~

\* Indicates a line inserted, at the pointing of an arrow, from the top
of the page.

The 'old saints a thousand years before Christ, sitting under the palms' I take to be a reference to the priests of, first, Apollo and, secondly, Buddha. In the drafts of 'The Statues', a poem whose composition partially overlapped with 'Under Ben Bulben', occurs the sentence 'Appolo had taken the name of Buddha'.[3] In Yeats's cyclic view of history one religion rises as another falls. Apollo and Dionysus prefigure Buddha, who prefigures Christ, who prefigures the 'rough beast' of 'The Second Coming', 'slouching towards Bethlehem to be born'. So here, the priests of pre-Christian eras are followed by 'the old saints about the Mareotic sea'. It is almost certain that Yeats first read of Saint Anthony and Egyptian monasticism of the third and fourth centuries in two books by J. O. Hannay: *The Spirit and Origin of Christian Monasticism* (1903) and *The Wisdom of the Desert* (1904). From the beliefs of the early Christian monks, Yeats turns in this first prose draft to the beliefs of 'the men upon the road . . . old women and beggar men'. The road, of course, is an Irish road, and he is affirming his faith in the pagan mythology of Ireland. So from the drafts of 'The Statues' it is clear that Yeats regarded Cuchulain as the spiritual descendant of Apollo. Where the Christian begins his Creed 'I believe in one God', Yeats is sympathetic to any religion that believes in a life of the soul after death.

F. 2r continues the first prose draft:

*where (  .  .  .  .  .  ) becomes (  .  .  .  )*

*armed philosophers seek each other in*

*air, where the conflict is has be*

*becomes nobility of body*

*Neither for those who die in bed who die at*

*battle field. I believe that if there was*

*anything to fear that great will of the*

*world could not exist with the eternal laughter*

> *eternal joy. To that joy & that laughter*
> *I gave my life – I am old & ill*
> *my flesh is heavy it weighs upon my*
> *heart but I shall soon cast it off*
> *be ~~as light as~~ if god wills I shall*
> *be as light as a bird (  .  .  ).*

Yeats cancelled this page with diagonal lines. From his contemplation of the life to come, he glances momentarily aside to
examine his present position. 'I am old & ill': he quotes directly
from 'The Man and the Echo'. 'My flesh is heavy it weighs upon
my heart but I shall soon cast it off' expresses an idea found also
in the first draft of 'Sailing to Byzantium': 'For many loves have I
taken off my clothes . . . but now I will take off my body.' The
simile 'as light as a bird', far from being idle decoration, introduces an important symbol that recurs frequently in Yeats's
work. He commonly depicts the souls of the dead as birds. In
*Deirdre* the First Musician makes his ominous prophecy of the
lovers' union in death, 'Eagles have gone into their cloudy
bed.'[4]

On F. 2v the poet asserts his belief in the immanence of God in
all things, but at the same time refuses to yield allegiance to the
Christian Godhead.

### III

> *God is in all things, ~~yet~~ but*
> *is all is a way of putting*
> *"thinking masks" – ~~I will have~~ (——  .  )*
> *I shut him out. I call to me Cuchulain*
> *~~from~~ years that seemed so new 30 yrs*
> *ago as I (  .  .  .  .  .  )*
> *(  .  .  .  .  .  )*

As in the last stanza of 'The Statues' he invokes, in the great
shade of Cuchulain, a proudly pagan ideal of man's heroic self-
reliance. On F. 3*r* he makes the contrast more explicit in his
redrafting of section III.

### III

*God comes to us in all things – in our*

*passing thoughts in the sun in the leaves*

*he is in all this morning & (    .    ) Yet I*
        *I would*                    *could*
~~*would*~~ *not ask him for anything & I* ~~*will*~~

*be satisfied by death did I not know*

*that it he who asks who refuses to ask.*

*But I throw from my heart all images of*

*submission – I have found the great*

*Cuchullain in my arrogant heart. There*

*is nothing that I have not* ~~*will*~~ *willed*

The second prose draft opens on F. 3*v* with recapitulation, but
section II introduces a new variation on the theme of death's
unimportance.

### I

*First principles*

*"Eternity to Eternity" etc*

*The common people and their women*

### II

*Death nothing – if the sky falls &*

*falling bombs – children hands & dance –*

*The soul out lives all things &*

*makes itself today as it pleases*

### III

*Let the bombs fall – let them destroy the*

*hateful cities –* ⟨ . ⟩

The talk of falling bombs recalls the opening of 'Lapis Lazuli', a poem written in 1936, but first published in March 1938:

> if nothing drastic is done
> Aeroplane and Zeppelin will come out,
> Pitch like King Billy bomb-balls in
> Until the town lie beaten flat.

The vision of physical disorder caused by falling bombs he contrasts with an image of children dancing. As in 'The Double Vision of Michael Robartes' and 'Long-legged Fly', Yeats uses a child's dance as a symbol of bodily and spiritual harmony. 'The soul out lives all things' – even the falling bombs. Indeed, in an outburst of rage against 'the hateful cities' of the materialistic age he so despised, like a vengeful prophet he bids the bombs fall.

The third prose draft begins on F. *4r*. Though structurally it has much in common with F. *1r*, the differences are significant.

### I

*I believe as did the old sages*

*who sat under the palm trees*

*the banyan trees, or among*

*those snow bound rocks, and*

*a thousand years before Chri Christ*

*was born; I believe as did the*

> monks of the Mareotic sea,
>
> as do ~~every n~~ country men
>
> who see the old fighting men
>
> & their fine women coming out
>
> of the mountain, moving from
>
> mountain to mountain

### II
> And this is what I believe that
>
> ~~man~~ man stands between two

The 'old saints' are now – more sensibly – 'the old sages'; 'saint' having predominantly Christian overtones. That some sit under banyan-trees identifies them as Buddhists: though Gautama Buddha, in fact, lived in the sixth century B.C. The Sidhe, or spirit population of Irish folk-lore, are more clearly delineated in this draft. 'The old fighting men & their fine women . . . moving from mountain to mountain' appear in the haunting refrain to 'Three Songs to the One Burden': 'From mountain to mountain ride the fierce horsemen.' An early version of the first song is to be found on F. 13*v*.

F. 5*r* follows on directly from F. 4*r*.

> eternities, that of ~~this family~~, his
>
> race that of his soul. Further
>
> I declare that man serves there
>
> sword in hand ~~or with armed~~
>
> ~~mind~~ & with an armoured mind That
>
> ~~a race is born~~ only so armed does
>
> man pick the right mate, & only
>
> ~~when~~ only in the midst in the midst

*of a conflict, not straining all his*

*mind & his body & to the utmost*

*has he wisdom enough to choose*

*his right mate. The wisdom I*

*seek is written on a sword, mirrored*

*on a sword ~~who wrapped in a pie~~*

*on Sato's sword, a sword wrapped*

Yeats's train of thought here enters the philosophical jungle of *A Vision.* Briefly, he believed with Blake that: 'Without Contraries there is no Progression. Attraction and Repulsion, Reason and Energy, Love and Hate are necessary to Human Existence.' Happiness, wisdom, and perfection are attained only by preserving the tension between these opposites. Richard Ellmann tells how Yeats upset the Indian Professor Bose, who came to see him in 1937, when he replied to Bose's request for a message to India: 'Let 100,000 men of one side meet the other. That is my message to India.' He then, as Bose described the scene, 'strode swiftly across the room, took up Sato's sword, and unsheathed it dramatically and shouted, "Conflict, more conflict" '.[5] Of Sato's sword, given to Yeats as a present, we hear in 'A Dialogue of Self and Soul':

> *My Self.*   Montashigi, third of his family, fashioned it
> Five hundred years ago, about it lie
> Flowers from I know not what embroidery –
> Heart's purple – and all these I set
> For emblems of the day against the tower
> Emblematical of the night,
> And claim as by a soldier's right
> A charter to commit the crime once more.

In section III on F. *6r* God is not mentioned as on F. *2v* and F. *3r*: attention instead is concentrated on the soul.

*in a woman's old embroidery.*

### III

*I declare that no evil*

*can happen to the soul except*

*from the soul – that death*
 *a brief      brief*
*is parting & ~~a passing sickness~~*

*What matter though the skies*

*drop for – children take hands*

*& dance*

At this point it would seem that Yeats turned back to F. 5*v* and considered not the living but the dead, who (as described in book IV of *A Vision*) 'recreate their old lives'.

              *writhe in remorse*
*I think the dead suffer remorse*

*for as I have described &*

*re create their old lives for*

*as I have described. There are*

*modern popular plays upon the*

*subject & much in the folk lore*

*of all countries. In it they*

*play & sport suffer remorse*

*because of its share while (   .   ) living*

*humans in the destruction of the*

*ancient houses. That destruction*

H

> *is taking place all over Ireland*
>
> *today. In a few cases the*
>
> *cause has been very much what*
>
> *I have described but in more*
>
> *cases (  • ) for power or because the*
>
> \* *new Governments have lost interest. I know that*
>
> \* *when old family ~~pictu have been sold~~*
>
> \* *silver, pictures furniture have been sold*

Yeats cancelled all but the last three lines with a diagonal stroke of his pen. The dead he is concerned with here suffer remorse for their part in the betrayal of Ireland's heroic heritage to what in 'In the Seven Woods' he calls the 'new commonness . . . crying about the streets'. This for him is typified by 'the destruction of the ancient houses', a theme to which he often returns – notably in his poems about Coole.

## II

This ends the prose drafts and on F. 7r rhyme enters the poem with the early version of the final epitaph already mentioned: 'Cast a cold eye' is a marked improvement on 'Turn that indifferent eye'.

> *Draw rain. Draw breath.*
> *Cast a cold*
> *~~Turn that indifferent~~ eye*
>
> *On life, on death.*
>
> *Horse man pass by*
>
> *Drop bombs & blow the pavement etc*

\* Indicates a line inserted from the top of the page.

> *What the great forefathers did*
>    *Measurement began our*
> ~~*Here the origin of our*~~ *might*
>
> *Forms a stark Egyptian thought*
>         (  .  )
> ~~*Forms a* (  .  ) *Phideas wrought*~~
>
> *That this purpose had been set*
>
> *Let children should an airplane*
>       ~~*Bomb the Drop bombs, & blow the city*~~ *etc*
>
> ~~*Bombs upon the city rain*~~
>
> *Or the deafening cannon sound*
>
> *Catch hands & dance in round*
>         *that*
> *explosion on* ~~*their*~~ (  .  ) *rain*
>
> *Bombs upon this* (  .  )
>
> *Or*

A new and important theme emerges from this page. With 'Here the origin of our might', corrected to 'Measurement began our might', Yeats introduces a theme central also to 'The Statues' and elaborated in *On the Boiler*:

There are moments when I am certain that art must once again accept those Greek proportions which carry into plastic art the Pythagorean numbers, those faces which are divine because all there is empty and measured.[6]

The subsequent jottings show him toying with the curious image – found first on F. 3*v* and later to be abandoned – of children dancing in a symbolic circle while 'cannon sound' and bombs fall. This idea he continues and expands on F. 8*r*:

> *Before he can accomplish fate*

* Having reached the foot of this page, Yeats turned it on its side and wrote five words along the right-hand edge.

*He recovers all his mind*
                    *stand*
*For an instant is at ease*
*Or*

*Laughs aloud as though in peace.*

*Let children should an airplane*
~~*Children that is an airplane*~~
            *Some neighbouring city pavement stain*
~~*Bombs upon the city rain.*~~
                            *Or the deadly cannon sound*
~~*That is the cannon's deafening sound*~~
~~*Hand in hand dance in a round.*~~
            *Catch their hands & dance in a round*

*That passing moment makes it sweet*
*When male & female organ meet*
~~*When*~~ *or enemy looks on enemy*
*Timeless man's this honey bee*

Now it is not only children who discover peace at the centre of conflict, but also lovers and soldiers. The sexual act was, of course, closely associated in Yeats's mind with the perpetual motion of the interpenetrating gyres described in *A Vision*.

### III

Ff. 9r to 13r constitute the third phase of the poem's composition: the first complete, but rough, verse draft. I have a strong suspicion that it was preceded by other, incomplete fragments of rough verse draft, but having found no trace of these I move now to F. 9r.

~~*His*~~

~~*Creed Convictions*~~
*Under Ben Bulben*

## I

              *sages*
Swear by what the ~~sages~~ spoke
Round the Mareotic Lake,
That the Witch of Atlas knew;
    Spoke and set all the
~~Swear before a~~ cock ~~can~~ crow.

            *by*         *swear by horsemen, swear by women*
By those horsemen or those women
Complexions lift above the human,
~~All those faces that appear in~~
~~Tuatha de Dananan of Erin,~~
    *That*
~~Pale~~ long visaged company
That airs an immortality
         *in*
Completeness ~~of~~ their passions won.
Now they ride the wintry dawn
Where Ben Bulben sets the scene;
Here's the gist of ~~th~~ what they mean.


## II

Many times man lives & dies,
Between his two eternities
    That of race & that of soul;
*and*    *Ireland*
Ancient ~~Erin~~ knew it all.
    Whether ~~a~~ man die in his bed

This draft shows the evolution of the poem's title from 'Creed' to 'His Convictions' and, finally, the impersonal 'Under Ben Bulben'. A similar movement from the subjective to the objective is visible in the first line, where the statement 'I believe . . .' has given place to the terse imperative 'Swear . . .'. Shelley's Witch of Atlas, who here makes her first appearance, knows – as 'the sages spoke' – of the immortality of the soul:

> She, all those human figures breathing there
>     Beheld as living spirits – to her eyes
> The naked beauty of the soul lay bare,
>     And often through a rude and worn disguise
> She saw the inner form most bright and fair . . .
>
>                                         (St. LXVI)

The opening of 'Under Ben Bulben' would seem to have its roots in Yeats's researches of almost forty years before. His essay, dated 1900, on 'The Philosophy of Shelley's Poetry' contains many references to the Witch of Atlas, as, for example: ,When the Witch has passed in her boat from the caverned river, that is doubtless her own destiny, she passes along the Nile 'by Moeris and the Mareotid lakes . . .".' At the essay's eloquent end he speaks of 'that far household where the undying gods await all whose souls have become simple as flame, whose bodies have become quiet as an agate lamp'.

The opening sentence of the finished poem has puzzled many people, since it sounds as if the Witch of Atlas 'Spoke and set the cocks a-crow'. No cocks crow in Shelley's poem. This draft shows that Yeats wrote at first 'Swear before a cock can crow'. In changing it to 'Spoke and set all the cock crow', he intended, I believe, the sages rather than the Witch to be the subject of 'Spoke'. The cock as a symbol of resurrection appears in 'Two Kings', 'Solomon and the Witch', and 'Byzantium', and is conceivably related to the cock that crowed over Saint Peter.

The 'old fighting men' of F. 4r here become, significantly, 'horsemen': the horse for Yeats was a symbol of spirited and courageous nobility, and time and again in his poems he refers to the good horsemanship of those whom he admires – such as Robert Gregory, Con Markiewicz, and George Pollexfen. In a note to 'The Hosting of the Sidhe' he explains the 'long visaged company':

The gods of ancient Ireland, the Tuatha de Danaan, or the tribes of the goddess Danu, or the Sidhe, from Aes Sidhe, or Sluagh Sidhe, the people of the Faery Hills, as these words are usually explained, still ride the country as of old. Sidhe is also Gaelic for wind, and certainly the Sidhe have much to do with the wind.[7]

Section II of the poem is continued on F. 10*r*.

*rifle* ~~shoot~~ *knock*

*Or the* ~~cannon strike~~ *him dead,*

*A brief parting from those dear*

*Is the worst man has to fear.*
 *Those           toil be*
*Though*  ~~Though~~ *grave diggers* ~~work is~~ *long*
  ~~his~~  *their     their*
*Sharp* ~~is~~ *spade s,* ~~his~~ *muscle strong*
*can       lay               ~~their~~*
~~have~~ *they* ~~laid~~ *Where* ~~can he lay his~~ *buried men?*
*their*

*Back in the human mind again.*


### III

~~knew heard~~
~~You that heard John Mitchell pray ed heard John Mitchel pray~~
~~might        in his day~~
~~That God might send war in his day before he died:~~

\* *You that Mitchell's prayer have heard*

\* *'Send war in our time O Lord',*

*Know that when all words are said*

*And a man is fighting mad,*

*Something drops from eyes long blind,*

*He recovers his whole mind,*

*For an instant stands at ease,*

~~*and*~~ *his heart's*

*Laughs aloud* ~~*and seems*~~ *at peace.*

*Even the wisest man grows tense*

*With some sort of violence*

*Before he can accomplish fate*

*Know his work or choose his mate*

~~*So what's the odds if war must come*~~

~~*From Moscow, from Berlin, or Rome.*~~

~~*From London, Moscow, Berlin, Rome.*~~

*So*

~~*Let children should an aeroplane*~~

~~*Some neighbouring city pavement stain,*~~

~~*Or Should the deafening cannon sound*~~

The 'cannon' that gave Yeats so much trouble on Ff. 7*r* and 8*r* is superseded by the more modern and appropriate 'rifle'. The grave-diggers must surely be related to those in *Hamlet*, a play that we know to have been in his mind at this time as the Prince is twice mentioned in the poem 'Lapis Lazuli'. The image of

\* Indicates a line inserted, at the pointing of an arrow, from the top of the page.

them burying their dead in the *anima mundi* appears also in *On the Boiler* which Yeats was writing at about this time:

No educated man to-day accepts the objective matter and space of popular science, and yet deductions made by those who believed in both dominate the world . . . [and] . . . compel denial of the immortality of the soul by hiding from the mass of the people that the grave diggers have no place to bury us but in the human mind.[8]

The same train of thought that led Yeats to entitle this poem 'Creed' and begin it 'I believe' prompts him to introduce section II with John Mitchel's terrible parody of the sentence from the Order for Evening Prayer; 'Give us peace in our time, O Lord.' Mitchel* wrote in his *Jail Journal*: 'Give us war in our time, O Lord.'[9] Yeats, of course, takes this plea for conflict out of its nationalistic context and uses it to support his philosophic doctrine. At the foot of this page he crosses out his reference to an impending international conflict, perhaps lest this distract attention from the dominant philosophic meaning.

F. 11r follows on directly from F. 10r:

*Clasp*

~~*Lay hand in hand and*~~

~~*and*~~

~~*Clasp their hands & dance a ro in a round.*~~

*or*

*The passing moment makes it sweet*

*When male & female organ meet*

*at*

*Or enemy looks ~~on~~ enemy,*

*Timeless man's this honey bee.*

---

* 1815–75: he founded *United Irishmen*, was tried for sedition and transported, but returned to Ireland and became an M.P.

~~III~~ IV

Poet ~~s~~ & sculptor ~~s~~ do the work,
    the
Nor let ~~the~~ modish painter ~~s~~ shirk
    his ~~their~~
What ~~his~~ great forefathers did,
Bring the soul of man to God
Make him fill the cradles right.

Measurement began our might.
Forms a stark Egyptian thought,
Forms that gentler Phideas wrought.

Michael Angelo left a proof
On the Sistine chapel roof
    but half awakened
Where ~~his homo-sexual~~ Adam
Can disturb globe-trotting madam
Till her bowels are in heat,
    ~~a~~
~~That this purpose had been set~~   Proof what purpose had been set
Before the secret working ~~min~~ mind:
Profane perfection of man kind.
Quatro cento put in paint
On backgrounds for a God or saint,

Here, for the first time, Yeats names the specific audience he has
in mind: 'Poet & sculptor do the work, Nor let the modish
painter shirk What his great forefathers did.' An artist is passing
on the tenets of his artistic creed to the artists who will follow

him. Though I use the word 'artist' in its widest sense, it should be remembered that not only were Yeats's father and brother celebrated painters, but that he himself at one time went to art school. So now, tracing the history of proportion in the visual arts from the ancient Egyptians to the Greeks to Michael Angelo, he returns to a theme already handled in 'Michael Robartes and the Dancer' and the last stanza of 'Long-legged Fly':

> That girls at puberty may find
> The first Adam in their thought,
> Shut the door of the Pope's chapel,
> Keep those children out.
> There on the scaffolding reclines
> Michael Angelo.

In short, Yeats sees it as an artist's duty to provide true heroic and sexual images to kindle the imagination of generations to come. He it is who must 'Bring the soul of man to God, Make him fill the cradles right'. The curious image of the cradles is also found in the drafts – though not the final version – of 'In Memory of Eva Gore-Booth and Con Markiewicz' as:

> For widow Nature still
> Has those cradles left to fill.[10]

On F. 12r Yeats outlines the history of art, as applicable to his 'system', from the Quattrocento painters to those of the English Romantic period.

> *Gardens where a soul's at ease;*
>
> *The soul's perfection is from peace;*
>
> *Where everything that meets the eye,*
>
> *Flowers & grass & cloudless sky*
>
> *Resembles forms that are or seem*
>
> *When sleepers wake & yet still dream*
>
> *And when it's vanished still declare*

*~~That~~ with only bed & bed stead there*

*That heaven had opened.*

                              *run*
                    *Gyres ran on:*
          *When that greater dream*
          *~~And all man's holiest thought~~ had gone,*

                              *and*
          *Calvert & Palmer, Wilson, Claude*
             *Prepared*
          *~~Made~~ a rest for the people of God*

          *Palmer's phrase but after that*

          *Confusion fell upon our thought*


                         *V*

          *Irish poets learn your trade,*

          *Sing whatever is well made,*

          *Scorn the sort now growing up,*

          *All out of shape from toe to ~~±~~ top*

          *Their unremembering hearts & heads*

          *Base born products of base beds,*

          *Sing the peasantry & then*

          *hardriding country gentlemen,*

It is interesting to see him change the line 'And all man's holiest thought had gone' to 'When that greater dream had gone'. I suspect he was loth to suggest that medieval Christianity had a monopoly of 'man's holiest thought'. Yeats almost certainly came to be acquainted with the work of Calvert and Palmer while preparing his 1893 edition of *The Poems of William Blake*.

At one time we know he considered writing a book on Calvert.
Raymond Lister writes that

> Calvert's engravings, and to a lesser extent his pictures, depict
> a symbolic world, a place of dreamy peacefulness. . . . It is a
> world perceived by Yeats, who, apropos of Blake's wood-
> engravings for Thornton's *Virgil*, wrote:
> '. . . always in his [Blake's] boys and girls walking or dancing on
> smooth grass and in golden light, as in pastoral scenes cut upon
> wood or copper by his disciples Palmer and Calvert, one notices
> the peaceful Swedenborgian heaven.'[11]

A heaven indeed, but hardly a Christian one. Calvert, like
Yeats, could never bring himself to accept Christianity in its
entirety.[12]

> Calvert & Palmer, Wilson and Claude
> Prepared a rest for the people of God
> Palmer's phrase

As with the prayer ascribed to John Mitchel at the start of section
III, Yeats does not quote 'Palmer's phrase' exactly. In fact Palmer
had said that Blake's work shows us 'the drawing aside of the
fleshly curtain and the glimpse which all the most holy, studious
saints and sages[13] have enjoyed of that rest which remaineth to
the people of God'.[14] Yeats had quoted this passage in 1896 in his
essay entitled 'William Blake and his Illustrations to the *Divine
Comedy*'.[15]

   Whereas sections I and III of 'Under Ben Bulben' open with a
general audience directly addressed ('Swear by what the sages
spoke' and 'You that Mitchel's prayer have heard'), section IV is
more specific ('Poet and sculptor, do the work,'); and section V
more specific still ('Irish poets, learn your trade,'). As might
have been expected, his last message is for the poets: let them
preserve order, proportion, and good craftsmanship. His own
language changes subtly here; becomes less colloquial, more
measured and literary. This is typified by the rhetorical repetition
of the imperative 'Sing' – a bardic, classical usage as in Virgil's
*Arma virumque cano*. The 'last romantic' bids his successors

praise peasant and country gentleman, monk, drunkard, and
aristocrat; figures beyond the perimeter of unromantic, bourgeois
society.

F. 13r concludes the complete verse draft.

> *The holiness of monks & after*
>
> *Porter drinkers randy laughter;*
>
> *Sing the lords and ladies gay*
>
> *That were beaten into the clay*
>
> *Through seven heroic centuries*
>     *Cast your mind*
> ~~*Set your thought*~~ *on other days*
>
> *That we in coming days may be*
>
> *Still the indomitable ~~Irishry~~ Irishry.*

> *VI*
>
>      *bare*
> *Under Benbulben's ~~Western~~ head*
>
> *In Drumcliff Churchyard Yeats is laid*
>     *ancestor*
> *An ~~cestor~~ was rector there*
>
> *Long years ago, a church stands near*
>      *side*
> *By the road an ancient cross.*
>         *~~to lie about our loss~~ braggs of ~~the country's~~ loss*
> *No marble ~~lies public man, lies lie about man's~~ loss,*
>                 *the braggs of ~~the country's~~ loss*
> *On limestone quarried near ~~that~~ spot Ireland's loss*
> *By his command these words are cut*
>        *Cast a cold eye*

> *On life, on death;*
>
> *Horse man pass by.*
>
> ## *W B Y*
>
> *Sept 4*
>
> *1938*

The lines 'Sing the lords and ladies gay That were beaten into the clay' suggest the influence – no doubt subconscious – of Frank O'Connor's translation 'Kilcash': 'The earls, the lady, the people Beaten into the clay.'[16] Yeats had earlier echoed O'Connor's translation in 'The Curse of Cromwell' ('The lovers and the dancers are beaten into the clay'), a poem that he published in his Cuala *Broadsides* in August 1937, three months after 'Kilcash' had appeared in the same series. O'Connor has written that the translation 'was one of [Yeats's] favourite poems, and there is a good bit of his work in it'.[17]

We see from this page that section VI gave Yeats trouble. Ben Bulben, whose back he so often climbed 'in boyhood . . . with rod and fly, Or the humbler worm', had set the scene at the start of the poem; and to this mountain at life's end and poem's end he returns. The cyclic movement that dominated his later thought brings him to cross and churchyard where his great-grandfather, the Reverend John Yeats, was rector:

> He that in Sligo at Drumcliff
> Set up the old stone Cross,
> That red-headed rector in County Down,
> A good man on a horse.

While Lister is correct in saying that Yeats 'could never bring himself to accept Christianity in its entirety',[18] 'Under Ben Bulben' shows how deeply Christian history and images had interpenetrated his thought. In the last analysis, however, he has the courage of his pagan convictions. His epitaph is addressed to a horseman who may be one of the Sidhe, or one of the 'Hard-riding country gentlemen'; either the living or the dead – or both.

> Cast a cold eye
> On life, on death;
> Horse man pass by.

The line 'Draw rein, draw breath' has been dropped: why?
Only the living draw breath and Yeats's omission of these
beautifully balanced imperatives suggests that he had a spiritual
horseman in mind, or at any rate wanted to preserve the ambiguity.[19] Drumcliffe churchyard may be seen as a symbolic
crossroads, for there the Sligo–Lissadell road that carries its
'hard-riding country gentlemen' intersects at right angles with
the route of the 'fierce horsemen' who ride 'from mountain to
mountain', from Knocknarea to Ben Bulben.[20]

   This at first sight may seem a surprising epitaph for a poet who
could elsewhere

> pray – for fashion's word is out
> And prayer comes round again –
> That I may seem, though I die old,
> A foolish, passionate man.

The paradox is stated more explicitly in the closing lines of 'The
Fisherman', where the poet imagined

> A man who does not exist,
> A man who is but a dream;
> And cried, 'Before I am old
> I shall have written him one
> Poem maybe as cold
> And passionate as the dawn.'

In his drafts of 'The Statues' he had written of 'cold marble forms'
and 'doric marble cold as moon or star',[21] but (in the words of
the finished poem)

> boys and girls, pale from the imagined love
> Of solitary beds, knew what they were,
> That passion could bring character enough . . .

Great statues, great paintings – all time-resisting works of art –
are in their technical perfection 'cold', but at the same time products of an artist's passionate integrity. By 'Cast a cold eye'
Yeats means on one level (of many) in this context, I believe, not
so much a passionless as an artist's discerning eye; one – like his

own – fixed equally on the natural and supernatural, 'On life, on death'. The ghostly horsemen of the Sidhe are said in section 1 of the poem to have won 'completeness of their passions' and this, Yeats was convinced, only the dead could do. To win complete-ness of one's passions, however, is not to reject them. Again, if he was addressing a phantom, its eye might well be described as cold.

The lines immediately preceding the epitaph, which we can see Yeats struggling over on F. 13r, he recasts on F. 12v:

> *A century ago, a church stands near*
>
> *By the roadside an ancient cross.*
>
> *No marble, no conventional phrase*
>
> *On limestone quarried near the spot*
>
> *By his command etc*

The first line here moves one stage further from its final form of 'Long years ago, a church stands near': while the third line reaches its final form. 'No marble, no conventional phrase' is much more appropriate than 'No marble brags of Ireland's loss', which has more than a hint of a forced rhyme.

It will by now be clear that the fourth phase of the poem's composition – the typescript stage – saw fewer changes than any other. Of the three typescripts, each of three pages, I consider only that which from its alterations I deduce to be the last. I therefore pass over Ff. 14r to 19r and come to F. 20r, on which the following lines differ from the previous manuscript drafts. (I give the line numbers of the final text.)

| | |
|---|---|
| Line 4. | Spoke and set all the cock crow. |
| | *becomes* |
| | Spoke and set all the cocks a-crow. |
| Lines 5–9. | Swear by horseman, swear by women, |
| | Complexions lift above the human, |
| | That long visaged company |
| | That airs an immortality |
| | Completeness in their passions won. |

*become*
Swear by those horsemen, by those women,
Complexion and form prove superhuman,
That pale, long visaged company
That airs an immortality
Completeness of their passions won;

Line 18.     ... rifle knock ...
             *becomes*
             ... rifle knocks ...

Line 21.     ... toil be long
             *becomes*
             ... toil is long

Line 23 – originally a rhetorical question –

             Where can they lay their buried men?
             *becomes*
             They but thrust their buried men

Line 30.     He recovers his whole mind,
             *becomes*
             He completes his partial mind,

F. 21r: Line 45.   Michael Angelo ...
             *becomes*
             Michaelangelo ...

Line 50.     Proof what purpose had been set
             *becomes*
             Proof that there's a purpose set

Line 64.     Calvert & Palmer, Wilson, and Claude
             *becomes*
             Calvert and Wilson, Blake and Claude

F. 22r: Line 84.   ... Benbulben's head
             *becomes*
             ... Ben Bulben's head

Line 87.     A century ago, ...
             *becomes*
             Long years ago; ...

Line 88.     By the roadside ...
             *becomes*
             By the road ...

This typescript is undated, but on an earlier one Yeats has set below his initials: 'Correct. Sept 23'.

The version of 'Under Ben Bulben' that Yeats, on his last night in Dublin, read to Higgins would presumably be that of the final typescript. The alterations that Mrs Yeats received from her husband on the day before he died might have been that to line 4, whereby '. . . set all the cocks a-crow' became '. . . set the cocks a-crow'; and that to line 8, whereby '. . . airs an immortality, became '. . . air in immortality'. The only other changes between typescript and final text are minor improvements of spelling and punctuation, which were probably made by Mrs Yeats or a publisher rather than by Yeats himself.

'Under Ben Bulben' is a fitting conclusion to the life and work of a poet whose lifelong concern was to 'hammer [his] thoughts into unity'. It brings full circle the poetic career of one for whom the circle was a dominant symbol. The themes and interests of his early manhood – Irish folk-lore and history, the occult, Shelley, Blake, and the English Romantic painters of the late nineteenth century – fit like tessarae into the mosaic pattern of his later 'system'. As Michael Angelo, though dead, continues to influence the living with heroic images 'On the Sistine Chapel roof', so Yeats still speaks from 'Under Ben Bulben'.

## NOTES

1. Joseph Hone, *W. B. Yeats, 1865–1939* (1962) p. 477.
2. *The Letters of W. B. Yeats* ed. Allan Wade (1954) p. 913.
3. See Jon Stallworthy, 'Two of Yeats's Last Poems', in *A Review of English Literature*, IV 3 (1963) 55 ff.
4. *Collected Plays of W. B. Yeats* (1953) p. 202.
5. Richard Ellmann, *The Identity of Yeats* (1954) p. 8.
6. *On the Boiler* (Dublin, 1939) p. 37.
7. *The Variorum Edition of the Poems of W. B. Yeats*, ed. Peter Allt and Russell K. Alspach (New York and London, 1957) p. 802.
8. *On the Boiler*, p. 26.
9. *Jail Journal, or Five Years in British Prisons* (Glasgow, 1856) p. 315.

10. See Jon Stallworthy, *Between the Lines: W. B. Yeats's Poetry in the Making* (1963) p. 171.

11. *Explorations* (1962) p. 44.

12. 'W. B. Yeats and Edward Calvert', in *The Irish Book*, II 3/4 (1963) p. 75.

13. Compare Yeats's interchange of these nouns in his drafts of the first line of 'Under Ben Bulben'.

14. A. H. Palmer, *Life and Letters of Samuel Palmer* (1892) p. 16. The phrase, in fact, is first found in St Paul's Epistle to the Hebrews IV 9: 'There remaineth therefore a rest to the people of God.'

15. *Essays and Introductions* (1961) p. 125.

16. *The Wild Bird's Nest: Poems from the Irish* (Dublin, 1932) p. 24.

17. Frank O'Conner, *Kings, Lords, & Commons* (1959) p. 100.

18. Loc. cit.

19. My view that this omission is necessary and an improvement supersedes a contrary opinion in *Between the Lines: W. B. Yeats's Poetry in the Making*, p. 6.

20. I am indebted to Dr Oliver Edwards for this suggestion.

21. Jon Stallworthy, 'Two of Yeats's Last Poems', in *A Review of English Literature*, IV 3 (1963) 56, 58.

*Peter Ure*

*PURGATORY* (1963)*

' "AND another time I saw Purgatory. It seemed to be in a level place, and no walls around it, but it all in one bright blaze, and the souls standing in it. And they suffer near as much as in Hell, only there are no devils with them there, and they have the hope of Heaven." ' So spoke the old Galway villager, commemorated in *The Celtic Twilight*, 'who can see nothing but wickedness. Some think him very holy, and others think him a little crazed'. For his last play on this theme Yeats chose an image which goes back to his younger years, to Castle Dargan, and the 'ruined castle lit up'.[1] From a ghost-story that Yeats himself told, about a family ruined by drink, a castle burnt down, and an 'ashen woman' repeatedly seen by her descendants living through her act of suicide, Yeats borrowed other main themes for *Purgatory*,[2] weaving the diffuseness of the old story into a tight dramatic narrative. The shades in this play, haunting the ruined mansion, are nearer to the audience than the mythological and historical figures of Dermot, Dervorgilla, and Swift, because they derive from the popular tale.

The scene is 'a ruined house and a bare tree in the back ground'.[3] A wandering pedlar and his bastard son stand in the moonlight before the ruin, while the old man reveals its history to the boy. In this house the pedlar had been born, the son of a great lady who had married a drunken groom. After his wife's death in child-birth, the groom had squandered the estate, but his son had been taught to read and had got a haphazard education. The boy listens enviously to the tale of riches and learning.

* This and the following essay are extracts taken from *Yeats the Playwright: A Commentary on Character and Design in the Major Plays*, which was first published in 1963.

When the old man was sixteen, the groom had burned down the house in a drunken frenzy and his son had stabbed him to death in the ruins and fled to escape trial. When this exposition is finished, the action begins.

It is the anniversary of the mother's wedding-night. Her remorseful shade must act the occasion through again and again, tortured by her knowledge of the ruinous consequences of her marriage. The old man hears the hoof-beats of the bridegroom's horse on the gravelled drive, and the figure of the bride appears at a lighted window of the ruin. The boy his son, meanwhile, can see and hear nothing, and mockingly accuses the old man of madness. A long speech from the old man divides the play into two portions, as he describes the wedding-night, cries out vainly to his mother's shade 'Do not let him touch you!', and meditates on the mystery of her re-enactment of the sexual act. But his meditation is interrupted by the boy, who had seized the chance of stealing the bag of money from the pedlar's pack and is making off with it. The catastrophe approaches in intensifying violence.

They struggle for the money, which is scattered on the ground, and the boy threatens to kill his father. While this is going on, the figure of the bridegroom appears at the window, leaning there like 'a tired beast'. The boy can see this apparition;* as, filled with horror, he hides his eyes, the old man stabs him to death. The window in which the apparition stands now darkens, and it seems as if the phantom, the 'nothing' that is the 'impression on my mother's mind', has been exorcized. Another stage-effect (which is seen to be equally ironic when the true catastrophe occurs) follows: the dry tree that emblematized when it was green the rich life of the prosperous family now appears bathed in white light on the darkened stage. As the old man looks at it standing there 'like a purified soul' he explains why he killed the boy. It was to put an end to the chain of consequence, the

* The boy can see this second apparition perhaps because he, like his grandfather the groom, represents the evil, degenerate element in the family-story. He cannot see the apparition of his grandmother because his evil nature cannot 'dramatize' it.

polluted blood that would have 'Begot, and passed pollution on'.
As he bends to pick up the scattered money, the bridegroom's
hoof-beats are heard again. The old man realizes in despair that
the dream of the dead woman cannot come to an end:

> Twice a murderer and all for nothing,
> And she must animate that dead night
> Not once but many times!

The play ends with his prayer to God to release the tormented
soul from its dream, for 'Mankind can do no more'.

In this play, the conscience of the shade compels her to re-
enact her transgression at that moment when it initiated the chain
of consequence that fills her with remorse: the begetting of a
child. This is the knot the old man strives to cut. The souls in
Purgatory, he says, that 'come back to habitations and familiar
spots'

> know at last
> The consequence of those transgressions
> Whether upon others or upon themselves;
> Upon others, others may bring help,
> For when the consequence is at an end
> The dream must end; upon themselves,
> There is no help but in themselves
> And in the mercy of God.

The consequence of her crime upon 'others' that is most
vividly presented in the play is the dynastic one, represented
especially by the character of the boy. He is ignorant, amoral,
thieving, a potential parricide, and – it is hinted – lecher. The
boy, then, is to be killed, to be 'exorcized' like the grandfather,
and the degenerate stock wiped out. Otherwise, he will repeat
the pattern of his polluted father's career, which began at sixteen,
the boy's age, with the murder of the groom, and went on to the
begetting of a bastard 'Upon a tinker's daughter in a ditch'. And
so on to generations unborn. When the boy is killed, the mother's
spirit is momentarily assuaged. This is emblematized by the
tree's becoming 'like a purified soul';

> All cold, sweet, glistening light.
> Dear mother, the window is dark again,

> But you are in the light because
> I finished all that consequence.*

But, after the death of the boy, there yet remains the consequence of the crime 'upon themselves'. This is also a ground of
the remorse that the spirit suffers. The crime that the woman
committed upon herself was the fouling of her own nature by
lust, as the old man explains in the central speech of the play
when he imagines the bridal night:

> She has gone down to open the door.
> This night she is no better than her man
> And does not mind that he is half drunk,
> She is mad about him. They mount the stairs,
> She brings him into her own chamber . . .

This, and the meditation that follows, is an extremely crucial part
of the play, to which I shall return. For the moment, it must be
clear to the audience that into *this* re-enactment no action of the
old man, of the living 'others', can possibly enter in order to cut
its knot. The point is stressed by the old man's ineffectual cry
'Do not let him touch you! . . . Deaf! Both deaf!' The woman
cannot be freed from that aspect of her crime which is equivalent
to her self-degradation. For this act, even after death, brings with
it pleasure as well as remorse, as the old man suggests. The remorseful spirit must, in order to be free of it, repeat, explore, or
dream through the crime which it committed during life; but in

---

* The tree is a family-'tree' and also stands for the condition of the
shade's soul. Fifty years ago it had 'Green leaves, ripe leaves, leaves
thick as butter, Fat greasy life'. Then it was blasted and became the
bare tree of the play, which resembles the image of the tree seen in the
bitter glass held up by demons before the woman who barters her
beauty in 'The Two Trees'. Through its branches fly the 'ravens of
unresting thought':

> For there a fatal image grows
> That the stormy night receives,
> Roots half-hidden under snows,
> Broken boughs and blackened leaves.
> For all things turn to barrenness
> In the dim glass the demons hold.
>                         (*Variorum Edition*, p. 135)

this case the renewal of the act, because of the nature of the act, renews the self-degrading pleasure that accompanied it. Thus the very consequence from which release is sought – self-degradation – is entailed upon the mother's spirit each time she lives through her transgression. It is as pretty an entanglement as Yeats ever devised. There is none like it in *A Vision*, perhaps because he had not yet seen, when he wrote that work, into what complexities his notion of the dead who are obliged to live through their transgressions might be developed if only the transgressions were complicated enough. The case is one, as the old man at length perceives, which only the 'mercy of God' can solve. Hence his final prayer. Yeats – can it be said? – has at last found a use for God. He is called in because the Yeatsian dead can no longer manage by themselves, so extraordinary has their private purgatory become. There is no God amongst the discarnate spirits of *A Vision*.

The subject of *Purgatory* is an extension of one that had been touched upon in *The Dreaming of the Bones*. Both plays are concerned with the remorse of the dead, and in the earlier one there is a hint that the living, the 'others' who suffer the consequences of the crimes of the dead, may help them. In *The Dreaming of the Bones* the soldier's forgiveness might have assuaged the torment of Dermot and Dervorgilla. The whole subject of *Purgatory* is such an assuagement, which is indeed accomplished, although under the conditions making for final frustration that have just been examined. That in this play the act of intervention is a murder, not pardon, is necessitated by the story chosen. It affords a measure of the difference between the finished, melancholy and somewhat self-conscious beauty of *The Dreaming of the Bones* and the squalor, sexuality and violence of *Purgatory*.

The development on this scale of a theme which *The Dreaming of the Bones* merely sketches meant that Yeats had to find a fresh dramatic form. The making of a self-subsistent image of phantasmic suffering such as he gives us in *The Dreaming of the Bones* and at the centre of *The Words upon the Window-pane* can no longer be his aim. His subject, which is now chiefly about an attempt at intervention by the living in the life of the dead,

requires that he concern himself with the living, with the unfinished life, not with the intense rendering of an unearthly
suffering. The story told in *Purgatory* is one that leaves on the
ears of the audience a cry reaching outside the play to God,
unlike the final words of both *The Dreaming of the Bones* and *The
Words upon the Window-pane*, which fold the plays back upon
themselves so that they contemplate their own stories. *Purgatory*
is an image deliberately left incomplete, a human image, rather
than one that shows the dead trapped in the vortex of their own
suffering. Compared with the earlier plays, it is, as it were,
slewed round; ghosts and men have exchanged positions. In
*Purgatory* the man is what we see first, and beyond and through
him the voiceless shades pose in a window like lantern-slides
upon which he discourses. This is very different from *The
Dreaming of the Bones*, where Dermot and Dervorgilla dominate
a human being whose representative status matters more than his
individuality, and from *The Words upon the Window-pane*, where
Mrs Henderson, asleep in her chair, mediates to us the full force
of the passionate shade. In *Purgatory* we are deeply engaged
with the old man.

One of his functions is to tell us what the apparitions mean and
to what realm they belong. He thus performs the task allotted to
Dr Trench in *The Words upon the Window-pane* and to the con-
versation between the soldier and the lovers about the different
kinds of hauntings in the first portion of *The Dreaming of the
Bones*. His speech, therefore, part of which I have quoted on
page 247, explains all that the spectator needs to know about the
condition of the dead in the play. But it could not have been
spoken by an entirely naturalistic character. If the old man really
'knew' all that, he would not have acted as he does, or at least
would not have been surprised that his action was ultimately
without effect in releasing his mother's shade from its dream.
This is one of those carelessnesses about orthodox realism that
also occur in *The Death of Cuchulain* and convey, however
mysteriously, a sense of theatrical power. This does not mean
that the old man and his whole situation are not sharply in-
dividualized with the aid of as much graphic detail as the minia-

ture size of the play permits. His description of the groom's murder,[4] for example, carries conviction: just so might the brutal country tragedy have happened. When the old man speaks of it, possessed though his mind is with heredity and phantoms, he looks round to make sure that no one can overhear, and similarly, when he kills the boy, he makes certain that nobody, except the phantom groom, is watching.

There are things, then, which the old man both 'knows' and does not *know*, and what he does not *know*, or does not fully understand, is an important element in his tragedy. He has learning, which he obtained in spite of his polluted origin, and he cherishes the things of learning and ancestral beauty. He speaks of the 'great people' of the old estate, their love of the demesne and the flowering trees that were cut down by the degenerate inheritor, and of his own education:

> some
> Half-loved me for my half of her:
> A gamekeeper's wife taught me to read,
> A Catholic curate taught me Latin.
> There were old books and books made fine
> By eighteenth-century French binding, books
> Modern and ancient, books by the ton.

But at a crucial moment this sort of learning becomes a crazy parody of itself. In the long central speech, during which the consummation of the fatal marriage is re-enacted, the old man tells the audience enough for them to understand the nature of the mother's self-degradation, the consequence that she commits upon herself; but he does not understand it himself.

> she must live
> Through everything in exact detail,
> Driven to it by remorse, and yet
> Can she renew the sexual act
> And find no pleasure in it, and if not,
> If pleasure and remorse must both be there,
> Which is the greater?
> I lack schooling.
> Go fetch Tertullian; he and I

> Will ravel all that problem out
> Whilst those two lie upon the mattress
> Begetting me.

The call for Tertullian is a kind of witless joke on his part.
F. A. C. Wilson's straight-faced comment that he 'refers to
Tertullian's treatise on the mixed nature of the soul, *de Anima*'s
seems to me to miss the point. The point is that the old man is
unable to relate what is happening with what as a character inside
the play's action he does not *know*, namely, that the dead

> know at last
> The consequence of those transgressions
> Whether upon others or upon themselves ...
> upon themselves,
> There is no help but in themselves
> And in the mercy of God.

If he were able to collate his two kinds of knowledge, which
being in a state of crazy half-knowledge he is not, he would
know his mother's condition to its depths; he would not suppose
that the killing of the boy could do more than momentarily
assuage her torment. This state of half-knowledge is his heredi-
tary condition entailed upon him by his polluted blood. It is his
tragic fate. It is that which engineers the catastrophe, just as
Cuchulain's movement of courage in *At the Hawk's Well* frus-
trates itself because of his fate. The old man, the son of a groom,
conceived in drunkenness, cannot be a sage, although there are
moments when he pathetically tries to behave like one.

All the old man's qualities are quartered with his vices in this
way. He acts to save his mother, but has brutalized his son, and
given him, as he tells him:

> the education that befits
> A bastard that a pedlar got
> Upon a tinker's daughter in a ditch.

He is capable of vision, but breaks away from it to struggle with
the boy for the bag of money. His past is like this, too: the gently

nurtured boy who killed his father and hid the body in the burning house. That he can say that he is 'a wretched foul old man' is
his noble trait, because it expresses his awareness of degradation,
which is not present in the boy his son yet further degenerated
from the stock; but it is also the truth.

The central figure is thus hereditarily endowed with worth
and vileness, and these are interlocked in his nature as Othello's
nobility is interlocked with his crime or Coriolanus's manhood
with his childishness. I think that we are meant to be aware of
this when we contemplate his final acts. He kills the boy in order
to break the links of consequence, but the act itself partakes of his
double nature. It is done by all that is good in him, but it is done
in the condition of half-knowledge necessitated by what he is,
and it is also a horrible crime. This last is true if I am right in
thinking that the dramatist did not mean us to regard it in a
coldly theoretical way simply as something done by the living
for the sake of the dead and therefore justifiable even if largely
ineffectual. The image of the father killing his son duplicates too
dreadfully the earlier image of the son killing the father; the knife
with which it is done is the same knife, the vile knife which 'cuts
my dinner', like the Blind Man's knife in *The Death of Cuchulain*;
the hand which drives it is the same hand:

> My father and my son on the same jack-knife!

'He stabs again and again', says the stage-direction. The act is a
crime because it explicitly shares features with the parricide
which, when he was sixteen, was the old man's first manifestation
in action of his tainted stock. The nursery-rhyme which he
chants as he murders the boy adds a special ghastliness. The
sacrifice turns out to be murder after all.

There is great irony in it, too. For this act, which is designed
to finish 'all that consequence', and indeed does so, is also a fresh
addition to the links of consequence. Instead of a lengthening
chain, it makes of them a circular band of horror, a wheel of fire:
the son kills the father, the father kills the son. And all this has
failed to break the suffering spirit's bondage. Thus the old man,
as this realization breaks upon him and he turns away from his

acts to pray, does rightly in that he prays for the living as well as
for the dead:

O God,
Release my mother's soul from its dream!
Mankind can do no more. Appease
The misery of the living and the remorse of the dead.

*Purgatory* is the most successful of Yeats's three attempts to
dramatize one stage of the progress of the soul from grave to
cradle, or from grave to beatitude. He chose the only one of the
visionary phases which could be adapted for human theatrical
life. The imagination that conceived the 'dreaming back' had
that much in common with the dramatic imagination. The purga-
torial state was made to fit forms so different from one another
as the Noh, the naturalistic play in prose, and a Shakespearian
tragedy in miniature.

There is room for another comment on the relation between
playwright and philosopher. In *The Words upon the Window-pane*
Yeats has suspended his own convictions for the play's sake, and
we are invited to put our own interpretation on what we have
seen. But the convictions remain there rigidly in the centre of the
play in the image of Swift's ghost and its suffering and re-enactment. This makes the rest of the play seem merely the scaffolding
for the central event, the mystery. The human observers are
grouped in a circle round the appalling, unreachable voice; the
construction of the play mirrors the arrangements for a séance,
or a revelation. As in *The Resurrection*, Yeats has turned the
tables upon the naturalistic drama by exploding it from inside;
from its shattered ruins there arises the terrible image of an
utterly different kind of life. But in *Purgatory* the convictions are
dissolved into the life of the protagonist; our attention is fixed
upon the old man's story and his divided nature. The dead of *A
Vision* and of the other plays live, although their condition is
vividly enough rendered, a schematic life, each in the appropriate
circle of their purgatory; but in the last play the old man's
attempt to break into the circle, driven by furious pity and by
jealous hatred of his own evil as embodied in his son, is his own
story and no ghost shares it.

## NOTES

1. *Autobiographies* (1926) p. 66; *Wheels and Butterflies* (1934) p. 37.
2. See Hone, *W. B. Yeats, 1865–1939* (1942) pp. 283–4.
3. *Last Poems and Plays* (1940) p. 97.
4. Ibid. p. 102.
5. *W. B. Yeats and Tradition* (1958) p. 152.

# Peter Ure

# THE DEATH OF CUCHULAIN (1963)

*The Death of Cuchulain* is based upon the version of the story contained in the last two chapters of Lady Gregory's *Cuchulain of Muirthemne*. It makes special use of three key-incidents in it: the war-goddess's device of a treacherous message, delivered by Cuchulain's mistress, to the beleaguered hero; the death itself against the 'pillar-stone west of the lake' on the plain of Muirthemne; and the lamentation of Emer, who 'took the head of Cuchulain in her hands, and she washed it clean, and put a silk cloth about it, and she held it to her breast; and she began to cry heavily over it'.[1]

Yeats wrote to Ethel Mannin in October, 1938:

Goethe said that the poet needs all philosophy but must keep it out of his work. I am writing a play on the death of Cuchulain, an episode or two from the old epic. My 'private philosophy' is there but there must be no sign of it; all must be like an old faery tale. It guided me to certain conclusions but I do not write it.[2]

I would draw a different inference from this passage than does F. A. C. Wilson who in his *W. B. Yeats and Tradition* has written at greater length on this play than any other scholar. It clearly affirms the continuing primacy, so far as the Cuchulain plays are concerned, of a theatrical rather than a symbolist strategy. Yeats still desires to 'show events' and still needs that roomful of people sharing one lofty emotion,[3] not puzzled by being presented with a chart they cannot decipher. He is ready, as in the closing song of *The Only Jealousy*, to weight his style and give strength to his imagery with obscure intimations of the philosophy. He does so, though, only when this is theatrically appropriate, as it is in this play for the song of the harlot and the beggar-man. This is detached from the play in the manner of the Noh choruses. It leads away from the event and generalizes the emotion so that the curtain is folded upon a distancing echo, the stage empty and ready to fade into silence. But the song is not the key to the play, which remains stubbornly a matter of interlocked character and plot dramatically realized, and Mr Wilson, for all his efforts, cannot make it look as if it were. It is only by means of a formidably selective treatment of it that he is able to reach his verdict that 'the play, a play of rejoicing, centres about [Cuchulain's] transfiguration'.[4] This misrepresents the structure of a play in which I see not transfiguration, and certainly not rejoicing – though there is a kind of grim joy in it – but the death of the hero seen as the final irony of his fate.

When Eithne Inguba enters (playing the role assigned to Niamh in Lady Gregory's version) she tells him that she has been charged by Emer to urge him to go forth at once and do battle with the troops of Maeve. Cuchulain is ready, but he notices that Eithne carries a letter in her hand. It is from Emer, and when he reads it he finds that she has written something quite different:

> I am not to move
> Until to-morrow morning, for, if now,
> I must face odds no man can face and live.[5]

In the morning Conall will come to his aid. The discrepancy is explained a few moments later when the Morrigu, goddess of war, appears and stands silently between the pair. Eithne realizes that when she spoke she had been bewitched into acting as the mouthpiece of the goddess, who wishes to destroy Cuchulain. Out of this situation the first episode develops.

Eithne, restored to her faithful self after the trance of deception, cannot save Cuchulain, who is blind to his fate. Although he has Emer's true message, his heart is set upon the grand, heroical gesture, the fight in the face of treachery and against great odds. This, indeed, is the only right way for a hero of his kind to die, unless he is caught up to heaven by the gods:

> I much prefer
> Your own unwritten words. I am for the fight,

I                                                                S.Y.L.P.

> I and my handful are set upon the fight;
> We have faced great odds before, a straw decided.

Although, by describing Maeve and the Morrigu, Eithne gives him the unmistakable clue that magic is at work, he does not see it, but ascribes the false message to what he thinks is her natural desire to get rid of a lover of whom she is tired. He exclaims in scorn:

> A woman that has an eye in the middle of her forehead!
> A woman that is headed like a crow!

All this, he implies, is fabulous nonsense. But had he not chosen to be blind, he would have recognized the baleful stigmata of the goddess. Despite his conviction that Eithne has sought to betray him, he adopts a role of heroic magnanimity towards her, pointing out how natural her behaviour is in a mistress who longs for a younger man, and how unsurprising, since she failed him in another great crisis, when it was his wife who saved him from the sea. The irony is intensified by his failure to understand that that is precisely what Eithne is trying to do now. Eithne, in despair, accuses him of wanting to die:

> You're not the man I loved,
> That violent man forgave no treachery.
> If, thinking what you think, you can forgive,
> It is because you are about to die.

But he mistakes her horror for exultation at the prospect:

> Spoken too loudly and too near the door;
> Speak low if you would speak about my death,
> Or not in that strange voice exulting in it.
> Who knows what ears listen behind the door?

Eithne cries that, if the servants are listening, at least they won't indulge in this disgusting charade of forgiveness; they have what Cuchulain seems to have lost, 'the passion necessary to life'. When he is dead she will denounce herself for treachery to the 'cooks, scullions, armourers, bed-makers, and messengers'. They are not heroes blinded by their own stories; they will put her to death

> So that my shade can stand among the shades
> And greet your shade and prove it is no traitor.

Cuchulain, unconvinced, answers 'Women have spoken so, plotting a man's death', and his last act before he goes to battle is to ensure that Eithne is drugged in order to prevent her condemning herself, and to charge a servant to 'protect her life As if it were your own'.

It has been necessary to follow the scene in this detailed way in order to show why I cannot see in the episode any sign of a Cuchulain who goes to his last battle in bitterness of heart at Eithne's defection and 'because the death-wish has come upon him'.[6] We have, instead, a dramatization of the reckless energy of the hero, seeking glory in a fight against the odds and behaving with generous forbearance to the woman whom he thinks has tried to bring about his death. Cuchulain of course acknowledges that he may perish in the battle, but he is not, like Lady Gregory's hero, ready to say: 'there is no reason for me to care for my life from this out, for my time is at an end'.[7] That is not the feeling of the scene at all. The 'pardon' granted to Eithne – indeed, the whole elaborate and intimate scene with her – is amongst the material that Yeats did not find in his source and is intended to enhance his portrait of the great-souled man.

The irony, plain to be seen by the audience, derives from the tangle of misunderstandings that is netted about these fine attitudes and drags the hero down. Because his eyes are dazzled by the vision of heroic strife, he cannot recognize the goddess of death standing before him, who makes a doom out of the adventure. Nor can he recognize the faithfulness of Eithne, who has to suffer the worst of horrors in being forgiven for a crime which she has not committed. Cuchulain's end is being determined by his own desire and by his fixed interpretation of his hero's role. The Morrigu is the presiding deity of the play (she claims later to have 'arranged the dance', the dance of death that the drama is, and Emer's dance of mourning that follows it); but, although she presides over the sequences of mortality, she does not directly implement them. Her false message is quickly seen for what it is, even by Cuchulain, who is otherwise incapable of distinguishing the false from the true. Yet plainly, Yeats seems to imply, the hero blinded by the vision of his story, tangled in error and giving those who love him bitter pain, still astonishes us with his majesty.

What is done to this majesty when Cuchulain comes to the moment of dying? The second part of the play is constructed of two antithetical episodes, and the second of these continually looks back towards the first. Cuchulain re-enters, wounded to death. He is followed by Aoife, who has come to kill him, and who helps him to bind himself to the standing-stone so that he may die, like Vespasian and Bussy d'Ambois, upon his feet. The intensely moving dialogue between the masterful, aged Aoife, whose cruelty is full of reminiscent wonder, and Cuchulain, whose voice and rhythms have stilled and melted into the weakness and confusion of the dying, slowly shapes a pattern in which the tragedies of Baile's strand and the hawk's well are remembered. The old story of love mixed with hatred, frustration and tragic error builds up towards what is plainly its one right ending – that Aoife should at last revenge upon his father the death of Conlaoch. Cuchulain admits that she has 'the right to kill me'. 'You have the right', he repeats, and her purpose remains unaltered despite all that they remember of their common history.

But this mounting tension is suddenly diverted; the pattern, just as it is about to become complete, is suddenly abandoned and rubbed out. Aoife's leaving the stage is contrived, awkward, and feebly explained. This is a master-stroke which draws attention to what is being done by the dramatist. It reminds us, with some boldness, as does Shakespeare's occasional use of the technical terms of dramaturgy, that we are in the theatre:

> Somebody comes,
> Some countryman, and when he finds you here,
> And none to protect him, will be terrified.
> I will keep out of his sight, for I have things
> That I must ask questions on before I kill you.

A fine reason for a fine queen to give for the suspension of so vital – or so mortal – a pattern! The Blind Man, who enters now, belongs to that part of the Cuchulain story that owns to ironic commentary on the doings of these great ones:

> Somebody said that I was in Maeve's tent,
> And somebody else, a big man by his voice,
> That if I brought Cuchulain's head in a bag
> I would be given twelve pennies; I had the bag
> To carry what I get at kitchen doors,
> Somebody told me how to find the place;
> I thought it would have taken till the night,
> But this has been my lucky day.

The clown's 'lucky day' is the day on which the hero dies. This, like the final episode in *On Baile's Strand*, is a deliberate trailing of the story in the refuse-dump of 'The Circus Animals' Desertion', the foul rag-and-bone shop of the heart. Cuchulain's own comment is almost his last comment on the heroic adventure, and a total denial of all its glorious rationale:

> Twelve pennies! What better reason for killing a man?

This is an acceptance, but it is not a transfiguration, and Aoife who had all the reason in the heroic world for killing Cuchulain is cheated. The story in which revenge would have meaningfully completed work, life, and death is carefully built up but does not resolve into its climax; the actual ending runs against it. Such is the construction of the play's second part, and it embodies a resounding irony. This is heard again in Cuchulain's vision of his soul after death ('a soft feathery shape . . . a strange shape for the soul / Of a great fighting man'), and in the juxtaposition of our last glimpse of the heroic woman (Emer, as she dances before the severed heads – an episode very dependent upon Lady Gregory's account) with that of the harlot-musician from the street fair.

*The Death of Cuchulain* is the most majestically designed and the most perfect of the five plays.* Yeats has moved a long way from the altogether more obscurely rendered antinomies of *On Baile's Strand*. In the last play he contrived more explicitly than

* On the life and death of Cuchulain [*Editor's note*].

ever before, and with a bold disregard for the timider realisms which it is not absurd to compare with the methods of Shakespeare's last plays, the acting out of the ironies attendant upon the hero's nature and fate. This is done by the characteristic Yeatsian method, which has operated in all the plays, of building up episode against episode and character against character so that the antitheses they form permit the ironic inference to be drawn, or culminate in a moment of revealingly double-natured action: the heroic decision that is also a mistaking (*On Baile's Strand, The Death of Cuchulain*), the love or courage whose expression in action unties the knot one way only to tighten it in another (*The Only Jealousy, At the Hawk's Well*). Yeats's strategy for putting the mythological hero on to the modern stage was cautious and full of ironic reserve in this series of plays. This saved his subject from the Pre-Raphaelite and rhapsodic air that dates the earlier Abbey plays, and from other perishable simplicities, Ossianic or patriotic. But he is never mean or malicious to his hero, and did not permit his audiences to look upon him with a levelling or a rancorous eye or 'pull established honour down'.

## NOTES

1. Lady Gregory, *Cuchulain of Muirthemne* (1903) p. 344.
2. *The Letters of W. B. Yeats*, ed. Allan Wade (1954) pp. 917–18.
3. *Four Plays for Dancers* (1921) p. 86.
4. *W. B. Yeats and Tradition* (1958) p. 163.
5. *Last Poems and Plays* (1940) pp. 113–14.
6. F. A. C. Wilson, op. cit. p. 170.
7. *Cuchulain of Muirthemne*, p. 332.

# QUESTIONS

1. What do you think Auden had in mind when he wrote that Yeats 'was silly like us'?

2. Is it fair to say that the poems of Yeats's later years were 'out of key with his time' and, if so, do you consider this a criticism?

3. Compare Yeats's social and political views, as evidenced in *Last Poems*, with those displayed in the poetry of Auden, or Pound, or Eliot.

4. From your reading of *Last Poems*, what do you deduce Yeats's attitude to Christianity and the supernatural to have been in the closing years of his life?

5. Write either your own review of *Last Poems and Plays*, or a review of the reviews quoted in this Casebook.

6. For what reasons do you think Yeats did not include 'Why should not Old Men be Mad?', 'The Statesman's Holiday', and 'Crazy Jane on the Mountain' in *Last Poems and Two Plays*?

7. If you were Yeats's publisher, would you now restore the original sequence of *Last Poems*?

8. How interrelated and interdependent are Yeats's poems? To what extent is a poet justified in making one poem the key to the full meaning of another?

9. What evidence, if any, do you find for the charge that certain *Last Poems* degenerate into doggerel?

10. Consider Yeats's use of the ballad refrain, and explain why you find it successful or unsuccessful.

11. Compare the poetic attitudes and methods of one of the following pairs:

(*a*) 'The Ballad of the Foxhunter' and 'The Three Bushes'.
(*b*) 'Nineteen Hundred and Nineteen' and 'Lapis Lazuli'.
(*c*) 'When You are Old' and 'A Bronze Head'.
(*d*) 'The Second Coming' and 'The Gyres'.

12. What stylistic differences do you detect between *The Winding Stair and Other Poems* and *Last Poems*? Do you consider that the later book shows a development or a falling-off?

13. Examine the metrical structure (rhythms, rhymes and half-rhymes) of 'Lapis Lazuli' and 'The Three Bushes' in such a way as to illustrate the differing techniques of Yeats's early, and his later, poetry.

14. What did Yeats mean when he wrote: 'And say my glory was I had such friends'; and how right do you think he was?

15. Consider the poet's attitude, or attitudes, to women in *Last Poems*.

16. Examine Yeats's use, or misuse, of history in *Last Poems*.

# SELECT BIBLIOGRAPHY

WORKS BY W. B. YEATS

*Autobiographies* (Macmillan, 1955).

*Essays and Introductions* (Macmillan, 1961).

*The Letters of W. B. Yeats*, ed. Allan Wade (Hart-Davis, 1954).

*Letters on Poetry from W. B. Yeats to Dorothy Wellesley*, ed. Dorothy Wellesley (Oxford University Press, reissued 1964).

*On the Boiler* (Cuala Press, 1939).

*The Variorum Edition of the Plays of W. B. Yeats*, ed. Russell K. Alspach (Macmillan, 1966).

*The Variorum Edition of the Poems of W. B. Yeats*, ed. Peter Allt and Russell K. Alspach (Macmillan, 1957).
*A Vision*, 2nd ed. reissued with corrections (Macmillan, 1962).

BOOKS RELEVANT TO THE STUDY OF *Last Poems and Plays*

Curtis Bradford, *Yeats at Work* (Southern Illinois University Press, 1965).

Richard Ellmann, *The Identity of Yeats*, 2nd ed. (Macmillan, 1964).

—— *Yeats: The Man and the Masks* (Macmillan, 1949).

Edward Engelberg, *The Vast Design: Patterns in W. B. Yeats's Aesthetic* (University of Toronto Press, 1964).

T. R. Henn, *The Lonely Tower*, 2nd ed. (Methuen, 1965).

Joseph Hone, *W. B. Yeats 1865–1939*, 2nd ed. (Macmillan, 1962).

*In Excited Reverie: A Centenary Tribute*, ed. A. N. Jeffares and K. G. W. Cross (Macmillan, 1965).

A. N. Jeffares, *W. B. Yeats: Man and Poet*, reissued with corrections (Routledge, 1962).

Sheelah Kirby, *The Yeats Country* (Dolmen Press, 1962).

Vivienne Koch, *W. B. Yeats: The Tragic Phase. A Study of the Last Poems* (Routledge, 1951).

Thomas Parkinson, *W. B. Yeats: The Later Poetry* (University of California Press, 1964).

B. Rajan, *W. B. Yeats: A Critical Introduction* (Hutchinson, 1965).

George Brandon Saul, *Prolegomena to the Study of Yeats's Poems* (University of Pennsylvania Press, 1957).

Jon Stallworthy, *Between the Lines: W. B. Yeats's Poetry in the Making*, 2nd imp. with corrections (Clarendon Press, 1965).

A. G. Stock, *W. B. Yeats: His Poetry and Thought* (Cambridge University Press, 1961).

Donald Torchiana, *W. B. Yeats and Georgian Ireland* (Northwestern University Press, 1966).

John Unterecker, *A Reader's Guide to W. B. Yeats* (Thames and Hudson, 1959).

ARTICLES RELEVANT TO THE STUDY OF *Last Poems and Plays*

Louise Bogan, 'William Butler Yeats', in *Atlantic Monthly*, CLXI, 5 (1938) 637–44.

Patrick Diskin, 'A Source for Yeats's "The Black Tower" ', in *Notes and Queries*, VIII 3 (1961) 107–8.

A. E. Dyson, 'An Analysis of Yeats's "Long-legged Fly" ', in *The Critical Survey*, ii 2 (1965), 101–3.

Arra M. Garab, 'Fabulous Artifice: Yeats's "Three Bushes" Sequence' in *Criticism*, VII 3 (1965) 235–49.

—— 'Yeats and *The Forged Casement Diaries*', in *English Language Notes*, II (1965) 289–92.

A. N. Jeffares, ' "Gyres" in the Poetry of W. B. Yeats', in *English Studies*, XXVII (1946) 65–74.

W. J. Keith, 'Yeats's Arthurian Black Tower', in *Modern Language Notes*, LXXXV I (1960) 119–23.

Marion Lobistour, 'Lapis Lazuli', in *The Critical Survey*, III I (1966) 13–16.

F. R. Leavis, 'The Great Yeats and the Latest', in *Scrutiny*, VIII 4 (March 1940) 437–40.

S. Mendel, 'Yeats's "Lapis Lazuli" ', in *Explicator*, XIX 9 (1961) item 64.

E. B. Partridge, 'Yeats's "The Three Bushes" – Genesis and Structure', in *Accent*, XVII (1957) 67–80.

L. Perrine, 'Yeats's "An Acre of Grass" ', in *Explicator*, XXII 8 (1964) item 64.

E. M. Sickels, 'Yeats's "The Gyres", 6', in *Explicator*, XV 9 (1957) item 60.

Jon Stallworthy, 'Two of Yeats's Last Poems', in *A Review of English Literature*, IV (1963) 48–69.

Peter Ure, ' "The Statues": A Note on the Meaning of Yeats's Poem', in *Review of English Studies*, XV 99 (1949) 254–7.

# NOTES ON CONTRIBUTORS

W. H. Auden, the most original and influential poet of his generation, made his reputation with *Poems* (1930), *On this Island* (1937), and *Selected Poems* (1938). Since 1939, when he became an American citizen, he published several more collections of poetry. A distinguished anthologist, editor, and critic, he taught and lectured at many universities and was Professor of Poetry at Oxford from 1956 to 1961. He died in 1973.

Curtis Bradford was, at the time of his death, Professor of English at Grinnell College, Iowa; his publications include *Yeats at Work* (1965).

Arra M. Garab is Professor of English at Northern Illinois University. In addition to his studies on Yeats, he is co-editor (with Russel Nye) of *Modern Essays*.

Thomas Rice Henn, who died in 1974, was Emeritus Fellow of St Catharine's College, Cambridge, and an Honorary Doctor of Letters of Trinity College, Dublin. His numerous publications include *Longinus and English Criticism* (1934), *The Lonely Tower* (1950; 2nd ed. 1965), *The Apple and the Spectroscope* (1951), and *Shooting a Bat and Other Poems* (1964).

J. J. Hogan was President of University College, Dublin, until his retirement in 1972, and the author of several books; among them *The English Language in Ireland* (1927) and *An Outline of English Philology chiefly for Irish Students* (1934).

A. NORMAN JEFFARES is Professor of English in the University of Stirling. His publications include *W. B. Yeats: Man and Poet* (2nd edn 1962) and editions of Yeats's poems, plays, prose and criticism. He is editor of the New Oxford English Series, the Writers and Critics series, and the Macmillan History of English Literature series (in preparation).

LOUIS MACNEICE made his name as a poet with *Poems* (1935), *Autumn Journal* (1939), *Collected Poems* (1949), *Ten Burnt Offerings* (1952), and *Autumn Sequel* (1954). He lectured in Classics from 1930 to 1940, and between 1941 and 1949 worked as a feature-writer and producer for the BBC, becoming Director of the British Institute at Athens in 1950. He died in 1963. *The Burning Perch* (1963), *The Strings are False*, an unfinished autobiography (1966), and *The Collected Poems of Louis MacNeice* (1967), ed. E. R. Dodds, were published posthumously.

J. R. MULRYNE is Professor of English in the University of Warwick, and a general editor of the Revels Plays; with Denis Donoghue he edited *An Honoured Guest: New Essays on W. B. Yeats* (1965).

FREDERIC PROKOSCH is known both for his novels – which include *The Skies of Europe* (1942), *The Conspirators* (1943), *A Ballad of Love* (1960) and *The Wreck of the Cassandra* (1966) – and for his poetry. His *Chosen Poems* were published in 1944.

KATHLEEN RAINE is a former Fellow of Girton College, Cambridge. Her *Collected Poems* were published in 1956, *The Hollow Hill* in 1965, and her critical writings include *William Blake and Traditional Mythology* (1963) and *Defending Ancient Springs* (1967).

JOHN CROWE RANSOM was for many years Professor of Poetry at Kenyon College, where he founded the *Kenyon Review*. He died in 1974. An influential critic, his many books include two major critical studies: *The World's Body* (1938) and *The New Criticism* (1941). An enlarged and revised edition of his *Selected Poems* appeared in 1963.

WINFIELD TOWNLEY SCOTT worked on the staff of the *Providence Journal* for twenty years and many volumes of his verse were published in his lifetime, including *Collected Poems* (1962).

JON STALLWORTHY was appointed Anderson Professor of English at Cornell University in 1978. He has published five books of poetry, two critical studies of the poetry of W. B. Yeats, and a biography of Wilfred Owen.

PETER URE was Joseph Cowen Professor of English Language and Literature in the University of Newcastle upon Tyne until his death in 1970. He was the author of *Towards a Mythology: Studies in the Poetry of W. B. Yeats* (1946), *Yeats* in the Writers and Critics series (1963), and *Yeats the Playwright* (1963) as well as two books on Shakespeare. He also edited several books, among them *Richard II* in the New Arden Shakespeare series (1956) and the volume on *Julius Caesar* in the present series (1969).

F. A. C. WILSON has written *W. B. Yeats and Tradition* (1958) and *Yeats's Iconography* (1960) and has been teaching English at the University of North Dakota.

# INDEX